Wiccan:

the Ultimate Starter Kit to Wicca Religion Beliefs, Rituals, Altars, Witchcraft, with Moon and Candle Spells

(This book Includes: Wicca for Beginners, Wiccan Spell Book, Wicca Herbal Magic)

by Gaia J. Mellor

prolonged validity or interim quality. Trademarks that are mentioned are done without written consent and can in no way be considered an endorsement from the trademark holder.

Table Of Contents

Wicca for Beginners:

A Witchcraft Guide for Every Wiccan Aspirant, Made Easy for the Solitary Practitioner.

by Gaia J. Mellor

Introduction

Wicca is a wonderful way to bring the power of all life into your heart, home, and healing. If you have ever wanted to go down the path of magic or embrace the culture surrounding the Wiccan holiday, festivals, and celebrations, then this book is a wonderful way for you to experience what it is that makes Wicca so unique and a great way to manifest the life of your dreams.

As many Wiccans can tell you, the power inherent in these practices has changed their lives for the better, bringing together the world of nature, the cosmos, the power of the moon and the sun, the elements, and all of the divine creation within these qualities, to support a vibrant, colorful, and abundant lifestyle.

For some Wiccans, it is all about the harvest, the cycles, and the seasons of change. For others, it is about magic, ritual, spell crafting, and the wisdom of the tools on the altar of your making. For every Wiccan, there are a set of beliefs, ideas, and philosophies that help them to create the practice of their choosing while giving them a great foundation to support their devotion to the divine in all life.

Wicca for Beginners: A Witchcraft Guide for Every Wiccan Aspirant, Made Easy for the Solitary Practitioner is a beautiful beginning for you to taste the beauty and understand the joy of what Wicca is and what it can bring into your life. The book contains a variety of helpful aspects for you to become acquainted with in your search for spiritual openness and abundance.

You will learn about the history of Wicca and where the philosophies are derived from. You will also find a chapter that covers the common beliefs and devotions, including deities, the elements and why they are so important to your practice, the holidays and festival celebrations that mark the Wiccan year, and astrological influences of the craft.

You will also discover some of the more interesting qualities of what it means to become a Wiccan, especially as a solitary practitioner, in comparison to working with a Coven or a Circle. There is a chapter devoted to helping you learn about The Book of Shadows, why it is important to have your own, and how to get started designing your very own Book.

Additionally, you will find chapters dedicated to the various tools and implements used for altars, rituals, and spells and will be able to reference a set of correspondence tables that will give you easy access to the different meanings behind colors, crystals, herbs, and runes.

Enjoy a beautiful journey through what Wicca can do for you! This book is your beginning to developing the practice that is right for you. If you are looking for answers about Wicca, then look no further. You are about to embark on a deeply magical journey. So mote it be!

Chapter 1: The Philosophy and History of the Wiccan Religion

Welcome to Wicca! This first chapter is designed to give you a foundation to understanding where it came from, how it has evolved, and what makes it different from other ways of life and spiritual practices.

The history of Wicca is more recent than many people may think when they are first learning about it, but even still, it has its practices steeped in ancient history. The philosophies of Wicca come from those ancient places and Pagan ways of life, coming together in our modern world as an offering to continue the life practice of working with nature and the divine in all things.

The History of Wicca

You are here to become acquainted with the magic and mystery of this ancient and beautiful craft. The origins of this specific form of Pagan worship come from a long line of ritual and devotion from a variety of periods and versions of historical Witchcraft. The fully formed basis for this practice, termed Wicca by its founder, came from the organization of a core system of beliefs and ideologies, created and made public by one Gerald Gardner in the 1950s in Great Britain.

Today's historians might call Wicca a Neo-Pagan religion, however, there are distinct characteristics and properties to this practice that set it apart from other forms of esoteric spirituality, including Pagan worship, Witchcraft, and others. Wicca is practiced by a wide range of cultures and people all over the world today, and as it continues to grow in a number of practitioners, it continues to evolve in unique ways.

Before Gerald Gardner introduced the formal concept of Wicca to the public in the 1950s, the ideas and beliefs of the practice could be traced back to a feminist folklorist, Egyptologist and anthropologist named Margaret Murray. She was renowned for her work in documenting cultural-historical background in certain subjects, specifically that of Pagan Witch-cults, and the traditions and cultures surrounding those beliefs.

Murray's publications on medieval religious practices, specifically on European Witchcraft, inspired readers to rekindle a relationship to the pagan arts by forming their own covens, structuring their practices around the concepts and descriptions in Murray's books. At this time, the 1920s, Occultism had already been a popular practice or cultural fad, popularized by Queen Victoria herself, in the mid-1850s.

By the time of Murray's publications, people were eager for new forms of spirituality outside of Christian doctrine and wanted to find new ways of connecting to the divine. Her research and writings were likely a catalyst for people like Aleister Crowley, and Gerald Gardner, to write and form their purposeful religious movements to help others connect to the lost art of Witchcraft and nature worship.

In *Witchcraft Today*, written by Gardner, he explains the origin of the word 'Wicca' and what it means to the spiritual practice. Originally, in his book, he spells Wicca with only one 'c' (Wica) based on the Scots-English word that means 'wise-people.' According to studies, the extra 'c' was added a decade later in the 1960s and stuck for the remainder of the decades following. Gardner's worship of Pagan rituals and practices included him becoming an initiate into a coven in the late 1930s, but by the 1940s he had formed his own coven and established a Folklore Center on his property, where he held his coven rituals and considered it his occult headquarters. This was where he continued to write and develop the concept of Wicca.

Sometime in the 1940s while Gardner was still compiling his words to practice Wicca, he met famed occultist, magician, and poet, Aleister Crowley. The two had a good deal in common about their beliefs in magic and the occult, and it is suggested that Gardener was influenced by Crowley's publications when he decided to write his book of Wicca.

His novel, entitled *High Magic's Aid*, became the first standard idea of Wicca, describing many of the practices and rituals he promoted in the book. It wasn't until he published his *Book of Shadows* that the practices of Wicca and the concepts and beliefs were officially made public, providing insight and specific understanding about the rituals, spells, beliefs, and devotions of the craft.

The *Book of Shadows* remains to this day one of the most important books relating to the original concepts of Wicca, containing within it all of Gardner's personal spells and rituals. Over time, it was added to and edited to be more accessible to a wider audience. Even with his publication, the concepts of Wicca are that it remains flexible and is allowed to evolve as a spiritual practice, based on the choice of the practitioner.

Doreen Valiente, an initiate into Gardner's coven, was the person who helped him to prepare the *Book of Shadows* for publication. Her interest in Wicca came from seeing a magazine article about covens and the way of life of ritual worshippers of nature. She personally contacted Gardener and ended up being his editor on his *Book of Shadows*, bringing it to the public and giving Wicca a 'coming out' into society.

The history of Wicca may not seem like much when you think about the great history behind Witchcraft and ancient Paganism, however when you take a deeper look, the formation of Wicca by one man, and its evolution over the years and across the world, has had a major impact on the way people see magic, Witchcraft and the exploration of Neo-Pagan spirituality. Witchcraft has had its history of being incredibly taboo and evil, but with the introduction of Wicca in the mid-twentieth century, Gardner helped a whole world of Witches find a way to practice faith in nature and the divine in a way that felt like magic to them and was allowed to be accessed in a much more public way than ever before.

Wicca has always existed in some way, but it was Gardner and the time of his work on these practices that gave it a name and brought it into a favorable cultural light. Paganism is a great umbrella for many devotions, practices, rituals, and denominations, and within that umbrella, Wicca stands alone and apart as something wonderfully unique and open-ended.

So, what is the philosophy of Wicca that makes it a different kind of worship? The next section will provide a basic philosophy that will lead to the formation of all of Wicca's core beliefs and devotions.

Philosophies Behind Wicca

Modern day Wicca approaches a connection to the divine through simple and elaborate rituals, spells, festivals, herbalism, worship of certain deities, Sabbats, Esbats, and a deliberate code of ethics and magical morals, as well as a belief in reincarnation and the afterlife.

It has been noted that Wicca is a modern-day interpretation of many other, old Pagan religions that formed before the Christian faith could

18

exist and take over the world as a main religious force. Paganism has its origins in Europe, and in today's Wicca, other concepts from all over the world are incorporated, such as Shamanism and other forms of esoteric spirituality from Eastern religious practices. Wicca has also been strongly associated with Druidism, but it is hard to know for sure exactly how Druids practiced and why.

Many Wiccans are considered duotheistic in their worship. This means that they will practice rituals and devotions through a belief in a male and a female god-force. In the case of Wicca, the male god-force is the Horned God, and the female god-force is the Triple Goddess or some form of Mother Earth. It is not always true that Wiccans worship with this dynamic and many solitary practitioners and coven members will choose a very specific deity to worship throughout their rituals, rather than focusing on a variety of gods/goddesses. The philosophy, however, is that Wicca worships the balance of all life. It brings into focus the patterns of duality and the partnership between the shadow and the light of all life.

Other forms of Wicca might practice atheism, polytheism, and pantheism, and Wicca supports all beliefs due to its practice of equality with all people and all beliefs. Wicca is unique in this way, allowing members of this culture to choose their beliefs while still adhering to the basic foundation of ethical practices and devotions. The foundation remains, while the practitioner decides the structure of the house.

Earth worship has always been a major component of Wicca, even in its earliest forms. This is why Wicca has often been termed as a nature-based religion and why there is a devotion to working within the rhythms of all life on Earth. In a connection to the Earth through this worship, a majority of Wiccans will use herbs and plants to work with spells and rituals, not to mention a regular devotion to the seasons of the year or the Wheel of the Year as it is called, through festivals, harvests, and celebrations.

The main philosophy of Wicca comes from this idea of nature: that we are all one with it and that we all have a responsibility to access the powers within it to manifest more powerful energies of love and light. The presence of magic in these ideas is only a conduit to celebrate and worship the divine quality of life's main elements, rhythms, and cycles.

When you break it down, the philosophy of Wicca is a concept arising from the understanding of and correlation with these major energies and rhythms. Stemming off of that philosophy, the core beliefs and devotions can be built and worked out. When you are in accordance with the rhythms of life, then you are in a responsibility to it, exchanging your devotional energy to the worship of the Moon, Sun, Earth, Heavens and all creative energies that lie within that Universe, for the gift of it coming back to you through your rituals and spells.

Wicca is about life-force energy and how to be creative with that true reality through a specific wielding of that power through thoughtful and mindful attention to the Earth, her beings, elements, and directions.

Your experiences with Wicca will revolve around these philosophies, and as you read more into the next chapter, you will see how that core idea relates to all of the beliefs and devotions that come from the rhythm of life and leads to practicing a sacred balance within that rhythm.

Chapter 2: Wiccan Beliefs and Devotions

There are so many different perspectives and beliefs in Wicca, making it a very broad way of life. Aside from the ability to practice in such a wide variety of ways, Wicca includes a set of major core beliefs that are practiced by a majority of Wiccans and are a structure based on the main philosophies behind it.

These beliefs and concepts are regularly utilized and taken into account for anyone working in the Wiccan way and should be considered as the platform for any sect of Wicca you are interested in. These beliefs are the basis of successful Wiccan worship, ritual, and spellcraft.

Basic Beliefs and Devotions

Nature Is a Divine Force

A fundamental philosophy and core belief of Wicca, the concept of "nature as divine law" is heavily practiced and explored. It is what controls the elements and the sacred rhythms that are incorporated in all life and most rituals. Every member of this Earth, down to the moss, rocks, and algae, are a part of the magic of all life and as we are in alignment with our attention to the divine in nature, we are in a relationship with all of these parts of life.

Our sacred home is the Earth and the stars, Moon and Sun that surround it. It is the place that we find our true nature and power. A devotion to nature and worship of all contained in it is to belong to all life and all matter. This belief is what all of the festivals, celebrations, rituals, and spells are based on. It's all about cycles, rhythms, and the energy in between.

In nature, there is the celebration of opposing forces, and this leads to the concept of worshipping the deities, both masculine and feminine. These gods and goddesses are represented through the forms of nature we celebrate through the seasons. It is the yin and the yang, and that is the very structure of all nature.

Devotion to nature is a long-standing aspect of the Wiccan creed. It is not a demand of Wicca, but it would be hard to embody the philosophies of a Wiccan practice without some nature worship.

Call Upon the Ancestors

All those that came before you, no matter how ancient, or how close to your cultural line, the ancestors are a spiritual force of humanity that brought to light a great deal of what we now know today. In Wicca, it is common to bring the energy of ancestors into your worship. It is a sacred honoring of where the path led to bring you to the place that you know today.

Ancestors are guides on the journey, and unlike deities that are regularly worshipped in several denominations of Wicca, the ancestors are a closer link to our spiritual humanity and the work of all souls to bring more knowledge and wisdom down the line of life through the heritage of all people on Earth and our great connection to all people throughout time.

Calling upon the ancestors' calls upon the past Witches and wizards who brought this knowledge of worshipping nature into the fibers of our very being. It is an excellent practice to honor that invisible guidance, wisdom, and support.

Seasons of the Year: The Great Wheel of Time

Wicca celebrates and worships all of the cycles of the year. Every Equinox with every solstice, every moon cycle and every season, rituals and celebrations throughout the great wheel of time mark crucial moments in the rhythm and cycles of the God and Goddess aspects of nature. The seasons of a year illustrate the great birth, death, and rebirth cycle that is also present in the nature of the God and Goddess energy worshipped by so many Wiccans.

This reality supports and promotes the waxing and waning of all energies, and that life brings death, which recreates life again and again and again.

In addition to the Equinoxes and Solstices, which are markers of the Sun's energy (God aspect), the Moon has her variations and cycles that incorporate into the bigger elemental shifts of season. The Moon and the Sun are great connecting points and road markers for the whole wheel of the year.

The belief in worshipping nature invests in this seasonal devotion, and it will always be a significant part of the practice of Wicca. You are closest to nature and the divine, when you are celebrating her rhythms.

Responsibility in Magic

Wicca requires honesty with personal power. Working with the elements and energies of all life and all beings requires an understanding that you have an impact; you have an influence, and you are giving and receiving power when you are practicing Wicca.

There are laws and creeds that make up a part of this responsibility, but the basic idea is that as you hold the power of all life in your hands through rituals, spells, and worship, you have a great responsibility to use that power wisely and to keep an intention of truth, integrity and a desire to harm no one.

You are responsible for more than just YOU when you practice Wicca. Your connection to the divine and to all life bridges a considerable gap and connects you the energy of everything. You want to be sure that what you do is something you are okay with coming back to you in the end.

Wicca will help you embrace this responsibility and help you avoid conflict with the universal energies that bind us all in the endless cycles, ebbs, and flows of nature and her divine law.

The Wiccan Rede

The basic concept of the Wiccan Rede is this: harm none. Any way that you worship and practice should be in accordance with this idea. It is an essential part of honoring that we are all one together and that any spell or ritual you perform should honor that when you harm another, you hurt yourself in the process.

Wicca is a practice to benefit all energies and life rhythms, and so when you are learning how to practice, it is essential to regard your experience as having high power. When you are responsible with that power, you choose the path of good for all beings and all life.

Equality

There are many religions that will attempt to coerce followers or proselytize to people, creating an energy of fear if you do not practice it a certain way, or live by that creed. Wicca is not a coercive practice and chooses a mentality of equality. There are too many ways to worship, and too many individuals to all bring the same work to our worship.

Wicca follows an idea that as long as you are responsible with your worship and that you are compassionate to another's, then you are in accordance with the divine law of nature: that when we are different, we are also equal.

Wicca may be unique in that way, compared to other spiritual practices or religions; you are not required to practice exactly like another, and all people have a right to celebrate the divine in their own way, within the basic ideas of harming no one and being responsible for your spiritual actions and choices.

This creative way of life embraces all versions of sacred nature worship and allows an opening for people to have uniqueness within their spiritual truth.

The Threefold Law

The Threefold Law is a familiar concept in a majority of Wiccan circles; it simply states that whatever magic you perform through ritual intention, spell work, celebration, or practice, will return to you threefold.

The law of three, as it is also called, will keep you in good standing with the Wiccan Rede of 'Harm None.' If you should choose to cast magic that would have a negative intention to another person, be careful what you wish for because it will come back to you three times. The energy you create gains in power, so make sure it is energy that you want to return to you in some way.

Deities

The deities worshipped in Wicca are broad and varied. The concept of worshipping nature deities is more prominently practiced, although some classes of Wicca will incorporate other types of gods and goddesses into their way of working with nature.

For the Beginner Wiccan, the following deities are a more mainstream concept and will help you get started identifying some of the bigger ideas in Wiccan worship and how they are reflected throughout the Wheel of the Year.

The Horned God

The Horned God is the masculine life force represented in Wicca by the horned animals of the forest. He is also seen and regarded as the Sun energy and embodies all male or masculine aspects of the greater whole in nature. He can sometimes appear as a man dressed in antlers and horns and is usually depicted as a goat, or sometimes a stag. He is the provider of the feast and the protector of the animals in nature. He is the great God of the Hunt, ensuring the life balance in natural ways.

Wicca's earliest associations with the Horned God show him as a fertility god and is sometimes regarded as the offering of marriage to the maiden in Spring who consummates the sacred marriage between the divine masculine and feminine life forces to give birth to the fertile abundance of Summer. He is regularly seen as a Pan-like God and even as a forest man, or Green Man, as he is often coined, covered in the natural foliage of Earth and her bounty.

He is also a reflection of the energy of the Sun, which is the other strength of the male aspect of Wiccan worship. The Sun is the masculine force necessary for all life to grow, and he inhabits this energy through his bright, light power. Some cultures called this male aspect 'Sky Father' to go along with the feminine 'Earth Mother.' The beautiful story of the male and female deities revolves around the yearly cycle and how they come together in a sacred union to give birth to all life before returning to the wise, old forms, resting in the darkness.

The Earth-Moon Mother

The balance and contradiction to the Horned Sun God and male energy is the feminine essence and power represented by the Earth herself and the quality of the Moon. She is what helps life take root in the soils, helping it to flourish. She is the tenderness and nurturing waters of all life that allows for flexibility and change. She is the mother and wife of God and encourages the flowing of the cycles of the year in conjunction with the Father Sky.

As the energy of the Moon as well, she moves the water of all life, especially the tides, connecting more to the internal richness of emotion, feeling, and intuition. She is the inner journey, while the masculine God is the external journey. The Moon has a powerful effect on our natural rhythms, and as it controls the waters of the world, it also controls our internal waters, pulling and pushing us in a life of ebb and flow as we pass through the seasons of the Sun and the male energy of all life.

The Earth has a unique relationship with the Moon that is different from its journey around the male Sun. Earth revolves around Sun; Moon revolves around Earth. This is something to consider in your worship of the divine masculine and feminine energy in all things and the relationship to the greater whole.

The Triple Goddess comes into play here and will be discussed further in the next section. Essentially, the Triple Goddess is the phases of the moon in one lunar cycle, and also throughout the entire year's Sun cycle. It is the connection of the waxing and waning or birth-death-rebirth cycle of every moon and of the whole wheel of the year.

The God and Goddess unite in a variety of ways and are also very separate in their aspects. Devotion to both is a highly common practice in many forms of nature worship, and it goes hand in hand with celebrating the divine in nature and all of its rhythms.

There are several ways that this devotion is represented. You can decorate your altar to bring both energies into practice, depending on your personal preferences. The Horned God can be represented with antlers or horns found in nature, or with the masculine candle colors of yellow, orange, red, and gold. Other objects to represent the divine masculine might include arrows, spears, swords and wands, all phallic and piercing strengths.

The Goddess energy is represented by colors like white, green, silver, and black. Objects are vessels like cauldrons and chalices, like the watery womb and carrier of all depths of feeling. Flowers and plants are common options as well. The best way for you to find what energy you want to bring to your altar to represent these aspects is to go out in nature and see what resonates most for you with the God and the Goddess. Meditate on their energies in your practice and find the best representation for your solitary practice.

The Triple Goddess: Maiden, Mother, Crone

The phases of the Moon are what give this aspect of the Goddess her Triple form name: Maiden, Mother, and Crone. This is depictive of the three phases of feminine life. Women have their youthful maiden phase that exists before they become fertile and give birth to life and becoming Mother. The final stage of life is after the child-bearing years are ended and spent, and the wise old woman continues to flourish as Crone.

These phases may be literal to a woman's actual life. However, the worship of the Triple Goddess in Wicca is symbolic for both male and female life forms, as we all have these cycles and phases in our transformation and growth. It can be said that this Triple-Goddess aspect is a reflection of the human psyche and all of the periods of life on Earth, for all living things.

The aspects of the Triple-Goddess connect to a part of the Wheel of the year, or a season and its natural rhythms, connecting with the very same cycles and rhythms of a person's life on Earth. Each aspect of the Goddess, therefore, is a useful bridge of connection to call upon in certain rituals, spells, and practices. Let's break it down and look at each aspect of the Triple Goddess to get a more in-depth idea of how to incorporate them into your magic practice.

- *The Maiden*

  This is the youthful phase of a woman's life, the cycle of the moon, or the season of the year. Imbolc usually marks the return of the Maiden at the beginning of February, heralding the emergence of Spring. This is the Crescent moon that moves into a waxing phase, growing pregnant with life. She is the dawn and the sunrise.

  Hers is the energy of new life, potential, possibility, beauty, and freshness. She is youth, innocence, independence, self-expression, creative life force, confidence. Associated goddesses are Brigid, Artemis, Persephone, Freya, and many others.

- *The Mother*

  This is the phase of giving birth and the abundance of life as represented by the light of the moon at its fullest. She is the season of Summertime when life is at its most luscious and bountiful. All of the flowers and foods are in full bloom and growth, and all of the animals are maturing and thriving.

  This is responsibility, maturity, living as the adult, and celebrating the fullness and abundance of giving birth to life. This is the light of the entire day shining brightly on the fields and meadows. She is the quality of manifestation and is sometimes considered by Wiccans to be the most powerful aspect of the Triple goddess because of this power. Her common forms in mythology are Demeter, Selene, Ceres, and Danu, among many others.

- *The Crone*

    This is the phase of the waning moon into its darkness. Here reality is in the time of no longer bearing fruit and being in the post-childbearing years of the life cycle. Her season is the Autumn and Winter, and she represents the setting sun and the darkness of the night. She is the grandmother and oversees the energies of endings, deaths, transformations, dreams and visions, prophecy, past lives, guidance, and the opening of a great rebirth with the coming dawn.

    She is an excellent reminder that death is a part of life and that death transforms into a new life with the waking of the New moon into Maiden light. Some of the typical representations of the Crone aspect are Hecate, Morrigan, Baba Yaga ad Cailleach Bear.

This view of the Earth Mother or the sacred feminine polarity in nature is a complex portrayal of the deeper levels of the human psyche in accordance with the rhythms of life. She provides an excellent opportunity for growth and transformation as you practice Wicca and as you work with the sacred feminine and the Moon energies, you may want to dig a little deeper into this feminine aspect of nature.

The Elements

In Wiccan belief and philosophy, there are five sacred elements, and they are as follows: Earth, Air, Fire, Water, Spirit (Ether). These elements are a significant aspect, like the seasons, or the celebration of the deities, in the practice of worshiping the wisdom and vibrational energy of all things in nature.

The elements are the material life force energies as a symbol of specific mental, emotional, physical and spiritual life experiences and rhythms, as well as a true definition of the ingredients that create and sustain all life. They are considered the building blocks of everything that surrounds us, and they are ultimately responsible for the cycles, seasons, and structure of nature as we know it. They are the literal force that binds our connection to the Earth and spiritual planes of existence.

Throughout time and history, almost all cultures at one point or another have celebrated or incorporated the essence of these elements in their religious, spiritual, and healing methodologies. They are one of the essential tools to sustain all life and to connect the dots of our integration into all of its cycles.

Another critical aspect of the Classical Elements, as they are sometimes referred, is the connection to the cycle of rebirth and destruction, or the life-death-life cycle present in the seasons and the aspect of the triple Goddess.

The elements are also representative of that cycle in that each one of them carries the quality of all three aspects or cycles. Fire brings life as much as it destroys. Water gives life as much as it washes it away. The earth grows life, as much as it returns it to the soils. The air breathes life as much as it snuffs it out. This aspect of the elements is in close connection to the overall philosophy of worshipping the power of nature and all of its rhythms and forces.

Elemental Magic in Wicca

The Elements are each a distinct spiritual energy, and each will play an important part in the sacred rites and rituals of Wicca. Overall, they are 'called upon' at the beginning of a ceremony and invoked as an opening and an introduction to whatever work is about to be performed.

Each of the elements is represented by the Cardinal Directions. The Cardinal Directions are the Four Quarters of the Earth, or what you would find on a standard compass: North, East, South, and West. The corresponding elements are as follows: North is Earth; East is Air; South is Fire; West is Water. When you call upon the Elements in your rituals and circle, you are also calling upon the cardinal directions and will often face each direction while you ask the Elements into your rite.

The Elements will also have a corresponding tool on your altar. You will learn more about these tools in a later chapter, but for the sake of this subject, an example of 'elemental' tools might look something like this: Earth is a Pentacle; Air is a Wand; Fire is a Candle; Water is a Chalice (empty or filled). Each tool will hold a dynamic, elemental quality and as such, will be used in accordance with that element throughout your ritual practice.

Even the herbs you use will have an elemental association, as well as other objects you find in nature to decorate your altar with or for your rituals, as well as crystals, gemstones, and even the representation of colors in your magic and casting.

As you can see, the Elements are in everything and all life and so to use Wiccan practices and rituals, you are going to have a close relationship with these five elements.

The Element of Spirit, which is here discussed separately from the Cardinal directional elements, is what is above. When you are casting a circle, and you face each direction to call in the corresponding elements, your last calling is to that of spirit, which is represented by the great divine, deities that support your practice, or whatever the essence and energy of spirit mean for you. It is where you point above the circle in the center of the four directions. It is the cross point of the earthly elements and what connects your spiritual practice to the Earth.

There are Elemental influences in other Wiccan tools and practices, such as in the astrological signs of the Zodiac and as is represented in the symbols and archetypes of the Tarot. Again, the Elements are in all things and to practice Wicca is to join forces with the forces of nature as represented by these sacred energies.

Connection to the Elements

While you are practicing Wicca and working with these energies, you will spend time learning more about them through your rituals and spellcraft. It is like forming a new friendship and relationship with a person. You will use your intuition to truly get to know their characters, qualities, personalities, and purposes as you work with them.

Seek out a variety of sources informing you about all of these different qualities. Spend more time in nature, looking at each one separately and together as a Universal whole, working together side by side.

You will likely resonate more with one element than others, based on your own personality, or you may go through phases with each one. As you grow in your practice, you may need to spend quality time working more with one energy over the others in order to learn a lesson from the quality of life it harbors and seeks to teach you. You will understand each one more deeply as you work with them more intimately on your journey. Let them guide you and become a part of the wisdom of your work. They will always guide you forward, precisely as you need to be shown your path.

Sabbats and Esbats

In the Wheel of the Year, there are multiple celebrations that are considered the solar, or "sun holidays," marking the times of the year when the sun is shifting and transforming with the rotation of the Earth through the seasons. They are demonstrated by the two Equinoxes and the two Solstices that divide the year into quarters. Between each of these holidays is another celebration, one for every mid-way point between the Solstice and the Equinox. These holidays are known in Wicca as Sabbats.

Between the eight total Sabbats, some Wiccans will refer to them as the Greater and Lesser Sabbats, the greater ones being the actual Solstices and Equinoxes, marking the change in season, and the lesser Sabbats, marking the mid-way points.

Each of these times is an essential moment of reflection regarding the cycles of Mother Earth and her power as well as the rhythms of transformation and seasons of life, that are always ever-flowing. There are a variety of ways you can celebrate these rites of passage, and in your own solitary practice, you will learn what ideas feel the most abundant for you.

Let's take a look at the Sabbats to give you an idea of what they bring into focus and how best to celebrate these moments in the Wheel of Life.

Sabbat is the Sun Cycle

Samhain

To begin the Wheel of the Year, we start with what has been coined as the Witches New Year, or Samhain (pronounced sow-in). You may be familiar with this celebration time already by the name of All Hallows Eve, or Halloween. This is the time when the great veil of mystery between worlds is lifted, connecting us more deeply to the spirit plane.

Falling on October 31st, and sometimes celebrated by Wiccans on November 1st as well, Samhain is a holiday of mystery, symbolic of the great cycles of death and rebirth, when the Sun has waned in power and brings forward the times of reflection and inward thinking. Light is fading in the day and the nights are gaining in darkness, celebrating the Crone aspect of the Triple Goddess and the seasons of the year. It is the last harvest summer.

It is the time to honor the underworld, the ancestors, the death in all things, and transformation is the theme. It is the final harvest before winter and marks the storing of seeds, herbs, and foods to last through the winter months, marking the hibernation and preparation for the next journey of rebirth and abundance.

Altar and ritual spaces are decorated with gourds, pumpkins, mums and the abundant fruits of fall, as well as a variety of herbs and spices. Common herbs used for magical purposes at this time are deadly nightshades, allspice, catnip, mugwort, and sage. Crone Goddesses are worshiped, such as Hecate, and the aging, masculine Sun God is celebrated through the enjoyment of the last moments of full sunshine in the sky.

It is a valuable time to prepare for the dark days ahead and to prepare for the great reflection time as the coming Winter calls upon the period of great resting before replanting in Spring.

Yule

Between December 21st and 23rd marks the day of the Winter Solstice. This is the time called "the longest night" as it is the point in the cycle of the year when the sun is at its lowest length of shining in the daylight hours. The Winter Solstice heralds the return of the light, and after this celebration, the days begin to grow longer and longer with the approach of the new year and the bounty of refreshing Spring.

Because of its association to the celebration of the returning light after a long darkness, the Winter solstice is the time of burning the Yule log. The log itself is usually harvested from your own property, traditionally, or given as a gift, but any Yule log can be made sacred to the ritual through some charging and consecration at your altar. It is decorated with Winter evergreens, hollies and mistletoe, as is the rest of the home and the altar space.

Candles are lit all over to bring a festival of lights into the life of the dark, celebrating the great shift in the season and the growing strength of the masculine Sun, being reborn in the chill of Winter. The Yule log burns all night long in a ceremony of sacred appreciation for the coming light and traditionally, a piece of your Yule log is kept for the following year's celebration, to ignite the next record.

Feasting is common, and the following herbs, spices, and decorations are brought into the rituals and spells: frankincense, pine, sage, bayberry, spiced and warm drinks like mulled wine and cider, poinsettias and evergreens, holly and mistletoe.

It is a time to let go of the year behind you and prepare for the next cycle, welcoming the growing light and the energy of the Sun back into your life.

Imbolc

This day is a celebration, usually carried out around the first or second day of February, between the Winter Solstice and the Spring Equinox. It is the return of the Maiden and heralds the awakening of light, renewal, purity, and growth, as the elements of Spring begin to push through the snow and ice of Winter's chill. The maiden goddesses, such as Brigid, are widely celebrated at this time. In fact, many religions consider Imbolc, St. Brigid's day.

The Maiden is the essence of innocence and brand-new growth. She has the energy of a renewed walk through the Wheel of the Year and is opening and transformative. This is the way forward into the growing light, as the Maiden life force energy prepares to mate with the male God of Sun and the hunt, to give new life to the Great Mother.

Candle lighting, feasting, and decorating altar spaces with white flowers and objects is a standard practice. Common herbs to use for spells and rituals include coltsfoot, myrrh, angelica, basil, celandine, and more. Seeds and seeded loaves of bread are a favorite food and can be offered to the Maiden Goddess on your altar space.

It is a particular time to finally release the old of the year behind to embrace the new of the year ahead of you. Rebirth and renewal are the time of Imbolc as the Maiden creates the bridge to Spring.

Ostara

The word Ostara is the name for the Goddess of Spring and also comes from the term 'oestre,' which means "egg." The egg of spring is ready to be fertilized and will grow into the life of the Mother Goddess when it is ready to burst forth in abundance. This is the Spring, or Vernal Equinox, and will fall somewhere between March 20th and 23rd, depending on the year.

This is the moment when the dark of night and light of day are in perfect balance together. This is why this time of year is celebrated as the sacred union between the Horned, or sun God (the masculine energy) and the Maiden form of the Goddess (feminine energy). There is a perfect balance between the yin and yang of life, and so they may join together in an ideal marriage, preparing the Earth with light and the seeds of Summer growing.

Wiccans will practice rituals and spells devoted to these energies and their harmony by using certain herbs, foods, and celebrations. Spring flowers are used on altars, such as daffodils, irises, violets, and woodruff. Spring vegetables and meats are common for feasting, and all varieties of spring herbs are used for spells and rituals. Many will plant their magical gardens at this time, signaling that as sacred ritual for growing of the magic herbs for the ceremonies to come for the rest of the year.

It is a time of balance and harmony between the male and female energies of the Universe and connects you to the possibilities of renewal and rebirth.

Beltane

Beltane lands on May first and is often coined as 'May Day.' The sacred marriage of the Maiden and the Green Man has occurred, and now they can consummate their marriage. It is a festival of fire and passion and brings into effect the tradition of the maypole dance as the sacred act of love between God and the Goddess. People are often seen decorated with flowers and dancing around bonfires, celebrating this principal act in nature, before the Mother Goddess of Summer is full and pregnant with earthly life.

The masculine power of the Sun is getting stronger by the day and lasting longer into the night. Feasting and the use of masculine fire energy are very common in many circles and celebrations. It is the emergence of the Horned God into his manhood and the emergence of the Mother aspect of the Triple Goddess.

Honey and nectar, oatcakes and cookies, bread, and grains are all present in the festivities. Herbs like nettle, flax, marjoram, coriander, curry, elder, and rose are common in rituals and spells.

It is the time to embrace the power of the growing fire of sunlight and the Maiden becoming the Mother aspect, pregnant with the masculine energies of the Sun. It is a time of growing bounty and abundance, fertility, and growth.

Litha

Litha is light. This day marks the Summer Solstice and will fall somewhere between June 20th and 22nd. This is the moment of the Sun's full power and the most powerful Father force and Mother force. In a similar fashion to Beltane rituals, Litha celebrates the light through fires and candlelight rituals as well as playing outside in the heat of the sun.

The focus is on the fertility of the Earth Mother and her growing riches provided by the Sky Father. There is also a great link to the power and magic of the fairies, especially on this occasion, sometimes referred to as Mid-Summer

Night's Eve, when the link to faery magic is its most profound. This is a good time for divination practices or scrying rituals because of the connection to the faery realms. It is also a time to rededicate your purposes and intentions, set in the Spring months at the time of great rebirth.

There is a tradition of making an herb bundle to burn in your cauldron, and some of the following herbs are often combined to make this offering: lavender, mugwort, vervain, St. John's Wort, honeysuckle, chamomile, thyme, yarrow, meadowsweet, rosemary, roses, and heartsease.

This is a time of creating and manifestation through the power of greatest sunlight to bring a passion through the end of the season as you materialize future abundance and prosperity.

Lughnasadh

Between the Summer Solstice and the Autumnal Equinox, Lughnasadh falls. It is at the end of July and the opening of August and is the time of the first harvests. The sun is starting to wane in power and light, and the Mother Goddess is birthing her fertile abundance. It is reaping what was sown through the sacred union and consummation of the God and Goddess energy of all life and creation.

This is a time when people will begin to store their riches, setting aside herbs, foods, and other bounties to prepare for the long nights ahead.

The first harvest is a celebration of the birth of fruits and abundance of Summer's growing seasons. Feasts of fruits and vegetables are common for ceremony and rituals. Bee pollen, mugwort, oat, comfrey, Queen Ann's lace, elder, barley, and many more herbs are used at this time for feasting and for spells and rituals.

It is a time to honor the growing darkness by appreciating the fruits born of the Spring and Summer. It is the first of three harvest times that mark the lowering light and the celebration of Mother Earth's riches and Father Sky's forces.

Mabon

This is the second harvest and is also known as the Autumnal Equinox. The time of Samhain is the end of harvest and the beginning of the Crone time. The Equinox will land somewhere between September 21st and 23rd and marks the time when the light echoes the coming dark and the middle harvest of the season continue the decadence of Mother Earth's bounty.

Leaves will start to change color, signaling the return of Persephone to the underworld and the relationship to the night grows in significance. The cornucopia is a symbol at this time of year for the fruits of the harvest and the labor of love between the Mother Goddess and Father God, now both preparing for the older years before they return to the shadows and prepare for rebirth. It signifies security, balance, protection, confidence in the future ahead, and prosperity.

Apples, nuts, seeds, root vegetables, onions, and garlic are common foods at this time, and other foods like squashes, gourds, corn, acorns, and pomegranates are featured heavily in these celebrations and festivities, as well as rituals and spells. Herbs like sage, milkweed, marigold, myrrh, rose petals, thistles and honeysuckle compliment these foods and spells.

This waning time marks the mysteries of the aging deities coming to a head as the spirit world opens at the time of Samhain. It is the moment of reaping what was sown and is an excellent preparation and storing for the winter ahead. It is the final celebration of the light as the God aspect becomes older and walks the path of Grandfather time. It is a time of peace and harmony, as well as abundance from the Summer's ending time.

Esbat is the Moon Cycle

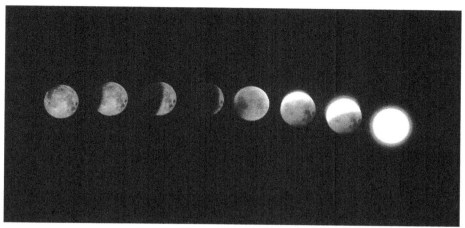

Within the Wheel of the Year and the cycles of the Sun marked by the Sabbats, there is the relationship of the Moon cycles within these rhythms. Within every Moon cycle (4 weeks), the Moon becomes pregnant with light and represents the fullness of the Mother. As you read in a previous section, the Triple Goddess aspect is greatly entrenched in the Moon cycles and should be considered when celebrating Esbats.

The Moon cycles work within the rhythms of the Sun cycles and yet take on a meaning of their own, representing a whole other quality of the Goddess energy in every season. An Esbat celebrates the quality of energy present in the current Moon phase. She is Maiden at the crescent and growing into the First Quarter, into the Full Moon Mother, and finally from Last Quarter to the darkened moon of the Crone.

However, you choose to celebrate your Esbats, considering the Triple Goddess is common in Wicca and bridges the energies of the seasons with the passing days and weeks of the Moon's sacred energy.

Ritual of the Full Moon

Many Wiccans will hold ritual or perform specific spells under the power of a Full Moon. Whatever work you are trying to do the Full Moon has a specific quality of energy to help you with your magical purposes. For some moons, you may only wish to honor the Moon alone, and not use the strength of the Moon for a specific spell. At any rate, the full celebration of this full power is a prominent part of working within Wicca's borders, and it will help you maintain focus and regain spiritual energy when fully celebrated and appreciated.

Full Moons are the beginning of a turning point and the closing of a cycle as she moves from fullness into the quiet darkness of the Crone phase. It is an excellent time to pull forward all of your energies to reflect on what you may be releasing or letting go of or to celebrate what you are giving birth to as the Moon wanes.
A full Moon is a significant point in time and will always have a significance in your partnership with Wicca. For the solitary practitioner, it will mean forming your own bond and relationship with the Full Moon that has meaning for you in your personal rituals and spells.

Ritual of the New Moon

The New Moon is at the end of a journey and marks the seed of new growth. Coming out of Full moonlight, the waning moon celebrates the crone phase, which is a time of preparation. When you think about it in relation to the Wheel of the Year, the Crone phase is also the time of year when Samhain hits and the Winter darkness enters, signaling the time of reflection and preparation for the Maiden Spring.

The New Moon is the opening, the gateway, to a new growth cycle and waxing energy. New moon rituals are the seed in the soil that will grow into fullness by the next Full Moon. Using that energy in your spells and rituals can be very powerful, and so if you are trying to grow something into abundance, the Esbat of the New Moon can be a very powerful time to set an intention.

New Moon Esbats are the last days of the Crone energy and the transformation into the Maiden, bringing forth a growing renewal and rebirth to help you charge your rituals, spells, and magic.

The Moons Between

Other aspects of the Moon's waxing and waning can also be celebrated as an Esbat. Some Wiccans will use the First and Last Quarter Moons as important moments for casting and honoring the Triple Goddess and the Horned God. Others will consider all phases of the Moon for every ritual, carefully planning in accordance with the passing energies.

Typically, within each Moon cycle, the Triple Goddess is given worship and devotion and all of the energies related to that part of the Moon phases assist in the celebration of the rhythms within the rhythms of magic and all life.

Astrology

Astrology can play a significant role in Wiccan practices because of the quality and nature of what is and what it represents with regard to nature and the cycles and rhythms of life. Astrology defined is the practice of understanding the positions of celestial bodies to interpret various aspects of human nature and symbolism through the connection to their movements and the effects of those movements on the Earth plane.

So basically, the planets and the stars have an impact on our Earth reality and our very make-up, including human attitude and personality. They can be tools of prediction and divination, as well as physical implications on Earth rhythms due to their relationship to our position in the Galaxy.

One of the core beliefs of astrology happens to fall in line with a common Wiccan belief and saying: as above, so below. The idea is that what happens above effects what is below, and vice versa. The 12-month annual cycle, celebrated in the Wheel of the Year, is also directly linked to the other planets in orbit around the Sun and the Zodiac symbols are brought to us through starlight and are ruled by specific planets, whose qualities and characteristics, prompt the concept of what kind of personality traits you will have if you are born under that zodiac sign and planetary energy.

Within the practice of Wicca, Zodiac signs and symbols are reflected and organized according to the concept of the Elements, gender (God/Goddess energy) and what planet rules your energy.

Elemental Astrology

Earth Signs

The Earth signs are Taurus, Virgo, and Capricorn. The personality traits invoked with this energy are practicality, stability, stubbornness, and groundedness. It is said that they are more interested in practical realities and mundane earth plane matters. They have a tendency to have a conflict with matters that cannot be seen or touched, like matters of the spirit plane.

Water Signs

The Water signs are Cancer, Scorpio, and Pisces. They are considered to be more emotional in life matters and will sometimes have trouble expressing their emotions through words and may need other forms of expression.

Fire Signs

The Fire signs are Aries, Leo, and Sagittarius. They are action-oriented, spirited, and have a strong vitality. They are warm even when it is cold (interpersonally) and have a tendency to insensitive to others.

Air Signs

The Air signs are Aquarius, Gemini, and Libra. They are thinkers and are good with thoughts and ideas and can have issues with emotions.

Each Sign, Broken down

1. Aries (March 21st- April 19th)

The symbol is the Ram; masculine; ruled by the head; herbs and oils are rosemary, marjoram, lemon, black pepper, frankincense;

ruled by Mars; Element is Air; associated with the magic of force, forward motion, war and conflict with resolve, beginnings, and birth, and openings.

2. Taurus (April 20th- May 20th)

The symbol is the Bull; feminine; ruled by the throat; herbs and oils are lemon, patchouli, rose and rosemary; ruled by Venus; Element is Earth; associated with the magic of groundedness, stability, stubbornness, relationships, practicality, empowerment.

3. Gemini (May 21st- June 20th)

The symbol is the Twins; masculine; ruled by the arms; herbs and oils are bergamot, basil, neroli, grapefruit, and ginger; ruled by Mercury; Element is Air; associated with the magic of balance, seeing both sides, compromise, thoughts and ideas, whimsy, duality.

4. Cancer (June 21st- July 22th)

The symbol is the Crab; feminine; ruled by the breasts and cancers; herbs and oils are chamomile, fennel, lavender, rosemary, ginger, juniper; ruled by the Moon; Element is Water; associated with the magic of nurturing, mothering, fertility, and protection, as well as compassion and empathy.

5. Leo (July 23rd- August 22nd)

The symbol is the Lion; masculine; ruled by the heart; herbs and oils are garlic, lemon, rosemary and rose; ruled by the Sun; Element is Fire; associated with the magic of courage, dramatic art, energy, affirmation, self-confidence, and loyalty.

6. Virgo (August 23rd- September 22nd)

The symbol is the Virgin; feminine; ruled by the stomach and bowels; herbs and oils are ginger, thyme, lemon, grapefruit, citrus; ruled by Mercury; Element is Earth; associated with the magic of practicality, domesticity, organization, and health.

7. Libra (September 23rd- October 22nd)

The symbol is the Scales; masculine; ruled by the kidneys and adrenals; herbs and oils are basil, melissa, frankincense, and bergamot; ruled by Venus; Element of Air; associated with the magic of relationships, justice, art, and social courteousness.

8. Scorpio (October 23rd- November 21st)

The symbol is the Scorpion; feminine; ruled by the sex organs; herbs and oils are sandalwood, clary sage, jasmine; ruled by Pluto; Element is Water; associated with the magic of death, sex, power, obsession, underworld matters, control, and stealth.

9. Sagittarius (November 22nd- December 21st)

The symbol is the Archer/Hunter; masculine; ruled by thighs and hips; herbs and oils are geranium, frankincense, rosemary, and tea tree; ruled by Jupiter; Element is Fire; associated with the magic of education, philosophy, traveling, language, sports, gambling, religions, foreign cultures.

10. Capricorn (December 22nd- January 20th)

The symbol is the Goat; feminine; ruled by knees and bones; herbs and oils are eucalyptus, ginger, chamomile; ruled by Saturn; Element is Earth; associated with the magic of advancement, history, tradition, climbing to the top.

Aquarius (January 21st- February 18th)

The symbol is the Water Bearer; masculine; ruled by the ankles, calves, circulatory system; herbs and oils are peppermint, rose, lemon, coriander; ruled by Uranus; Element is Fire; associated with the magic of independence, inspiration, freedom, and invention.

11. Pisces (February 19th- March 20th)

The symbol is the Fish; feminine; ruled by the feet; herbs and oils rose, lavender and sandalwood; ruled by Neptune; Element is Water;

associated with the magic of creativity, intuition, compassion, imagination.

The Zodiac as a tool of Wicca will help you connect with more than what lies on Earth. It is a greater connection to the whole world of celestial energies that are pushing and pulling us constantly. As you grow in your knowledge of Wicca, continue to dedicate more time and learning to the concepts of astrology and how they may influence your practice and ritual.

Moving Forward

All of the fundamental beliefs and devotions of Wicca are here to help guide you towards a better understanding of the best way to enjoy the concepts and ideas of what it means to be Wiccan. The practice of Wicca is creative and transformative, and so you can adopt some of these concepts, or all of them, and you may find that you are drawn more to some than others.

As a solitary practitioner, you will find the best methods for your practice and will incorporate the beliefs that resonate the most with you on your journey. Let it evolve with you and work on what makes you feel most aligned with your real power and purpose.

Chapter 3: Other Beliefs

After you have read some of the main beliefs, devotions traditions, and philosophies of Wicca, it is important to recognize some of the other beliefs that fall into many, but not all practices. As a solitary practitioner, it will be up to you to decide exactly what you choose to incorporate into your regular devotion and belief and having a broader idea of what many Wiccans consider as truth is a helpful jumping off point.

This chapter will delve into some of the other beliefs supported by many Wiccan sects. They all pertain to the greater forces and cosmic reality of what happens beyond the earthly life. The subjects of karma, reincarnation and the afterlife, all fit together like puzzle pieces of a greater whole, but you don't need to believe in all three to support your Wiccan practice.

Karma

Karma is an important position to take within your magical work. It has its echo in the concept of the Law of Three, which you read about in the last chapter. The Law of Three states that whatever you give or manifest through magic comes back to you threefold in this life.

With karma, whatever actions you take throughout the course of your life will come back to you in the next. It might not be with the power of three that karma comes back, but it could very well show up in a big way. Many believe in karma as a warning or an experience to help guide you on a positive and heartfelt life path, honoring that however you choose to live now will revisit you again when you come back as a soul in future life.

Karma poses that if you are not ready to achieve growth and acceptance of your faults or pride, then you will have to continue learning them over and over again. Therefore, karma is a teacher who helps you understand the benefit of processing your thoughts and actions, as well as emotions and choices so that you can release them and open yourself to a more fulfilling life in the next one.

Karma is a widely known concept and has appeared across culture and religion, and it is nothing new with Wicca. The concept has its origins in many Eastern thought beliefs, as well as in some ancient Pagan practices. The reality of karma and the belief in that possibility requires a belief in something else: if you believe in karma, then you will likely believe in reincarnation, because if you are going to experience the karma of your former lives revisiting you, then you will have to trust that there is another life to be lived in the future.

Reincarnation

Reincarnation is traditional Wiccan teaching, and it will vary amongst Wiccans, circles, and covens, as well as solitary practitioners. According to the idea of reincarnation, a soul will reincarnate into the same species throughout many lives in order to learn lessons to advance one's soul. This belief is not a Universal truth for those who believe in it. Some will suggest that your incarnate self will take many different forms, instead of staying limited to one species, throughout your many lives. Some Witches believe that they always reincarnate as a Witch.

Possibilities of what kind of life you will live in the future (where you will be, what you will do, what form you will take) are a favorite subject and some Wiccans who will make an effort to communicate with spirit to find out more information about what lies ahead in their path so that they can start preparing for it in this life, ensuring that there is no karmic debt to pay off.

As with all past life experiences, the lessons that can be learned from them in your present life are essential to your growth and education not only as a Wiccan but also as a soul on a journey. Many Wiccans practice past life readings to teach themselves where they have been so that they can heal the wounds of their very own past and progress more smoothly into their future.

Some Wiccans believe that before you reincarnate into the next life, you have a brief or long resting period in an afterlife post, but more on that in the next section. Other items of interest with regard to reincarnation is the ability to communicate with the souls of the spirit world, or those in the "resting place" before their return to Earth.

The practice of Spiritualism and the Occult in the early twentieth century saw a rise in conjuring spirits and Gardner himself, was known to be involved in these mystical séances.

There are a lot of varying beliefs amongst Wiccans about how reincarnation even works. There is an idea that you begin as a lower form of a human, as in fresh and new with a whole lot to learn, and will work to ascend into a higher order of human experience, climbing up the spiritual life pyramid, evolving through some kind of rank of awakening. Another case for reincarnation is that you will only ever just reincarnate as a human, and will likely only travel cyclically through all of your life's, like the concept of the seasons of the year, or the life-death-life cycle inherent in all significant Wiccan philosophies and practices.

Whether you decide to consider reincarnation as a spiritually progressive experience, or a simple cycle and wheel of life, you will find an understanding that connects you more deeply to the great unknown. You may choose to identify with a specific concept of reincarnation or take a broader view. Perhaps it is a totally random fate, or maybe you have a choice in what way you return. Your solitary practice in Wicca will help you answer these questions over time.

Afterlife

As with the concept of reincarnation, a view of the afterlife varies amongst the various Wiccan practices across the world, and there isn't a set doctrine or belief system about it. It seems to follow whatever rule of thumb is chosen by the coven, circle, or eclectic (solitary) Wiccan.

In general, even with a belief in reincarnating, a central idea in Wicca is that you choose to make the most of the current life you are living, and not spend too much time living in the future, or the past.

In Gardner's original Wiccan writings and practices, he demonstrated the belief that Witches will reincarnate as future Witches and also that you spend your eternal moments between lives in a realm coined as 'The Summerland.' There are many practicing Wiccans who take the viewpoint that the Summerland is the afterlife place that you can return to over and over again, as you prepare to reincarnate into your next phase of soul growth and ascension.

The Summerland has even been described by some Wiccan authors and practitioners. According to the description, it is "a place on the astral plane…a place of eternal summer, a pastoral place with woods, parks, and gardens… a place where souls meet between incarnations [to] assimilate what they have learned and decide where to go next."

With a description like that, it is no wonder that Witches seem to be notorious for having little fear of death, knowing that they will take repose in The Summerland before journeying ahead on their path into their next life.

There have also been some ideas drawn about the concept of an alternative resting place between lives, and that is more of a hellish place called 'The Winterland.' These ideas have origins in the ancient Pagan traditions that Wicca was built upon, but not all Wiccans honor the concept of a hell-like place to shiver and chill until their time finally comes to move forward into another human life. Whether or not you choose to believe in these contrasts, between the peaceful and harmonious Summerland, and the cold and icy retribution of a Winterland, your choice of belief in the afterlife will come from your own unique practice.

Where Do We Go?

Moving forward, you now have another idea to bolster your knowledge of Wicca and what it can mean to your practice to believe in these other concepts. So much of what you do here and now matters to your overall quality of life in the present one you are living.

To make amends with your past and carry more of your truth into the future, you don't have to believe in karma, reincarnation and an afterlife; but you may find as you begin your practice, that these concepts naturally find their way into to the work that you do and it is undoubtedly an excellent practice to ponder these matters.

If you are really curious about it, you can cast a circle and speak directly to spirit. Ask for advice, or ask questions about your past lives and if they even existed. Communicate with the divine and find out more about what it all will mean to your practice. Create a ritual to get answers to these questions so you know which way you will want to go with your personal magic.

Chapter 4: Introduction to Witchcraft

Now that you have more in-depth knowledge and understanding of what Wicca is and how it was born into being, you can begin to understand its relationship to the practices involved and how they are alike, or different, from the common beliefs about Witchcraft.

This chapter serves as an introduction to the basics of Witchcraft, and why if you are a practicing Wiccan, you will want to have a grasp and understanding about what that word actually means and why it will be vital for you to know it.

Witchcraft and Wicca: Are They the Same?

Are they the same? Yes and no: it depends on who you ask. The term "Wicca" was initially spelled as 'wica,' as you read in the chapter on the history of Wicca and its origins, the Old English, or Scots-English term for 'wica' meant 'wise people.' The Witches of any community, especially in pre-Christian Europe, were considered to be the wise people and the name 'wica' would be used as well as the word 'Witch' giving them both the same meaning. So basically, the word Wicca is a derivation of the word 'Witch.'

Many of the symbols and tools used in Witchcraft are strikingly similar to those used in Wicca, and they even will boast a similarity in their beliefs and worship. The term 'Witch' is a broad term to describe anyone who uses the energy and elements of nature to perform acts of devotion, worship, healing, and manifestation.

There are many people who are not Wiccan who call themselves Witches, and it goes without saying that the two are intertwined in some way. It really comes down to what you believe and how you choose to practice magic. Earlier, you learned that Paganism is an umbrella term to cover a lot of different practices and types of nature-based worship and devotion. Witchcraft could be seen in a similar way, covering a wide range of possible manifestations of what it means to be a Witch.

Witches have a dark history and have been called hideous old hags who work with the devil and perform evil magic in order to enslave men and cause disease. There is a great history of Witchcraft and the persecution of Witches all over Europe and the Americas for their knowledge and understanding of the world around them and how to use energy to manifest reality.

Fortunately for modern Witches, the arrival of Wiccan practices came at a time in history when you were less likely to be burned at the stake for dancing naked under a Full Moon, and today's Witch is lucky to have the freedom to practice without persecution.

Witchcraft is notorious for the practice of casting spells, creating and performing rituals and working with herbal plant medicine and magic. Today's Wiccans utilize a broad range of many of these practices with a specific devotion to nature, seasons, moon cycles, and more.

When you are devoting yourself to a form of Wicca, you are embracing the concept of Witchcraft and making it a part of how you work with your tools, spells, and intentional magical purposes. However, you may not want to practice any kind of magic and would prefer to engage more in worship and devotional practice that doesn't incorporate casting spells or manifesting outcomes through a craft. The next section will explain more about that.

Witchcraft and Wicca: The Difference Between Them

Not all Wiccans will identify as Witches and vice versa. There are a lot of different ideas and connotations between what each of these terms means, and it seems to be subjective to the practitioner or group. There is certainly a wide range of overlaps between the two, as you read in the last section. However, it is not a requirement that you identify as one and therefore automatically identify with the other.

Some Wiccans simply don't practice magic, and therein lies the difference between them. You can still be Wiccan and not practice magic, which is what a Witch does. Wiccans' primary choice of practice is to live in harmony with nature, worship a god/goddess deity, or group of deities, celebrate the seasons and cycles of the year and so forth. It is not a requirement of Wicca that you practice harnessing and manifesting the natural energies inherent in these cycles, rhythms, and seasons. You could argue then that Wiccans are not Witches and that the difference is that a Wiccan worships nature and a Witch practices magic.

Origins of Wicca are considered by many to be a form of Witchcraft, however. Gerald Gardner himself was one who associated the two together, through his own occult and spiritism practices. Witches and Wiccans have plenty of similarities. However, there are a lot of differences between them that is heavily dependent on what you choose to practice and how.

Bringing yourself forward into your work, you will know intuitively and instinctively what the differences might be for you and how you will choose to identify with your practice. If all you want to do is to party at the solstices and equinoxes, build an altar for the Sun God and the Moon Goddess and worship the divinity of nature, then you can call yourself a Wiccan. You can also call yourself a Wiccan who practices Witchcraft, enjoying all of the above-mentioned elements and incorporating spell work, and casting magic to manifest your life goals and purposes.

Magic, Rituals, Tools, and Preparations

There are so many different ways to celebrate Wicca and Witchcraft through various kinds of magic, rituals, and celebrations. The tools that you use and the way that you prepare for these experiences is a deeply personal form of art for each practitioner. From divination to charms, spells to constructing your own tools, the different forms of magical work you do will involve a variety of ingredients, set-ups, preparations, and actions. To give you an idea of some of these magical attributes, the following section is for you to get a grasp of what Wiccans might incorporate into their regular practices.

Candle Magic

An excellent place for a beginner to start casting and creating rituals, candle magic is a straightforward kind of spellcraft. It is effortless, simple, and elegant and requires a direct approach. These kinds of spells can really help you strengthen and build your confidence with performing magic.

The purpose of candle magic is to manifest the intention or magical request/ purpose. The flame of the candle is the medium, or conduit, of your plan and as the candle burns and slowly disappears, leaving the earth plane to become one with the spirit plane, it will carry with it your message of intention to make manifest in the energy of all life. This physical transformation is a creative tool to help a beginner visualize and witness the change from a candle to a manifestation through the burning of it on an altar.

Crystal Magic

Crystals are art forms in nature, minerals formed over time and possessing high energy and unique qualities and characteristics. Wiccans and Witches alike see these special tools as living objects that are a significant part of Earth's rhythms, and they are often used for healing, rebalancing, and magical intention and manifestation.

Crystals and gemstones are powerful conduits for energy and can be used often to help you manifest, celebrate, or perform rituals and devotions. The crystals that you use may be specific to particular spell work or rituals, or may simply be used as part of casting your circle of protection and calling on the elements.

Herbal Magic

This kind of magic is as ancient as agriculture and is often used not just for healing and health purposes, but also for incantations and empowering spells and rituals. A variety of herbs may be used throughout the year, and quite a few of them are already in your kitchen cabinet.

They are incredibly versatile and can be used in a great many ways. They can be used in Candle magic to anoint your candle before burning, inside of sachets and pillows as well as charms, you can use them to make your own incense and smudge sticks for burning in ritual or spell work, and you can also create tonics, elixirs and teas to ingest as part of your ritual celebrations. They are potent and powerful and have been around for as long as the Earth has helped them grow.

Incense Magic

You could consider incensing a simple tool for your rituals, but you can also perform magic with it. Incense comes from a long history of ritual across many cultures and continues to be utilized today as a great source of healing and purification. Swept through the air, it cleanses the area you are working in, helping to purify your space for magical intent.

It is often burned at the time of ritual or spell casting, and you could as ask it to be a part of your magical spell as the conduit for your intention and purpose. Most incense is made from a combination of herbs, spices, barks, and roots, and any of these herbs can be matched to whatever type of spell work or ritual you are doing.

Oil Magic

Magical oils are often used to enhance certain rituals and spells, and many Wiccans and Witches will make their own based on their specific needs. They are often used to consecrate or anoint other tools like charms, amulets, talismans, and candles. Depending on the spell you are casting, you might even use it on your own body, considering yourself the tool to be consecrated.

Essential oils are regularly used for their aromatic and healing, or magical properties and should be explored when working with magical oils.

An Overview of Rituals

Rituals are usually private, specific to a certain time of year or seasonal celebration, in devotion to a particular God or Goddess deity, or in celebration of a Sabbat or Esbat. Even when a ritual is practiced alone by a solitary practitioner, the energy and intention of creating ritual space around a particular cycle or event, adds to the collective power of everyone else celebrating the same thing over the same period of time; so even when you are practicing your rituals alone, you are adding to the collective consciousness of Earth Magic.

An essential ritual is a simple, elegant, and comforting experience that will incorporate many tools of magic, foods, herbs, beverages, candles, crystals, or other objects pertinent to the form of celebration. They can be very structured, organized, and elaborate, while other times they can be very easy going and intuitive at the moment.

As it is, a ritual will always be specific to what is being celebrated. However, there are elements to a typical ritual that appear across the board. Those standard elements are:

1. <u>Purification Process</u>- this first step is when you purify yourself and the space you are working in, to extinguish and remove any and all unwanted energies that might be present. This will usually involve smudging incense with sacred herbs. Sage, rosemary, and/or lavender are popular choices.

2. <u>Setting Up an Altar</u>- an altar can be permanently set up and redecorated over the course of the year for whatever Sabbat or Esbat you are celebrating. Your altar will contain your regularly used tools, as well as symbols, offerings, images of deities, and so on.

3. <u>Casting a Circle</u>- this is a step that opens up a circle of protection for you to safely enjoy your practice. It is a boundary between your sacred space and the mundane world around you, where you can openly connect to the divine energies.

   A circle will call in the Elements and the Cardinal directions. There are a variety of ways to physically mark a circle, including seas salt, crystals, tools from the altar, or other items; you can also just use visualization to see it as an orb of light around your workspace.

4. <u>Invocations</u>- invitations to the God/Goddess to join you in your ritual, you may use this time to speak more directly to the Elements, directions, and spirit for coming into your circle for your ritual.

5. <u>The Ritual Begins</u>- this stage is the ritual itself after all of the other preparation have been made. This is when you deliver your intention for the occasion and ritual (ex: the celebration of a Solstice, or asking for help manifesting abundance, etc.)

6. <u>Ritual Activities</u>- this stage of the ritual will include any specific actions you wish to carry out to honor, celebrate, invoke, or manifest your intentions.
   It depends on what kind of Wiccan you are but this part can include any, or all of the following possibilities: performance/drama, such as scenes from myths or folktales;

dancing; reading poetry or words from other texts pertaining to your purpose; chanting; singing; prayers; meditations; and so on.

7. The Offering- there may be a moment to offer food and drink to the gods/goddesses and to the self to partake of along with spirit. It is a symbolic gesture as well as a physical action to create an offering and an opening for your intentions to be fulfilled. It is a grounding act before closing the ritual.

8. Closing the Ritual- this stage is the time to offer gratitude to the deities called in and celebrated as well as an opportunity to prepare to return to life outside the circle.

These steps are just a typical outline and starting point to prepare you for what kinds of rituals you can create on your own, using a basic template. There are a variety of other tools that can be used in rituals, and you will learn more about them in *Chapter 7: Wiccan Tools.* All of the necessary magic, rituals, tools, and preparations are dependent upon what kind of magic you want to perform, what your solitary practice involves, and what types of tools and preparations you want to work with for your introduction to these practices.

The Balance Between Light and Dark

Throughout time and space, we have dealt with the concept of dueling forces of nature; however, from the perspective of a Wiccan point of view, they are never really dueling; they are always working together to achieve a greater balance in all things.

The balance between the light and the dark is a concept known throughout many religions, not just ancient and neo-Paganism, or Witchcraft. The properties of all matter in the universe straddle the concepts of 'without one, there is no other.' A perfect symbol of the attitude of balance between light and dark is the yin/yang symbol: two opposing forces, one white and one black, swirling in perfect unison and harmony. This symbol has been known as a part of the Wiccan culture and is also reflected in a variety of other beliefs and cultural identities.

Practicing Wicca or Witchcraft includes this understanding: you can't have one without the other, and as such, you must respect the balance of both and what each one will mean in your practice.

Let's look at the concept of the male and female energies in all things. In your reading so far, you have learned that a variety of celebrations and beliefs derive from an idea that there is a balance in all things, especially in the energies of the male God and female Goddess. All of the Sabbats and Esbats are celebrating this very concept: the balance of the light and the dark.

The light is masculine, Sun, action-oriented, visceral, stable, and potent. The dark is feminine, Moon, intuitive and emotional, mysterious, flowing, and connective. The two come together throughout the cycles of the year in a sacred union, each delivering their own potent energy that when brought together, creates the energetic balance required by nature.

In both Wicca and Witchcraft, there is the concept or practice of "white magic" and "black magic." Those without real understanding and knowledge of what Witchcraft will decide on the white equates with good, and the black equates with evil. This is not how white and black of magic work, and it is more often than not about the balance between the shadow and the light, and that one will not exist without the other.

Some Witches and Wiccans will alternate between the two, depending on the time of year or season, while others will devote their entire practice and ritual worship to embodying one side of it, performing either only to the light or only to the dark. This is not a bad thing, and all that matters is that the Wiccan or Witch in practice is honoring their deeper personal truths and harming none.

Some Witches have a gift for black magic, or shadow magic, while others are drawn to keeping in alignment with white, or light magic. Others will embrace both simultaneously to support another kind of balance. Any of these options is okay and is always the choice you have to make when you are honing in on your own magic and purpose.

Overall, you will decide what kind of Wiccan you are and how you want to practice these kinds of techniques on your own. There are so many different ways that you can be Wiccan, and for many, it will go hand in hand with working with magic and Witchcraft. Consider what you want from your practice and use the tools from what you have learned to develop your own unique craft.

Chapter 5: The Aspiring Wiccan

We are all looking for the right practice to support who we are and what we want to express through our own personal truth in this world. Wicca is a wonderful way for anyone interested in finding a group, coven, or just a personal expression of a deeper connection to the Earth and all of her beauty.

So much of what you have already learned in this book is a precursor to getting you started with creating and bonding to your own magical practice. You always have to start somewhere, and if you are an aspiring Wiccan, this book will give you all the basics you need to step more fully into living by these philosophies and practicing them in your everyday life.

When you are ready to choose a Wiccan approach to your spiritual journey, you will want to celebrate your opening to it through a form of initiation. After that, you will need to decide if a group or circle is more for you, or if you would like to support a more solitary practice. This book is geared more for the solitary practitioner and will give more insight into that reality as well as what some of the positive influences of Wicca can be for your life overall.

Initiation to Wicca

Newcomers to Wicca usually want to know if there is an initiation process, or if that is even necessary. What does it entail? Are there certain rituals to perform and is a requirement to consider yourself a truly Wiccan?

For anyone starting off on a spiritual journey, there will be a lot of questions to answer. Looking for answers within Wicca is a common way to start exploring the nature of what it involves and what it can mean to your life. You may not want to be initiated into it right away, doing more of quest or search to find what works best for you on your unique path. In several cases, people will adhere to many of the traditional beliefs while also exploring other attitudes and philosophies from other esoteric practices, not really fully embracing a totally Wiccan approach.

Somewhere on your path of discovery, you are likely going to find that you want to continue your practice and will feel called to perform some kind of ceremony to make a pact with your faith or practice. This is what is known as the initiation and how you approach that experience depends on a variety of factors, specifically whether or not you will belong to a coven or practice on your own.

A coven initiation is an elaborate process and may require a long period of preparation with the group itself, getting to know the members and practicing as an apprentice or initiate, before becoming a full coven member. This book focuses more on the solitary practitioner and so the initiation detained here will be about self-dedication.

The Solitary Initiate

For a solitary, or eclectic, as you will sometimes be called, the path into a Wiccan approach to life involves your own self-dedication. A ritual of this kind could have similarities to a typical coven ritual; however, it is essential that you create your own initiation based on your private unique practice.

Any self-dedication is a commitment to your craft, your inner-self, your magic, to the divine in the Universe, to the deities you will choose to worship, and anything else that feels appropriate to your initiation.

It must occur on your own terms and be designed through your dedication to yourself and spirit. Here are some basic guidelines to get you comfortable with self-dedication into Wicca:

Step 1: Spending Time with the Craft-

You will need to dedicate time to really exploring the elements, beliefs, and philosophies of Wicca before fully committing yourself to it. It might involve some research, practice with rituals, celebrating for a full year of Sabbats and Esbats and genuinely exploring all of the tools, herbs, concepts, and deities. This is a time of apprenticeship with Wicca, to give you a chance to decide if it is truly what you want to be celebrating and worshipping on your spiritual path.

Step 2: Planning Your Ritual of Initiation-

This is a critical moment and special occasion that should be carefully prepared for. For some, it might even feel like a rebirth into your true self or your new life, giving you the opening of a fresh start with abundant spirituality.

You may want to take a very structured approach to this ritual, and there are a variety of online resources that you can look at for ideas of what might be the best approach for you. You may want to follow an already established practice of Wicca, instead of forming your own, creative and eclectic version, in which case you will want to study the specific traditions of whatever Wicca practice you want to initiate yourself into and follow the specific instructions of that sect for your sacred ritual.

Eclectic Solitaries will most likely choose from a variety of sources to build their own magical ritual, or if you are really creative, you will invent it from your own knowledge and research, experience and exploration, of the Wiccan craft that you have undergone. If you are diligently studying all of the ins and out of Wicca for a while before your initiation, then you have already practiced a wide variety of rituals and spells and will likely have a good grasp on how you want to design your self-dedication.

Step 3: Commitment to Your Practice Through Sacred Ritual-

The ritual itself will be specific to you and will be an essential rite of passage in your journey. It will be a milestone and a turning point on your path, and you will need to be prepared for your whole life to shift to accommodate your new experience and dedication.

The ritual you choose to perform, either from trusted resources or teachers or of your own design, will begin your story as a Wiccan and will help you move forward to find an even deeper bond with your real power and magic.

At some point on your journey, you may want to rededicate yourself. You might choose to celebrate the original initiation date as an anniversary of your commitment to Wicca and can set up an annual ritual to honor that moment. You could also rededicate yourself every year to Wicca in order to feel a continued power and worship for your choice of self-dedication.

However, you choose to support your initiation, the ritual itself is a turning point in your life story and your quest for greater truth in celebration of the cycles and rhythms of all life.

Covens, Circles, and Solitary Eclectics

There are a ton of people practicing Wicca today, and they will either tell you that they are in a coven and circle or that they are solitary. So, what is the difference between all of these choices? This section will give a little more detail about some of the differences.

Covens

A traditional coven is typically comprised of 13 people who meet to secretly practice and worship according to their group's traditions. Early sects of Wicca had a High Priest and Priestess to represent the God and Goddess in their ceremonies and celebrations. Some covens are strictly devoted to the original Wicca formed by Gerald Gardner and prefer the traditional format, while other covens will adopt a more eclectic choice by developing their own rituals and processes.

Every new member will undergo a ritual of initiation, which will first have to spend a great deal of time studying the rituals and practices of the coven. Covens will often use degree systems to promote an initiate overtime through their devotion and study, as an achievement or advancement. Degrees start with the first degree and eventually go all the way up to the High Priest or Priestess, depending on the coven.

A coven will meet to celebrate Sabbats and Esbats, as well as to perform other rituals and practices. New coven members, before initiation, will be asked to spend a lot of time getting to know the group as many coven members will form very close bonds and connections and there needs to be a feeling of community between all members. The coven will usually decide together if a new initiate will be a good fit for their group.

Many people first starting out in Wicca take a solitary road before joining a coven. There will be plenty of time to explore on your own before dedicating yourself to a regular meeting group of Witches and Wiccans.

Circles

A circle is just a way of saying "community." Being in a coven might be too large a commitment, but you may still want to be involved in a community of other Wiccans to share experiences, tell stories, and celebrate Sabbats and other activities. It is a much more informal approach to connecting with other Wiccan practitioners that can give you a close circle of others like you. You may find that it is appreciated that you attend any Circle meetings and celebrations and make a commitment to being in that group, regardless if you are solitary, or in a coven.

Circles are loose and have a 'come and go as you please' attitude. You may find that it suits you for specific times and not others, and you will likely find a wide range of individuals at various levels of practice, so you may be able to gain some excellent knowledge through your bond and kinship with a circle.

Solitaries

When you can't find the right group, circle, or coven to meet your needs, it is alright to just appreciate Wicca on your own. Many Wiccans, in general, have their own personal relationship with the craft, even when they are in a coven and will likely still practice spells and rituals on their own time, outside of their group meetings.

It is a gratifying experience to do this work on your own and for many practicing Wiccans today getting started on their journeys, it is the best choice, as it will give you a lot of freedom to explore at your own pace, create your own plans and practices, use your own intuition and connection to the divine, and support your personal life as well as your commitment to the good of all life, through a personal and solitary devotion.

Eclectics

Eclectic Wicca is its own creative art form. A majority of Wiccans who are just learning are tempted to follow the rules and discover Wicca through the resources of all of the other traditions and practices, sometimes adhering to a more traditional practice and approach to stay in alignment with original work from the beginnings of Wicca.

These days, many people, especially solitary practitioners, are forming their own systems and creative rituals in order to bring forward an even broader range of concepts and ideas or to become more specific and pinpoint a practice that is written by their own Wiccan exploration and creative spiritual journey. It is up to you to decide what kind of worship is most suited to your style, personality, and desires.

Even though eclectic Wicca is more creatively free, it is still based on the philosophies, beliefs, and ideas of traditional Wiccan practice, as that is what really makes Wicca what it is.

For the Solitary Practitioner

There can be some obvious benefits to choosing a solitary practice to get started. Some of those benefits are:

Setting your Own Schedule

For many people, being able to set your own schedule is crucial. You can really work out a lot of opportunities with your magical practice when you don't have to organize a whole group to do it. In a lot of ways, Wiccans are all already celebrating certain times of the year and moon phases at the same moments, but if you are in your own practice, you can have a lot more control over the entire experience and the timing of all matters involved in your ritual.

Working at Your Own Pace

Being able to work at your own pace is an important part of any person's unique spiritual journey. If you are working with a group, you may be pushed farther than you are ready to be and will want more time to explore certain individual aspects of your practice. Not all groups will push or challenge enough either, and you may have an urgency to move forward more quickly.

When you are a solitary practitioner, you can set the pace for your study and growth, offering yourself the freedom to spend more time with certain practices, and less time with others.

Avoiding Uncomfortable Energies from Group, Circle and Coven Dynamics

Drama is inevitable in large groups. Even when all people involved are practicing similar beliefs, concepts, and ideals, there are always personalities to contend with and possible awkwardness and uncomfortable situations that can arise in a group dynamic. Not all groups will have these kinds of issues, and if you are choosing a Circle or a Coven, you will spend time with everyone in order to decide whether it is a good fit for you.

More often than not, those who are drawn to a solitary practice are looking for a different kind of energy and experience than what is offered in a larger group dynamic.

Eclectic and Artistic

In a solitary practice, there will often be fewer rules to follow that are often common among Covens or groups. You may want to have total authority and autonomy over your spiritual practice and will want to be able to explore a variety of options and avenue to support your craft.

Wicca is a creative journey, and the more you explore on your own, the more deeply you can embrace the artistic and eclectic qualities of bringing all you need into your craft. You may use a variety of sources to pull together a unique version of Wicca that is right for you, something you can usually only do if you are solitary.

Practical Tips for the Solitary Practitioner

Tip 1: Daily Routine

Working on your own and making your own schedule means creating time to practice. If you are working on your own, you are responsible for the energy you are putting into your daily routine and magic work. It can be anything, like reading about certain parts of the craft, studying herbs and their uses, cleaning and organizing your altar, simple daily meditation or ritual. All of these things are just possibilities to what will be in a daily routine you can create for your solitary work.

Tip 2: Write It Down

Keeping a journal such as a Book of Shadows, or even just a set of notes, is an incredibly useful tool while you build your practice. Keeping a diary of your progress will help you see what you have already done, how to improve upon it, what works, and what doesn't, it keeps track of everything you have already accomplished. It is also something you can return to later to repeat a process or a spell. It helps set the foundation and framework of your personal practice in writing so that it can grow with you.

You can have a record of how your craft evolves and make necessary notations and changes as little or as often as you like.

Tip 3: Meet Other Wiccans and Witches

Being alone is great when it's how you feel best in your practice, but at some point, you are going to need some solidarity. There are plenty of other solitary practitioners or even people who aren't Wiccans but explore all kinds of Pagan philosophies and esoteric religions. Having a community of like-minded people is a great resource and will help you stay excited about your own personal work. If you can't find anyone else in your local community, try finding some online groups that you can participate in from anywhere, just to give yourself the support and balance that comes from a group.

Tip 4: Always Ask Questions

There is a lot of information out there in the world, and when you are looking for clues or answers to your study of Wicca, be sure to ask plenty of questions to support your path. Many people will boast about only one way of doing things or will try to guide your mysterious journey through a prediction of how things will or should always unfold with a magical practice. Trust yourself to find your own answers by continually asking questions. The more you ask, the more secure you will feel in your own work as it develops over time.

Tip 5: Never Stop Learning

There truly is no endpoint to what you can discover. All of your research in Wicca won't stop with this book. There are so many pathways to explore and so many different modalities for making magic and Wicca work for you. Anytime you find information, online or in a book, it will usually lead you to other information that you can delve more deeply into. You will find a cornucopia of information out there to peruse and dig into, and it is vital that you can continue to teach yourself new information as you practice.

The Positive Influence of Wicca

What does Wicca do for you? What can it offer you that other practices cannot? Asking a question of this caliber begs another question: will Wicca be a positive influence on my life? The answer to that question is a resounding yes! Wicca may be a somewhat recent branch of more ancient Pagan traditions and ways, but it has also established a way for people who appreciate this kind of magic to practice it.

Wicca is a way for someone to truly connect to their personal power, innate wisdom, intuition, spirituality as well as nature an all of her bounty. The influences of Wicca are plentiful and varied, and you might say that its deepest resource is a connection to all of the living things in this world. When you are in alignment with the powerful forces of nature, you are guided to live a life of compassion and honesty, with yourself and others.

Wicca opens your heart to an approach to life that requires an ethical vision toward all beings, as well as the whole Earth and everything outside of it. To practice Wicca is to become connected to all things, and that is a huge benefit and positive influence on the overall joy you will experience in your life.

Have you ever just laid down under a starry night sky, looking at the moon and listening to the trees sway in the wind, or the waters of the stream babble by? What does it feel like for you when you sink your toes into the muddy Earth and squish your feet around? Do you take pleasure in a hot, salty bath by candlelight and soak in the aromas of flower petals during a rainstorm?

Anyone can do any of these things and not practice Wicca, but usually, if you are a practicing Wiccan, then you take greater pleasure in these moments. It helps you to spend more time appreciating the simple pleasures and the beauty of all things, which ultimately leads to a deeper and more divine connection with yourself.

The real magic of Wicca is that it balances your life in a significant way. When you are devoting time to celebrating the seasons and the cycles of the moon and sun, you are in great reverence to your own life as well, appreciating every moment and every day as though it is as sacred as the God and Goddess.

These are only some of the positive influences of Wicca, and as you work more in your own practice, growing your confidence with all of your work, you will start to feel those abundances spring up, like a well of fresh water after a gorgeous rain, from which you can eternally drink.

Wicca will always support you and keep you close to your intuition, your wisdom, and your journey through the earth plane as you connect to spirit in all things.

Black Magic

Black Magic doesn't get positive reviews, online and throughout history. The color black seems to have a negative connotation to it, and in comparison to White Magic, it sounds so much more sinister. Some say it is potent, while others call it 'evil,' but if you are a real Wiccan, then you agree to harm no one, so where is the logic in a magic that would do so? As you have already read in "The Balance Between Light and Dark" in chapter 4, there is nothing really sinister about black magic at all, and it has a negative reputation that has grown over time but is a gross miscalculation.

Black Magic in History

According to history and the Christian church, any non-Christian religion was considered "black magic." Anyone who was a healer, a seer, soothsayer, and the like, was considered guilty of causing harm through the use of black magic, spells, hexes, and other "evil forces."

People accused of Witchcraft and practicing black magic were often blamed for things that had happened and occurred naturally, such as an outbreak of smallpox or a herd of dead livestock who were likely poisoned by toxic water.

It was also sometimes reported that a person who might feel like that they were hexed or cursed, would seek the assistance of a "white Witch" to counteract the spell or enchantment. This idea suggests that even then, people saw a contrast between what was considered 'good' magic and what was considered 'bad.'

All of the histories of Witchcraft shows an overall obsession with the idea that women or men who had discovered a powerful path outside of Christian faith, or who were already practicing it from their heritage and ancestry, were deemed Witches and guilty of black magic and anything or everything terrible that happened in the village.

Fast forward to modern times, and we have all, for the most part, recognized that all of that heresy against the church was a deliberate method to accuse people of choosing alternative faith. Most Witches were herbal healers and midwives who toiled to save lives.

Learning what you have about Wicca, you have recognized the great balance in all things and that everything in nature is a combination of light and dark forces that requires excellent balance.

It's All Magic and Intention

There are Wiccans and Witches who will want to form a distinction between whether they are a White or a Black Witches. Others will say that there is no difference at all and that the two work in tandem to offer a great balance. With any kind of magic, it is always about your intentions, and so with black magic, your intentions may be the following:

- Power
- Protection
- Crone Phase
- Banishing negativity
- Reversing hexes
- Resilience
- Self-control
- Inner strength
- Healing from grief and loss

These are some of the things that the color black represents in Wicca. If your intentions to harm one are present in your practice and you are using "black magic," then you are merely calling upon the forces of the darker elements in all life and working with them to help you with your magical purposes.

Black magic is nothing more than a use of the divine force in the shadows of our reality. You could also view it as the deeper mysteries of the feminine form. The Crone is a part of this color, and so you can use this color of magic to help you understand the secrets of this phase in life.

Be wary of labels and ask more questions. Black magic is safe and is only about how your practice setting your intentions in magic, just like with any other color you are using.

The next chapter will offer some more insight and guidance about a very important about your start to Wicca and performing your own rituals and spells. You have all you need in just one book, and in Wicca, it is known as The Book of Shadows.

Chapter 6: Book of Shadows

Within the Wicca world, there are a variety of groups practicing, as well as several thousand solitary practitioners, all of whom need their recipe for ritual. Since not every single Wiccan or Witch has the exact same practice, there is a need to set some definition to what your magic looks like and how you like to celebrate it. For some other religious traditions, there are doctrines, one of the most famous being the Bible, a book that all practicing Christians will regularly read.

Unlike Christianity, Wicca does not have one specific book that determines the practice. There is, however, one specific kind of book that is a universally accepted tool in the Wiccan arts. The Book of Shadows is one of the main components of practicing this beautiful craft, and this chapter will shed some light on the Book of Shadows for you.

What Is It and Why Is It A Must-Have for a Wiccan?

The Book of Shadows was the name given originally by Gerald Gardner to the book that contains all of the traditions, ethics, philosophy, ritual texts, spells, and necessary information to practice Wicca. A Book of Shadows is akin to a personal diary or journal of magic, containing within it the more specific choices of each individual or coven practice.

In a coven, it is the sacred text for all members and will traditionally be copied by hand by each new initiate and will serve as the reference for all Wiccan and coven matters henceforth. For a solitary practitioner, the Book of Shadows is a more personal creation that you form on your own as you explore your craft and induction into the Wiccan arts.

Several different versions of a Book of Shadows have been published and are available for purchase online and in book stores, and many of them are consistent with the more traditional forms of Wicca.

A Book of Shadows is an invaluable tool in your practice. As you read earlier in the book, it is an amazing way to document your journey and witness your own progress with your work. A Book of Shadows is a method for organizing all of your rituals, spells, ideas, and beliefs so that you can have an easy reference for repeating spells and rituals and adding to them more and more as you grow.

Many Wiccans will start with the one that they acquire from a bookseller, which is an easy way to get started and help you find what practices you most want in your own Book. Others will start from scratch and simply write out their own creative spell and ritual ideas from an intuitive standpoint.

However, you choose to approach it, your book of spells is an ingredient that you must consider in your practice. Having your own personal reference guide for your practices will keep you closely connected to your worship and progress throughout life. These books are even something that can be handed down to another generation and are considered priceless family heirlooms of magic.

Your Book of Shadows is the only book you will really need, once you feel confident in your practice. It can start simply and can be built from a variety of different sources to help you get started.

Symbols, Signs, Runes, and Rituals

Within your Book of Shadows, you will have a reference of several different signs and symbols that are intended for use in spellcraft and rituals to help enhance and cultivate energy. The symbols and signs themselves are just tools and will vary depending on your practices.

All of the symbols listed here are just some of the possibilities. Additionally, Runes were a common tool to help receive guidance and were tossed out to land with specific information for the reader. A brief introduction of runes will help you get started with digging more deeply into their meanings and possibilities in your work.

Any of these signs and symbols can find their way into your rituals as you achieve a stronger connection to the best ways to honor and worship the Wiccan experience.

Ankh

From ancient Egypt, the ankh has stood the test of time as a symbol of eternal life. It has been considered 'the key to life' and even bears a resemblance to a key. The shape of the ankh has been thought to represent the male and female energy connected to the Sun. The curve at the top is the Sun while the long bar coming down is the feminine energy and the bar crossing that line is the male energy.

It has been incorporated into some Wiccan practices, especially those who celebrate Isis, the Egyptian Goddess, and is considered a symbol of protection and everlasting life. Others will use it to ward off evil.

Hecate's Wheel

This symbol represents a labyrinth within a circle and is named Hecate's Wheel because she was often seen connected to a maze, being known as the guardian of the crossroads, later evolving into the goddess of magic and sorcery. Hecate's Wheel has also been connected to the Triple Goddess and, in a few feminist traditions and practices, is heavily used for that reason.

When using this symbol, you will likely be calling in the power of the Maiden, Mother, and Crone, as well as honoring the time of year of Hecate (October 31st- Yule). You may also be honoring the symbol of the maze and the concept of the labyrinth we all must walk in life, to find the center and our true vision. Hecate's Wheel is a symbol of journeying and also of the wisdom of the Goddess.

The Horned God

You have already read about the presence of the Horned God in Wicca and that he represents the divine masculine energy present in all nature and life forces. The symbol itself is just a circle, or head shape, with horns, and is usually brought into rituals that are intending to honor the masculine energies. The symbol can add some power to your celebrations, calling in the strength of the Horned God and placing it on the altar or adding it to your spells and rituals.

Alternatively, in some more Goddess based Wiccan practices, the Horned God symbol has been used to celebrate a feminine sign, that is the 'Horn Moon' or blessing moon and will be utilized to celebrate lunar goddesses.

The Pentagram

The pentagram is a five-pointed star contained within a circle. Each point represents the classical elements, Earth, Air, Fire, Water, and Spirit. It is one of the best-known symbols of Wicca and is widely used as a symbol of protection and Earth when called a pentacle. The difference between a pentagram and a pentacle is that a pentacle is just a disc shape with a symbol carved into it or drawn. It could be another symbol, other than a pentagram. However, many people will call a pentagram a pentacle in general, as it is the most common.

It will often be traced in the air during rituals and incantations. It has also been called the 'Star of Wisdom' and the 'apple-star,' as when you cut an apple across instead of down and find a five-pointed star.

The Solar Cross

The basic solar cross is a circle with four lines in it, almost like a compass. It represents both the Sun and also the four seasons, as well as the four classical elements. You could also point out that its compass-like picture honors the cardinal directions as well. It can often be seen as an astrological symbol of Earth when portrayed with the other four three elements.

Despite being sometimes associated with earth energy, as a symbol of the sun, it is also connected to the element of fire. When you are casting circles or celebrating rituals in honor of fire, heat, sun, and power, you can work this symbol into your rituals. It is a symbol of masculine energy and purification. Some will use it in rituals for casting away the old and rebirthing the new (Litha and Yule).

Triple Goddess Symbol

This symbol represents the three phases of the moon and therefore the Triple Goddess. The center of the symbol is a full, round circle, flanked by crescent moons on either side, representing Maiden and Crone. This symbol is often present in Wiccan worship, and as the image suggests, it is about the phases of life and cycles of times through the power of the moon and the Goddess: waxing phase- rejuvenation, new life, beginnings; full phase- most potent and powerful time of magic; waning phase- sending things away, banishing. This symbol will always connect to the energies of the moon and the Triple Goddess and can be used in a variety of rituals and spells.

Runes

In addition to the standard symbols and signs that can be applied to the rituals you perform, there are also sacred alphabets that contain a whole group of symbols with various meanings. Runes are an ancient alphabet that has been used for centuries in Pagan worship and are considered tools of magic and divination.

When working with Runes, you simply ask a specific question and allow the symbols of the runes to give you an answer. There are several different symbols, one marked on each individual stone, or piece of wood. Some people even used animal bones to inscribe the rune symbols on.

Using the Runes: A Meditation for Your Book of Shadows

Rune stones are not useful for predicting the future. The function is more like a type of guidance to help you on your path. It is a tool, like the Tarot, to help you work on the mental aspects of your journey and help to bring to light some of the more profound unanswered questions.

A rune stone reading will usually involve calling on a spirit guide to help you and guide you in your quest for answers, as well as thanking them after they have aided you.

Here is how to perform this simple reading:

1. Put all of your rune stones in a bag.
2. Meditate and clear your mind.
3. Focus on a specific question
4. Hold your rune bag in your more magical, or receptive, hand.
5. Then, hold the bag and reach the fingers of your receptive hand into the bag, stirring them with your question in mind.
6. Ask your question, aloud or in your mind, and as you stir with your fingers, select one stone.
7. Read the symbol on the stone to answer your question.
8. If you need more clarification about what you have pulled, ask for more clarification and pull another stone from the bag to help you hone in on the deeper meaning.
9. Repeat as necessary with other questions.

Runes are an excellent tool for your Book of Shadows. You don't have to have the physical runes; you can simply use the symbols that can be carved into candles or drawn in the air during a ritual. The Runic Alphabet is its own language, and as you study Wicca, you may want to examine a more in-depth view of runes and how to enjoy them in your practice.

For a simple list of names and meanings of the Futhark Alphabet of Runes, see the Table of Correspondence at the end of the book.

Short Introduction to Spells and Magic

Your Book of Shadows, if nothing else, is a book of spells and rituals. When you are creating your own Book, you will fill its pages with a wide assortment of various rituals and incantations to help you manifest the energy you require within the balance of the energy of all things. So then, what exactly is a magic spell?

A magic spell is a simple or elaborate ritual carried out to elicit the desired change in your life. A typical spell will include some or all of the following: candles, herbs, charms, amulets, visualization, incantation, poetry, song, incense, magical tools and objects, and any other form of magic you choose to include.

They are a creative and beautiful way to communicate with spirit and influence that spiritual energy all around you. It is an act of manifestation, gratitude, prayer, and devotion to a personal or worldly cause. When we are affecting the energy of the spiritual plane with our spells and rituals, we are thusly bringing its impact into the physical plane.

Not all Wiccans practice magic, and so if you are deciding to center your practice on devotions to cycles, seasons, celebrations, and particular deities, without practicing any magic, you may not need to read about spells. It can be useful, however, to have a basic understanding of what spells are anyway, no matter how you choose to practice your craft.

How does a magic spell work exactly? Magic, for all intents and purposes, is very simply a concentration and channeling of energy. This channeling has the effect of moving and manipulating larger currents in any area in which you wish to see a change in your life, or in the world of energy. Any person can perform magic, and it is all just a matter of practicing your skills of focus, intention, and concentration. Being able to approach magic spells from your higher wisdom, specific needs, clear communication with spirit, and power of ethic and belief in the Wiccan Rede, will help you to practice successful spellcraft.

For many Solitary practitioners, you will approach spell casting from your own unique point of view, although you may start by finding any number of spells from the internet and other books.

For the Solitary building their Book of Shadows and wanting to explore the creative art of writing your own magic spells, here is a simple list of guidelines to help you get started with writing your own spells:

Creating Your Own Magic Spell

What is Your Intention and Magical Purpose?

The very first and most crucial step to creating a spell is deciding what the purpose of it is. Your spell's intention is what will help you achieve manifestation and practice successful magic. It will also determine how you will structure your spell and eventually write it out in your Book of Shadows.

Ask yourself some questions about your intentions: what do I want to achieve? What kind of magic am I looking to manifest? Is about love, money, health? There are several specific possibilities, while at other times, it might be an overall idea and concept. The best bet when determining your purpose for magic is to keep it simple and clear. If you want your spell to work well, then you need to be very aware of what you are trying to magically manifest.

Once you are clear about your intentions, then you can build your spell around your purpose. It is always the first step and should be carefully considered when preparing to cast a spell.

What Does This Spell Need to Work?

Some spells don't need much, while others will need a lot of special tools and objects in order to work the magic more effectively. It really all depends on what kind of practice you want to have, and what kind of tools you prefer to use. In general, you will always need a little something to call in the directions.

Lighting a candle, burning some incense, honoring the earth with a stone or some soil, a dish of water on the altar; all of these tools are commonplace and can have an added impact on your spell work when you set the stage well for your focused intentions.

Many spells will incorporate an elegant experience with other tools, whose energies represent the very thing you are working to manifest. Every color, herb, incense, aroma, and the object will have magical energy and meaning, and so with your intention and purpose decided, you will now determine what kind of tools will help your spell enhance.

If you have ever followed a cooking recipe, you will have noticed the list of ingredients followed by the preparation instructions. A spell has similar qualities, and as you write your spells out in your Book of Shadows, it may start to take on the appearance of a magical cookbook. Some of your ingredients might be:

- Candles
- Incense and smudge sticks
- Various Herbs
- Nature treasures
- Crystals and stones
- Magically charged and consecrated mixing bowls, spoons, etc.
- Special cloths or clothing

Not every spell will use the same instruments and ingredients, and this will be something creative and fun for you to play around with and enjoy.

When Is the Best Time to Cast a Magic Spell?

Timing is essential when it comes to casting a spell. It should not be done in a hurry, right before you are heading off to work unless you have planned in advance to do it that way. All spells require specific energies and focus and the time of day; you do it can matter just as much as what moon cycle you are in when you cast. Your spell might need night time energy, while another will need the full Sun of day.

Some Wiccans will use the power of the moon cycles, or seasonal cycles to cast their magic, while others find valuable times of day to do their magic work. Typically, you will probably find that you will have greater success and manifestation results when you are using the powers that be within the cycles of the Earth, Moon, and Sun.

Whatever time you are choosing to cast your spell, it will have an impact on the overall outcome and nature of your goal. The timing should be chosen based on what your intentions are. The crescent waxing moon in the Maiden form is about new beginnings and growth. This might be a perfect time to cast a love spell or a financial prosperity spell. From the full moon to a waxing crescent Crone moon, you may be wanting to banish or release something and can use the energy of that moon to help you empower your spell.

These timing specifics will be a part of the recipe you include in your Book of Shadows, and so you may need to play around with the timing of something in order to determine the best moment s for casting a particular spell. The great thing about a Book of Shadows is that it is a living project, meaning that it will change over time.

If the timing of a specific spell doesn't manifest as quickly or easily, you can go back and make some adjustments and try again, noting your progress in your book, until you hone in on the perfect timing for your magic manifestation.

What Words Should I Use to Bring the Spell to Life?

Words are significant, and they carry a lot of meaning. They constitute a considerable part of what takes your intentions and purposes into the energy of the Universe and all things to be received and heard, to help make them manifest. You want to be sure when writing or even practicing another Witch's spells that you are speaking the right words for the spell.

Getting started with spells, you may end up utilizing already existing spells from the great variety available online and in other sources, but if you are a solitary practitioner, you may decide to start coming up with your own poetic way of conjuring and manifesting. The right words to communicate your goal will make all the difference.

The lesson for a lot of Wiccans and Witches is that the universe can be receptive and takes things literally, or with a sense of humor, so whatever your words are, the Universe will deliver what is wished for, based on what you say. An old saying of "be careful what you wish for" is prominent in Wicca and in spell work. Whatever you wish for will come back to you, so be sure it is worded in the way that you want it to come to you.

How Do I plan and Organize a Spell?

After determining what you will need, taken from the first four key points listed above, you can take the time to really design and organize what you will be working with. If you are choosing a spell that has already been written in another published Book of Shadows, then you will be able to see exactly what this kind of organization will look like.

In most cases, it is a lot like a cooking recipe that you would find in an ordinary cookbook.

As the architect of your spell, you will have the power to decide what steps will work the best and in what order. You may reference other spells in the beginning, but as you become more confident in your craft, you will intuitively know precisely what direction to take in the construction of your spell.

This will include how to prepare your herbs, how many candles, and what symbols you want to carve into them, or what type of oil to anoint them with. You will decide on your words and incantations and at what point they will be needed to be stated in the process, for example, before or after the lighting of a candle, etc... You may want to include certain foods and beverages and will have to determine at what point those will be offered to the altar and/or consumed in your spell.

The craft of spellcasting includes the dynamic art of putting it together, like putting paint on a canvas. Designing your recipe will come with practice, and every spell you borrow or create will be added to your book of shadows to help you stay focused with your practice.

How Often Should I Use a Spell?

After you have started to build your Book of Shadows and are performing spells from your book, you may wonder about when and how often to use your spells. It will always depend on the type of spell, the intention behind it, and why it would be relevant to your life right now.

Take a love spell as an example. Love spells take a variety of forms and so in your Book you will have maybe five different love spells, one for every kind of love, or how to attract it or banish it. If you are working a love spell to call true love into your life and you perform it once under specific conditions, you may find that nothing has occurred yet and that you will want to perform the spell again. A general rule of thumb for repeating spells is that you can wait until the next moon cycle, or wait a full month before attempting it again.

Your spell will have a specific idea of when to perform a spell anyway, so if your love spell needs to occur on the New Moon, you will have to wait anyway for it to come back around.

Manifestation takes time, and so as with most things in life, patience and focus are required. If your spell isn't producing any results, try restructuring the spell and performing it at a different part of the moon cycle. Use your intuition to guide you.

It is exciting to make regular use of your spells, and it will be good practice to use your intuition to help you in the matters of how often to use certain ones. Asking for guidance from spirit can help you make those determinations as well.

There are so many spells out there to use, and you will want to explore a wide variety of them, instead of returning to the same ones over and over. Have fun trying new things, and if you are drawn to a particular spell over and over, it is likely a sign that you need to keep casting it. Trust your intuition.

Magic is "The Law of Attraction" in Spells

This term has become popular in today's culture. People of all backgrounds and life practices share a common desire: to manifest abundance, happiness, and prosperity in your life. There are a lot of perspectives and ideas about what the Law of Attraction is and how it works both in spiritual and esoteric communities, as well as the scientific communities.

It is really just a law of energy that states that 'like attracts like' and so when you are Wiccan and practicing spell work, you are practicing the Law of Attraction. It is essentially magic.

What is it and How Does it Work?

The idea of "like attracts like" could also be stated as "thoughts become things." The Law of Attraction is an umbrella term to explain the way that anything you think, feel, believe, and pronounce, has the energetic capacity and probability of becoming real in the physical. Everything is energy, and we have a vibrational frequency of energy; everything does. These frequencies are bumping into each other, touching, rejecting, and moving away from each other, and bonding.

As an energy yourself, your thoughts and feelings become the energy that promotes your life experience. An example of this would be: waking up I the wrong side of the bed after a bad dream and deciding that the rest of the day is going to go terribly. You always have the power to change that perspective, but when you decide that something is going to be a certain way, it is that way. This goes hand-in-hand with magic and what you cast becomes what your intention of manifestation are.

Basically, the Law of Attraction determines what will come into your life through intentions, thoughts, beliefs, and feelings. This can be very uncomfortable for some people to grasp because it assumes that you have total power to manifest the life that you want, instead of the one you don't. There are always unforeseen circumstances out of our control, but with the Law of Attraction, you can have greater control of the outcomes in your physical reality. The point of exploring this concept is to understand what kind of energy to bring into your spells. Your spell work is exactly this: thoughts become things. When you cast a magic spell, you are practicing the Law of Attraction. If you are using your focus to elaborately explain your focus and intentions, you will have greater success in manifesting what you want, and when you want it because your energy is in alignment with that outcome.

Manifesting Attraction and Magic

With the Law of Attraction as a concept of magic, you can now put into effect the way to make it work for you through your spells. There are three main components that can help with manifestation and magic, and they are:

Affirmation- your affirmation is what you speak to conjure your magical purpose. It is the poetry that brings your intention to life, and the clearer and more specific your words, the more abundant the return.

Affirmations can also be repeated throughout the timing of a spell. While you are waiting for your intention to manifest, you can use the words you cast as a reflection and a reminder to yourself about what it is you are trying to "magic into being."

Visualization- Using your creative imagination to spark the reality into focus is a huge help. Your ideas as pictures in your mind help you to truly see an outcome and will bring that outcome into the foreground of your experience.

Visualization is most often practiced with eyes shut, and can also be done with eyes open. It is the act of looking at what you want with your mind's eye. Truly seeing what you want instead of just saying what it is, brings even more possibility and enhancement to your goal.

Appreciation- Giving thanks to what is surrounding you and guiding you as you work, your magic is also a powerful tool to manifestation. In Wicca and Witchcraft, you are usually calling upon the directions and elements, as well as spirit.

Offering appreciation to these energies is what creates a balance and energetic opening and opportunity for you to realize your magical manifestation. The appreciation and gratitude provided is also a way to help shift your energy to be more available to what will come back to you in your life.

In short, magic is defined as bringing about the desired effect through focused intention. Magic is, in essence, The Law of Attraction. There are, of course, many layers to it, and when you are working within the framework of a specific practice, like Wicca, there are many more components to consider.

Spells and magic are what your Book of Shadows can become as you practice. Finding the right wording, tools, energies, and organization will be part of the joy and beauty of constructing your own Book of shadows and developing your spells and magic practice. All of your time and energy you will spend on creating your unique Book will become part of the magic with the Wiccan practice you are devoting yourself to. Building a Book of Shadows is part of casting magic, so have fun and get creative with it!

Chapter 7: Wiccan Tools

One of the most exciting parts of Wicca and working on your practice is utilizing your tools of devotion and worship. Whenever you use your special implements, whether it is for celebrating a Solstice or casting a spell, you feel an even closer connection to the divine and your own personal magic and love for your spirit.

Your tools can be varied and elaborate or as simple as you want them to be. As you continue developing your practice, your tools may change over time, and you may incorporate new ones to help you advance your magical intentions.

This chapter will give you some insight into the tools of practice, as well as the altar spaces you can use to bring these objects to life.

The Altar: Personal, Ritual, Working

What exactly is an altar? Altars are spaces of devotion. They can be organized to reflect a specific inspiration, deity, workspace of magic, or ever-changing and fluctuating celebration of the seasons and cycles.

Altars have been utilized all over the world throughout history and are still incredibly useful and used in a wide range of religions and cultural communities.

The altar that you choose is a physical reflection of your internal spiritual devotion, and it will be something that has a life of its own transforming with you and with the cycles you are going through, as well as the cycles and seasons of the Earth.

There are several ways to decorate your altar, and your specific needs will be a mark of what you are trying to work on in your practice. You can say that the altar is the centerpiece of your practice and so it will need to be somewhere where you can see it and be present with it regularly.

There are a few different kinds of altars, and depending on your needs, you may choose to have one of these in your home, or all three. Altars can be built to last for a short period of time, as in for a particular holiday, festival or celebration. They can also be built to last as a permanent fixture and will reflect certain aspects of your spiritual identity and your ritual practices.

Personal Altar

A personal altar is precisely what it says it is: devoted to you and your own beliefs and goals or spiritual preferences. A personal altar can take many forms and be decorated in a variety of ways. Some will choose certain types of incense, candle colors, aromas, and objects to display, that are significant and unique to them. Many will use a personal altar to honor their ancestors with photographs or paintings.

Personal altars can be built in your bedroom, living room, or anywhere else in the house that feels right for you. It has to be somewhere where you can see it and interact with it. The very nature of an altar is to call attention to the energies you want to display and promote in your life, and so they need to be available for you to spend time with and regard. It will usually stay set up and in one place for a long time and will only change as you do.

For your personal altar, you don't have to make it about Wicca, or any deities, unless you are called to do so. If you are identifying as a Wiccan or a Witch, showing that in some way on your altar may be an empowering experience and will be a daily reminder to you of what you have committed yourself to on your spiritual path.

Ritual Altar

A ritual altar is something that can come and go based on your ritual practices. It is used for the purpose of aligning you with your magical purposes, such as performing spells or honoring deities. You can do these things in front of your personal altar, but you may want to have a separate altar for specific ritual needs.

For this reason, you can make them a little more flexible, moveable, and changeable, and you can build them inside or outside, depending on what the ritual calls for. You will usually need some kind of surface, table top, counter top, or other, in order to have a place to lay out your tools, offerings, and magical ritual gifts.

For some, the ritual altar is another mainstay and will need to have a fixed and regular space in the home. It can be a prominently displayed, or private affair and will serve as offering space to the various Sabbats and Esbats. This can be an empowering way to incorporate your ritual practices into your life and your home and always having some kind of display honoring a season or cycle will keep you in a greater balance with nature.

The ritual altar should also be in a place where you feel comfortable performing a ritual. If you aren't willing to do that in the living room in front of your family, you may need to have it secured in a more personal location. The purpose of having a ritual altar is that you have a place to hold your tools for your casting of magic, as well as a place to perform the rites of each spell or process. You can achieve this same goal on a personal altar; however, you may want to have a separate space to do these kinds of tasks, keeping your own altar set up for another, more individual purpose.

A ritual altar might be needed to perform incantations and spells on behalf of another or the entire community. That is something you may not want to tie into your personal magic space. Furthermore, your ritual altar can act as a constant display or reminder of the current Esbat and Sabbat, which will have its own unique devotion and energy requirement, separate from another altar space.

Again, in your practice, you may choose to keep only one altar, and that is absolutely okay. All you have to do is set the right intention for the work you are doing with it. Ritual altars are present, whether built for the purpose of the ritual, or a permanent fixture that rotates seasonally, to help you create a space of devotion for your creative Wiccan work. They are the perfect place to keep your tools and implements for ritual purposes.

Working Altar

A working altar is something that can offer you a space to do the work prior to the ritual. If you have ever spent a lot of time in your kitchen, cutting up vegetables, pouring over recipes, and getting all of the ingredients put together to make a proper meal, then you can get a picture of what a working altar might look like.

When you are making preparations for your spells and rituals, you will need a sacred space to do your work. All materials need to be purified and charged with powerful intention, and all of your tools can be present to help you make the most of the workspace altar. It is the place where you may choose to store all of your ingredients like herbs, candles, various incenses, essential oils, and other items wanted for a particular ritual or spell.

Having a workspace altar is similar to the altar you would use for the actual ritual. It is still a sacred space and will need to be cleansed before and after use to make sure all of the energy you are using is pure.

Here, within the balance of energy, you can prepare the materials and tools you will need to perform rituals or to add consecrated objects to your personal altar. Your mixing bowls, spoons, and other tools of the working altar will help you keep everything you need for magical purposes in one location.

Think of it like your spell crafting workbench. Before you perform any ritual, you may need to mix your herbs, or anoint your candles; you may need to charge some stones and crystals and give magic to your ritual tools.

A working altar is a space to help you prepare the ingredients for the bigger ritual to come. You only need a little bit of space for this, and a kitchen countertop will work just fine. The point is that you make it sacred before using it or find a space in your kitchen where you can set up a permanent magical work altar so that you can have access whenever you need.

All-in-One Altar

If you are limited on space, you can combine all three altars to perform each set of ritual magic. There isn't a rule about how your altar looks or what you put on it. It is an original part of your practice that will transform and alter over time with everything that you do.

When you only have so much space to use, you may need to do all of your magical work in one altar space. Your altar will work as your personal devotion, your ritual devotion, and your sacred work to prepare for the bigger castings and magic moments.

There are always ways to support the experience in one magical spot, and your altar only needs to be a reflection of what matters to you in your practice of Wicca and Witchcraft.

The Set of Tools for the Altar

Your altar is your space for your magical tools. It is the best place to store all of the unique implements that you will use in your rituals and devotions. There are some tools that are more commonly used in Wicca than others, and this section will give brief descriptions of what those tools are and how they are used in your practice.

Pentacles

Pentacles are considered a tool of consecration (the act of imbuing with sacred intention). It is usually a round, disk shape and has some kind of magical symbol drawn or carved into it. The pentagram is the most common symbol, as you read about in the last chapter, and is the five-pointed star.

Any pentacle tends to be affiliated with the Earth element in rituals and will sometimes be placed in the North quadrant of the circle you are casting to pin down your cardinal direction and element.

Consecration is the primary use of this tool. As such, it has the power to bless certain items with magical energy and can also enhance or energize whatever tools or object you are trying to consecrate. This process will usually involve laying the object down on top of the pentacle while you allow your intentions to assist in consecrating it.

Symbols on your pentacle will vary and will be specific to your choice of practice and devotion.

Chalices

A chalice is a cup, goblet, or vessel used to represent the feminine energies, the West, and the element of Water. Wiccans do not always consider this a tool of ritual or spell work, and see it as more of a symbol of the Goddess; however, many will work it into their toolbox, depending on what kind of rituals are being performed.

It is a symbol of the womb and can either be full or empty as it sits on your altar. A full chalice might indicate that you are already full of life or that you are making an offering of some kind to the god/goddess. An empty chalice can work as an indication of being open to receiving and will allow the cup to be filled with whatever you are attempting to manifest.

Swords

In Wicca, a ritual blade or sword is often called the athame and is a ritual tool for metaphorically cutting energies or directing them, controlling spirits, and other uses. It also serves as a representation of the Fire element and the masculine form of the god. It has also been associated with Air in some practices.

It is usually black-handled with some kind of symbol(s) inscribed in the handle.

Wands

Like the sword, the element of the Wand has been known interchangeably between Air and Fire. Usually, it is associated with Air, according to Gardnerian Wicca. It is constructed of either, rock, wood or metal, and has also been made from crystal or gemstone.

The wand is another sacred tool of Wicca to help direct and manifest energies. It has a great connection to the spirit plane and can help with summoning or calling certain spirits into your rituals.

Candles

Candles are a commonly used tool in almost every ritual, spell, or altar space. The candle is used to represent fire because of the hot flame on top of it. Candles are also a fully balanced magic, representing all four elements in the following way: the wick is the Earth, grounding the candle and allowing it to burn; the wax is the water, which as it burns flows away into the atmosphere as a vapor; the air around is what allows the fire to burn; the flame is fire.

Candles are also necessary due to their ability to manifest over a long period of time. Once you are finished with your spell or ritual, instructions will sometimes require that you let the candle burn until it has gone out. This is to ensure that your intentions and manifestations are being carried all the way to spirit.

They come in a variety of colors, and each color represents a certain kind of magic, so whatever color candle you choose will have an impact on your spell. You will also carve symbols into the wax for added power, as well as roll it in herbs and anoint it with oils. All of these activities will enhance the quality of the magic you are working with.

Incense

Incense is often associated with the Air element and is used in a majority of Wiccan practices. It has been used in a variety of religious traditions across the world and has been identified as a purifying and cleansing agent, used to consecrate the space you are working it to make it more 'holy.'

It comes in a variety of aromas and scents and is also mainly made of herbs, barks, roots, and flowers; therefore, it can also be seen as an Earth element. The use of incense in any ritual or spell will offer an equally perfumed cleansing of the air in your circle and delicate connection to the divine and spiritual energies involved in your work.

Smudging is another term for burning a bundle of dried herbs and then smudging it out to prevent excessive burning. A smudge stick can be handmade with a few cuts of sage or rosemary from your garden, dried and wrapped before using in a ceremony. The aromatic smoke will help you to feel the sacredness of the space you are working in and can also be used to purify and cleanse all of your tools.

Crystals and Gemstones

Crystals and gemstones are not a requirement of Wicca and Witchcraft, but because of their powerful ability to harness energy, they are regularly used and revered for their magical qualities. Though they are classified as "in-organic" material, crystals and gemstones are very much alive, especially to anyone who has ever felt the power of their energy.

They are potent conduits and channels of frequency and vibration and will hold onto any intention or purpose that you need to consecrate this tool with. Because they are powerful at absorbing energy, they will likely need to be cleansed and purified regularly so that they don't retain unwanted energies as you work with them more and more.

Crystals and gemstones can be used in spell work, rituals, added to charms, act as an amulet or talisman and so much more. Below you will find some of the more common uses for crystals and gemstones in ritual magic.

Crystals and Gemstones: Common Uses

1. <u>Marking the Sacred Circle</u>- in ritual practices, crystals are often used to mark the circle you are casting prior to doing any spell work or ritual. Your circle is your sacred space of protection to work your magic in, and having crystals on the border of this circle is very powerful. They can be associated with cardinal directions or elements, or they can be specific to grounding and protection, or divination and communication with spirit. Within the circle or on the altar, they can be used to honor specific deities and are also often found as decoration and adornment for certain tools, like wands and chalices.

2. <u>Manifestation and Divination</u>- crystals and gemstones are widely used for the powers of manifestation and divination. Some Wiccans will use them as part of a spell or ritual and include it in the ingredients to perform certain casting. Placing a certain quality of stone or crystal on the third eye while lying down in your circle can have a major impact on opening your eye to "see" visions and receive input and downloads form spirit. This can also help as a tool of guidance so that you can "see" what to manifest.

3. <u>Talismans and Amulets</u>- crystals are a frequent component to a charm or amulet because of the nature of what they can bring to your energy. Worn as jewelry, they can be very opening and engaging, or very grounding and protective, depending on your needs. They pack a powerful punch and are regarded as an appropriate way to ward off or collect energy when used in this fashion.

4. <u>Charging and Consecrating</u>- gemstones and crystals can hold a lot of energy, as well as transmute energy. In ritual practices, crystals can be a great tool to help cleanse and purify other implements and instruments you are using, as well as infuse those tools and devices with the powerful energy of the crystal. You can bring them into any spell or ritual for this purpose and allow them to wield the energy as a conduit and channel of magic.

5. Color Correspondence- Color can play a significant role in your spells and rituals (see *Table of Correspondence: The Magic of Color*). With all crystals and gemstones, there is a unique color influence that can be coordinated with the type of work you are doing in your craft. Considering not only the personality and properties of each stone, but you can also use the magic of color to influence and enhance your spell work.

Welcoming Crystals and Gemstones into Your Practice

You can find thousands of different varieties of stones and crystals from a wide range of sources. Many can be found in New Age shops in your local community, and they can also be purchased online if you cannot find the one you are looking for in the local shops. One thing I will say, it is a fascinating experience to allow the crystal to choose you. When you are able to select your crystals in person, you have the option of holding them in your hand and feeling their energetic powers.

This can make all of the difference when choosing the right stone for you. Your own energy will have an impact on the stone as well, and so with some energies, you won't feel the "pull" as much as you will with others. This can be an indication that whatever stone you are looking for and are drawn to most is the one that is energetically right for you, right now.

Let your intuition be your guide and allow yourself to be pulled or drawn to certain stones. They may be communicating with you and letting you know that they are the right choice for your present magic.

Whenever you acquire new stones and crystals, be sure to cleanse them before using them for your spells and rituals, They carry so much energy, and if you are buying them from a retailer in your town, the one you take home may have been handled by a lot of people before coming home with you. It's best to be on the safe side and to give your crystals a warm salt water bath, a sunshine cleansing, and a smoke smudge.

Wrap-Up of Wiccan Tools

As you can see, there are a lot of options for what you can work with. All of the tools listed in this chapter are just the beginning of what you will find in your search and your practice of Wiccan arts. There will be a lot more for you to discovery, and as a beginner, these tools are a great place to start to help you get your altar ready and prepared for casting magic and devoting your heart to the energy of the divine.

Some of your tools will be purchased online or in a shop, while others may be given to you as gifts on your journey. One way for a solitary practitioner to have a good time with their craft is to make their own tools. Obviously, crystals and gemstones make themselves deep within the Earth, but there are other tools that you can make from scratch or embellish already existing items in your kitchen. Making an old kitchen knife into a sacred magical tool only requires intention, ritual, and casting a circle to honor the object.

You may also decide on your path that you will want to bring about your own candle making. Candle making can be a form of Witchcraft by itself, and you can support so many of your rituals and spells with homemade magical candles.

Have fun and explore the possibilities of what tools are for you. Begin building your altar and set your tools up in that space to show yourself your journey and what lies ahead!

Chapter 8: The Magic of Colors

Colors are symbolic of a wide range of things. Across time, colors have been associated with specific energies, like red being connected to passion, love, and romance, the redness of blood being the organ of the heart. The color green, on the other hand, has been associated with abundance and wealth, due to the color of some money, but also because of the connection to the growing verdant abundance of nature and Mother Earth. The qualities themselves might seem intangible, but when color is added into the mix, it is somehow much more visceral an expression.

Making use of these color correspondences with your magic practices reinforces and enhances the manifestation of your spell. Many of the candles that you use can take on these certain colors and will be integral to the overall quality of the spell work you are performing. Colorful tools, flowers, and decorations are also an exciting part of celebrations, festivals, and rituals, to demonstrate the time of year and the colors associated with it.

The Magic of Color

The list below is a demonstration of some of the magical color correspondences you will find commonly used in Wicca. You can also let your intuition or spirit guide you to help you make a color selection. Trust your inner knowing and guidance from the divine.

Red- Love, romance, passion, courage, intense emotion, willpower, strength, physical energy and vitality, health, root chakra, fire

Orange- Power, energy, vitality, attraction, stimulation, adaptability-especially with sudden change, sacral chakra

Yellow- Communication, confidence, study, divination, intellect, inspiration, knowledge, solar plexus chakra

Green- prosperity, wealth, growth, fertility, balance, health, luck, abundance, growth, renewal, heart chakra, Mother Earth, Mother Moon of Triple Goddess

Blue- healing, psychic ability, understanding, peace, wisdom, protection, patience, truth, understanding, harmony in the home, throat chakra

Violet- devotion, wisdom, spirituality, peace, enhancement of nurturing capability or quality, balancing sensitivities, divination, third eye/brow chakra

White- clarity, cleansing, spiritual growth, understanding, peace, innocence, illumination, establishing order, purity, crown chakra, Maiden of the Triple Moon

Black-Force, stability, protection, transformation, enlightenment, dignity, banishing and releasing negative energies, Crone of the Triple Moon

Silver- spiritual development, psychic ability, wisdom, intelligence, memory, meditation, warding off negative vibrations, psychic development, divine feminine/ female Goddess

Gold- Success, good fortune, ambition, self-realization, intuition, divination, inner-strength, health, finances, divine masculine/ male God

Brown- Balance, concentration, endurance, solidity, strength, grounding, concentration, material gain, companion animals, home, Earth, balance

Grey- contemplation, neutrality, stability, complex decisions, compromise, binding negative influences, complex decisions, balance

Indigo- clarity of purpose, spiritual healing, self-mastery, emotion, insight, fluidity, expressiveness, meditation, crown chakra

Pink- partnerships, friendship, affection, companionship, spiritual healing, child magic, spiritual awakening

Chapter 9: The Magic of Crystals and Gemstones

As you read in *Chapter 7: Wiccan Tools*, crystals, and gemstones have strong power and ability to wield energy. Each crystal and gemstone come from a unique process that takes time, and all of these unique aspects of the Earth are here as highly useful tools for manifesting or securing any kind of energy.

The work of crystals and gemstones will be an exciting part of your practice and becoming acquainted with the stones you will be using is vital to your journey. Each one possesses an individual essence and energy to be utilized in your practice. Get to know them like you are getting to know a new friend and spend quality time with each one. They will give you all of the energy and influence you need to understand their properties and qualities.

Take a look at the list below of some of the more common crystals and gemstone. You may find that you are already acquainted with a few. Practice various spell work and ritual with specific ones and decide which ones will be best for your particular needs. They can be used to consecrated tools, enhance spells, are added to charms, sachets, pillows, and potions, and are also great to sleep with under your pillow to improve your dream state, as well as many more options.

Get to know the crystals in your life and let them bring you even more magical abundance on your journey!

List of Crystals and Gemstones for Magical Use:

Amethyst: self-discipline, pride, sobriety, helps break habits and addictions, opens dreams and psychic visions, clear channel for communication with spirit, inner strength, calms fears or anxieties,

Black Tourmaline: shielding, protective, grounding, repels negativity, cleanses auras, breaks obsessions, heals anxiety, and prevents a psychic attack on the spiritual plane.

Black Onyx: booster of strength and confidence, banishing and releasing, wards of negativity and conflict, protection stone

Bloodstone: abundance, fertility, physical health and healing, relief from grief or loss

Blue Kyanite: One of a few stones that don't need regular cleansing, balances, promotes clear personal truth, new chapters, clears auras, and chakras.

Carnelian: passion, determination, courage, joy, warmth, motivation and individuality, success, inner fire, manifesting goals, productivity, directness, illumination.

Citrine: sun energy, joy, warmth, friendship, communication, dream manifestation, individuality.

Hematite: kinds of attraction, magic, protection, stability, grounding, clear understanding, and perspective.

Jade: protection from negative energies and influences, emotional balance, wisdom, harmony, grounding

Jet: protection from negativity or challenging emotions of others, supportive of transitions, grounding, centering

Lapis Lazuli: openness, insight, truth, inner power, universal spiritual truth, interpretation of intuitive thought, psychic ability, soul guide magic.

Malachite: emotional courage supportive during times of spiritual growth, helpful during significant life changes

Moonstone: moon magic, intuition, life cycles, empathy and clairvoyance, emotional love, connections of the heart, empathy, and kindness.

Quartz Crystal: all-purpose energy stone, personal power, and energy, clearing, balance, healing, spiritual growth, and enlightenment, amplifies intentions.

Rose Quartz: compassion, tolerance, love, peace, reveals inner beauty, self-confidence booster, relationships, and self-love.

Selenite- connection to spirit, a conduit between physical and spiritual realm, simultaneously cleanses and recharges, intuition, higher self, spirit guides, honesty, and purity, heightened personal vibration.

Sodalite- Cooperation, communication, knowledge, intelligence, rational mind, education, and learning, wisdom, study, logic and intellect, inner calm, clears mental noise, self-awareness, and self-improvement

Tiger's Eye: courage, willpower, loyalty, truth, luck, protection, truth-seeking, perception, cuts through illusions, brings to light manipulative or dishonest intentions.

Turquoise: healer stone, inner beauty, joy, relaxation, healing, contentment, positive vibrations, prosperity, happiness, friendship, protection, neutralize negativity, empath stone.

Chapter 10: The Magic of Herbs

Herbs are heavily used and highly symbolic in the world of magic and the work of Wicca. Every herb or plant has some remedy involved in its power, as well as a symbolic connection to one of the four elements and the directions. All plants and herbs begin as a seed in the earth, are fed by the soil, watered with the rain, and need air and the fire of sunlight to thrive and grow. They are imbued with all of these elements and like colors and crystals, have their own unique properties, qualities, and personalities to include in all of your ritual magic and spell work.

Working with herbs will always come up in your practice, and it is essential to know what you are handling and dealing with when you make selections for what herbs to use. There are tons of options, and depending on where you live, there may be some that are available to you on the land, while others would have to be acquired in a local shop or store.

Some herbs are sold at your local supermarket, while others need to be purchased at specialty shops. There will always be a source for them, and you can buy them, grow them, or harvest them from the wild.

Wildcrafting (collecting from the wild) is something that every Wiccan or Witch should explore. Being in a practice of devotion to nature and all her inhabitants, going out into the woods and meadows and identifying the sweet herbal and floral bounty and abundance, is part of being a Witch or Wiccan. You can collect them from wherever they grow and ask them what they are useful for.

As you develop your skills of psychic awareness and openness to the divine, you will have a better understanding of how to communicate with plant energies. They have their own quality of expression and are capable of informing you of who does and doesn't want to be picked. Trust your intuition.

One thing to keep in mind is that as you are learning and studying: you may want to have a field guide handy to make sure you are getting the right information and picking the right plant for your needs. A field guide for herbs is an excellent resource for getting you started in meeting the herbs in your native region.

Below is a list of commonly used herbs and their magical properties. There are hundreds more, and if you want to learn more about herbal magic and how to incorporate them as healing medicine and as a magical influence then you will need to dig more deeply into the realm of herbal magic on your path.

Basil- protection, wards of negative vibrations in the home, opens up loving feelings and vibrations

Bay Leaf- good fortune, money, success, protection, purification, strength, healing

Chamomile- relieves stress, relieves insomnia, sleep, peace, relaxation, healing, brings love

Cinnamon- prosperity, luck, success, love, increases spiritual vibrations

Dandelion- wishes, spirit world interaction, divination

Elecampane- luck, protection, plant spirit communications, dispelling negative energy and vibrations

Hibiscus- dreams, love, lust, divination

Lavender- clairvoyance, happiness, healing, love, peace, restful sleep, relief from grief, money, passion, longevity, protection, meditation

Mugwort- increase in fertility and lust, protection, powerful psychic healing, and enhancement.

Nutmeg- protection, luck, prosperity, money

Rosemary- healthy rest, love, lust

Sage- protection, dispels negative energy and vibrations, longevity, wisdom

Star Anise- magical power, psychic power, spiritual connection, and divination

Thyme- psychic abilities, loyalty, affection

Valerian- purifies sacred places, drives off negative energies and vibrations, protection, relaxation, calming of nerves, sleep

Yarrow- courage and confidence, healing, love, divination, blood

Appendix: Rune Names and Meanings

Fehu

English Alphabet: F

Meaning: Wealth, Fulfillment of Goals

Element: Fire

Uruz

English alphabet: U

Meaning: Invites creativity, wealth, strength

Element: Earth

Thurisaz

English Alphabet: TH

Meaning: facing a powerful enemy, facing difficulty, strength for facing a test, force, giant

Element: Fire

Ansuz

English Alphabet: A

Meaning: power, luck, inspiration, ancestors, God, divine

Element: Air

Raido

English Alphabet: R

Meaning: promotes safe journeys (physical or spiritual); wheel, journey

Element: Air

Kenaz

English Alphabet: K, C or Q

Meaning: light, fire, passion, torch, ignites or manifests personality and character

Element: Fire

Gifu

English Alphabet: G

Meaning: generosity, harmony, gifts, partnership, joy

Element: Air

Wunjo

English Alphabet: W or V

Meaning: invites wisdom, glory, perfection, joy, granting wishes

Element: Earth

Hagalaz

English Alphabet: H

Meaning: weapon of war, (carved into weapons of war)

Element: Ice

Nauthiz

English Alphabet: N

Meaning: destiny to accomplish impossible feats, necessity, need

Element: Fire

Isa

English Alphabet: I

Meaning: authority, power, masculinity, ice

Element: Ice

Jera

English Alphabet: Y or J

Meaning: luck and long-term success, harvest, year, gardener's rune

Element: Earth

Eihwaz

English Alphabet: EI, AE

Meaning: manifesting greatest potential, potential, yew tree

Element: Air

Pertho

English Alphabet: P

Meaning: birth of the new, chance, success in games of chance, secrets

Element: Water

Algiz

English Alphabet: Z or X

Meaning: health and happiness,

Element: Air

Sowulo

English Alphabet: S

Meaning: salvation, spiritual protection, sun

Element: Air

Teiwaz

English Alphabet: T

Meaning: strength of purpose, creator, will power, resolution in times of conflict, justice

Element: Air

Berkana

English Alphabet: B

Meaning: healing and protection, romance, beloved, birch tree

Element: Earth

Ehwaz

English Alphabet: E

Meaning: Bonds of friendship, horses

Element: Earth

Mannaz

English Alphabet: M

Meaning: manifestation of true self, self-knowledge, mankind,

Element: Air

Laguz

English Alphabet: L

Meaning: sustenance of life, water, lake, hope

Element: Water

Inguz

English Alphabet: NG or ing

Meaning: friendship, lasting partnerships, true love, romance

Element: Earth

Othila

English Alphabet: O

Meaning: strengthening family and partnerships, inheritance, homeland

Element: Earth

Dagaz

English Alphabet: D

Meaning: inviting spiritual growth, luck, good luck charm

Element: Fire/ Air

Conclusion

A magical journey it was, and now, you are all set to get started in your practice! There will be so many ways for you to begin engaging with your new tools and understanding of the Wiccan craft, and all you need is this book to guide you in your preparations. With all you have learned from these pages, you are now ready to begin setting up your altar, acquiring your tools, going out and communing with nature, and finding the best times for your practice.

As you go forward on your path with Wicca, you can add more understanding and knowledge to your practice. In my book, *Wicca Herbal Magic: A Practical Beginner's Herbal Guide for Wiccans and Modern Witches, Includes the Must-Have Natural Herbs for Baths, Oils, Teas and Spells,* you will learn even more about the power and benefit of working with herbs and how to bring them into your everyday practice through some recipes, spells, and rituals.

If you are looking for a way to get your Book of Shadows started and need some inspiration for your spells and enchantments, *Wiccan Spell Book: A Wicca Practical Magic Book of Shadows with Crystal, Candle, Moon Spells and Witchcraft for Beginners* is the perfect companion to going forward on your journey of learning the craft and working with your own spells and rituals.

There are so many exciting ways for you to teach yourself the art and magic of Wicca and this book is a guide for you anytime you need a reference on your spiritual path and devotion to the God and Goddess. Further study of your practice is always recommended, and as you continue on your path, don't stop asking questions and practice a little magic every day. Celebrate nature and worship the abundance and beauty of this great, green Earth we call home. Set up your altar and find your tools and objects to ground you in your magical practice.

I hope you have enjoyed this journey as much as I have enjoyed sharing it with you. If you have found this book helpful and inspiring, a review on Amazon.com is always appreciated.

May your path be full of magical inspiration, manifestation, and abundance. So mote it be!

Wiccan Spell Book:

A Wicca Practical Magic Book of Shadows with Crystal, Candle, Moon Spells, and Witchcraft for Beginners

By Gaia J. Mellor

Introduction

Welcome to a wonderful world of Wiccan Spells! What are spells? How do they work? What makes a Wiccan spell different from any other kind of spell? Are there wrong ways to cast one? How does it really work?

If you are reading this book, then you may be asking some of these questions. Spells are tools of manifestation. They are an act of powerful, creative, and energetic force and are managed and delivered to the Universe of possibilities by your very own hands. To work with a spell and cast it into the energy of all things is to work with the divine power of all life. A spell is a tool of connection to your practice, to yourself, to the God and Goddess, or whatever life-force energies you may worship and devote your energy to.

Whether you are Wiccan, Witch, Pagan, or otherwise, this book is a simple and effective tool to help you discover your power and path toward working more deeply with the magic of spell work in your practice.

This journey has everything to do with practicing safe and effective magic and will give you all of the guidance you need to take your trip to the next level. If you have been working with Wicca for a while now, you may be looking for some fresh spell ideas to add to your Book of Shadows. For the beginner, this is a great companion to start your spells and finding the ones that will help you explore and manifest possibilities in your everyday life.

Getting started with your spellcraft and casting can be one of the most exciting parts of your lessons in Witchcraft and Wicca. Your every day love spells and protection spells are what can help you gain confidence in writing and creating your own magic to continue your budding and blossoming Book of Shadows.

This book will offer you some necessary introductory information about Wiccan spells, as well as some guidelines to help you practice safely and effectively within your own practice. Because the energy you are working with is so powerful, it is crucial that you are prepared to handle the results of what you are working on manifesting into your reality.

Wiccan Spell Book will also give you in-depth information about your Book of Shadows. An essential part of any Wiccan or Witch's practice, your Book of Shadows is your personal reference guide to all of your spells and rituals and will contain all the knowledge that is important to your practice. This book will give you some background history, as well as provide some examples of what goes inside of a typical Book.

It will be an excellent resource for you for a variety of spells to include in your own Book to help you get going with your casting and craft. You will find an assortment of spells for love, prosperity, health, and luck. There is also a chapter explaining the moon phases and how the magic of the moon can significantly impact all of your spells and rituals. The section on moon magic will give you important insight into how and when to cast certain spells and what some of those spells might look like.

In another chapter, you will find in-depth explanations and expertise about candle magic and how it works. Using specific types of candles for certain kinds of spells can make all the difference in manifesting your goals and ambitions. You will discover the uses of candles and their magical properties, as well as some specific candle magic spells to get you started with your candle craft.

Another spell of importance is the kind that uses crystal magic. You will find information about how and why crystals are so magical and vital to your spell work and some of the most creative ways you can cast spells using these powerful conduits of energy and life force.

In short, *Wiccan Spell Book: A Wicca Practical Magic Book of Shadows With Crystal, Candle, Moon Spells, and Witchcraft for Beginners* is exactly what you need if you are a beginner Wiccan or Witch who is looking for a jumping off point for your spells and Book of Shadows.

It is a great resource that will hold your hand in whatever way you need to illuminate the brilliant aspects of learning how to use spells in your practice and the best ways to work them.

Whatever your practice may look like, this book is geared toward a beginner looking for a great resource to help you dive more deeply into the world of spells and the craft of magic. You are on a great path of personal and spiritual discovery, and casting spells is such a creative and expressive part of that journey.

Your beautiful power is waiting for you to express itself through spells, and as you become more aligned with the kind of Wiccan practice you want to have, you will know precisely what kind of spells you want to work with and add to your own personal Book of Shadows.

Give yourself the pleasure and joy of working with *Wiccan Spell Book* to find all of the answers to your questions, so you can start casting magic today! So mote it be!

Chapter 1: Introduction to Wicca Spells

What is a spell, anyway? In your practice or study of Wicca so far, you may have discovered that there are not always spells involved and that you don't have to cast them in order to practice the Wiccan religion. Even if you aren't Wiccan or are just wondering about Wicca, you may be curious and looking for answers about spells, what they do, and how to use them in your personal spiritual practice.

They are considered magic, or magick as you may sometimes see it spelled. Some say that if you practice magic, then you are a spell caster and, therefore, a Witch. Labels are common but not always needed or necessary to enjoy a magical life. Truthfully, every culture has practiced some form of what we call "witchcraft," or magic, and as it has developed with our species, we have developed with it.

Spells are an essential part of what magic involves. When you are talking to someone about how you want to improve your life or trying to think positive thoughts about your career shift, you are essentially casting a spell. So, what is a spell then?

A spell is any kind of experience that includes the intention to manifest something into your physical life experience. A spell is a direct line of communication between you and the cosmos to achieve a goal. A spell is your voice and action asking for what you want to occur and giving energy to the outcomes through creative expression.

Spells come in a variety of shapes, sizes, formats, colors, aromas, and they occur at different dates, times, moons, seasons, and so on. There are limitless possibilities when working with magic and manifestation, and that is really all it is: a way to show yourself and the energy of all life, who you are, and what you want.

A spell can be anything that you want it to be and is ultimately a creative process to give you insight and support in where you want to go in your practice. Once you get the hang of using a few simple spells from this book, you will gain the confidence to start creating and utilizing your spells. With any spell, you will always work with specific intentions and find the best methods that will work for you along the way.

What you may be thinking, at this point, is how does a spell work? As you have read, a spell is a tool of manifestation. It is a powerful way to take the time to set a focused goal or intention through the use of specific ingredients, timing, and clarity of thought.

Spells are a way for you to gain an energetic connection to the reality you are working to create and set into motion. For a lot of Wiccans who practice magic, spells are the gateway to link with spirits and the great divine. You can easily transport yourself into another realm when you are in a circle cast for protection, imbuing the space with your precise intentions and magic ritual. It is a sacred dance that calls upon the energies of all that is around you to hear your call for something relevant to your life.

A spell works as an opening and affirmation of what energy you want to promote, enhance, and delegate to the earthly plane of reality. It is energy that you hone and connect to so that it can be powerfully, elegantly, and eloquently delivered into the energy of everything around you. It is a ripple effect made possible by the stones you cast into the waters of life.

It's not just as simple as an affirmation that you repeat to yourself over and over, although words are heavily used in casting spells. So much of asking for what you want from the Universe includes a special time, space, ritual, ingredients, and connection to your deities and honoring of the elements, at least from the Wiccan point of view.

So then, what makes a Wiccan spell different from other types of spells? Wicca has everything to do with the worship of nature, the seasons, the cycles and rhythms of all life, and the God/Goddess relationship between all matter in the Universe. Wiccans have access to the natural world through their connection to Mother Nature and her supreme gifts; you will find that most of your spells, Wiccan or not, will contain tools and ingredients that are a part of the nature of life here on Earth. If you are looking to learn more about the practice of Wicca and what it involves, you can take a look at my book, *Wicca for Beginners: A Witchcraft Guide for Every Wiccan Aspirant, Made Easy for the Solitary Practitioner.*

All spells share some common qualities, steps, and ingredients, and they will always have an impact of some kind. The best way to practice casting Wiccan spells is to use your knowledge of nature, the elements, the directions, and the cycles of life. These aspects might be what sets a Wiccan spell apart from other practices.

If you are engaging in the moon cycles, seasonal celebrations, the balance of light and dark, and all of the life that exists in our cosmos, you will be in a format practiced by many Wiccans today.

There are several ways to treat a spell, and as you may already know from practicing Wicca, or learning about its beliefs and philosophies, there is a statement of power that has an impact on the right kind of energy to use when casting any magic, spell, ritual, or otherwise. The Wiccan Rede is a commonly known element of the craft and states that you should "harm none" in your work.

What this means is that if you are casting a spell and you are using your power and energy, along with the strength of all creation, to perform a spell of ill will on another person, you are not accessing it in the right way, according to Wiccan teachings. Spells are not used to hurt others, and what you do will come back to you three-fold.

Coming into an agreement with your magic that you will do no harm means that you are willing to work with magic and spells only to improve or benefit your life and the overall energy of other things, not the other way around.

The best way to enjoy Wiccan spellcasting is to embrace the elements and use all of the fun and exciting tools that help you empower your spells. You will have so much fun acquiring what you will need, and as you build your altar and collect your tools, you will get delightful ideas about how to create your unique spells.

Some people want to know if there is a wrong way to cast a spell, and the answer to that is no if you are harming no one. Spells are a creative experience, and many Wiccans and Witches find beautiful harmony and balance through aligning with their intuitions to craft the right spell for them and their practices. You can always branch out from what you have already learned from the other spells you have seen and practiced.

Several of the spells that are listed in this book are great methods to get you started, so you can understand how so many spells are crafted. The main thing about spells is understanding the energy you are working with and how to set your intentions clearly, but more on that in the next chapter.

Wiccan spells are a creative life force waiting for you to breathe them into existence. Your spells will hold the key to aligning with your own powerful, personal magic and will help you work more closely with the Wiccan beliefs of harmony, balance, and nature. Wiccan spells will introduce you to working with some or all of the following manifestation practices:

- Candle magic
- Herbal magic and remedy
- Honoring Gods, Goddesses, and Deities
- Moon cycle power
- Crystal magic
- Elemental magic
- Creative visualization
- Altar space and consecrated or charged tools for your work
- Sun cycles
- Seasonal celebrations
- Harvest
- Empowerment, wealth, prosperity, protection, love, abundance, good luck, and good health
- Spiritual awakening and communication with the divine
- And more!

Wiccan spells are a gateway to trusting your intuition, calling upon the universal energies and celebrating nature and the Goddess and God. It is performing a ritual of manifestation using all that is around you and choosing the path that is right for you through your relationship with Wicca.

All of the spells in this book are guidelines and ideas to get you started and help you understand more about Wiccan Spells and how to use them. In the next chapter, you will get a deeper understanding about how to cast spells safely and effectively, guidelines for casting a circle and preparing for a spell, and basic concepts and steps to what a successful spell looks like.

Chapter 2: Guidelines for Successful Spellcasting

Spellcasting is for anyone who wants to practice magic and the craft. It only takes a little bit of practice and some experimentation to feel comfortable and confident with any spell. Because there are so many different kinds and so many different ways to cast, this chapter will serve as an overview of guidelines to cast spells safely and effectively to get you on the right path.

As you are reading, you will appreciate how much you may already know about spells and casting. So much of this is innate knowledge and intuition, and as you grow your spiritual practice, you will learn how to be guided by your intuition so much more through all of your individual endeavors with magic.

The main thing with any spell is to be safe and to have fun while you set your clear goals and intentions. All spells are about the energy you put into them to create a positive outcome. Starting on the right foot with spellcasting will make all the difference on your journey.

Safe Spellcasting

Enjoying your spell work is easy, especially when you are taking the right precautions. Even when you aren't using any potentially dangerous tools or implements, it is still a good practice to go into your work with a mindset of feeling prepared, protected, and safe. Having a standard protocol for your witchcraft and spell work will help you remain respectful of yourself and all the energies that you choose to incorporate into your process.

Safety with Tools

You will find that a lot of the tools in this book and any that you find online or in other books will have a list of things you will need to accomplish the spell. Some of these tools will include flame, candles dripping hot wax, smoke for smudging, blades for cutting and other sharp tools for specific acts of manifestation, and many more.

The tools that you use will help you harness the energy and manipulate in the way that is required to achieve the final goal and outcome of your spell. All tools are sacred to your practice and should be properly cared for. Safety with tools isn't just about safe handling, which you will want to make sure of; it can also be about safe energy.

Consider how often you will be using these tools and how much energy they will accumulate over time. Cleansing and purifying your tools is an easy and effective way for you to keep your tools in a higher state of vibration and clarity for use in spell work. Sometimes, the energy of something can feel "off," and you aren't sure why. This can happen with your tools for Wiccan spell work, and a"funky-feeling" tool can cause you to fumble and could even cause some injury.

Safe handling of candles, matches, fire, blades, and smudging sticks is always highly recommended. Make sure you have the right dishes and containers to keep your candles standing upright and your smudge stick away from anything it could set fire. You may also want to make sure your altar and ritual space is well-ventilated while you use smoke for purification.

Practicing proper tool safety is a must, even when it means clearing and purifying the energy of your tools and implements regularly, to prevent them from collecting unwanted energies that could mar your spells and incantations or them make difficult.

Fire Safety

Fire safety should go without saying, but it bears mention here. However, fire comes into your rituals and spell work; it must be respected for the energy that it carries. Fire is a power of creation and destruction and has always been here to give us life and sometimes take it away. The reality is, fire is dangerous, and it needs to be used wisely.

Many spells call for candle magic for the lighting of sacred smoke and for burning of intentions, messages written on paper, and herbs. The use of fire and burning things is a very holy and magical practice and will give a great deal of power to any spell work you choose to do when performed safely.

When you are using fire in your spells, take necessary precautions:

- Use a sturdy candle holder for every candle.
- Keep your candles out of strong winds and away from things that can easily burst in flames.
- If you are letting your candles burn down, then you will need to monitor them or make sure they are in a safe container.
- Have a dish for your smudge sticks to lay them in while they burn out, as well as your incense.
- Use a cauldron or fire-safe bowl to burn your written words on paper, herbs, or other items. You may even want to do your burning outside during spells, depending on the space and ventilation.
- Keep flammable items away from anything burning until the flames are put out.

Fire is powerful, and so is the magic it adds to your spell. Use it wisely, and it will help you to manifest your goals and spells very effectively.

Harm None

As you have already read in Chapter 1, an essential aspect of the Wiccan philosophy is that you will cause no harm to another while you practice magic. This is a potent tool to help you stay safe from causing damage to yourself and others while you cast.

The Threefold Law states that anything you do can return to you three times, meaning your energetic impact through rituals and spells will return to you three times over. That is incredibly powerful energy to return to you, and if you are casting to bring more wealth and abundance into your life, that would be a good thing.

However, if you are casting a spell to make someone fall out of love with another person to fall in love with you, that is harmful to not only one, but two people. It will come back to you at some point by the power of three, according to Wiccan beliefs.

However it returns to you, it will likely feel bad and unpleasant, and so for the safety of your feelings and those of another, it is best to state the Wiccan Rede of "harm none," before you cast any spell to make sure you are not going to bring any hurt to you or another. This is a powerful way for you to engage with magic more positively and beneficially to the good of all.

Spiritual Safety

Preparing to cast a spell requires an opening to all of the energies and a connection with spirit. Becoming wide open as a channel of energy during your spells and incantations requires some protection on your part to make sure you only include positive and light vibrational energies into your spellcasting.

Sometimes, when we are doing our work, we forget that we can easily open to all different kinds of nature, both dark and light and that it will be necessary to consider protecting yourself from anything that might have a negative impact or effect on your energy or your spells.

All this means is that you set an intention of protection and invite only positive energies into your circle and your spell work. Some might even call upon a specific deity to act as a guardian during their spells to help them stay focused and keep any unwanted energies at bay.

Another excellent method of creating spiritual protection is through the casting of a circle (more on that later in the chapter).

Personal Safety and Well-Being

Your personal safety and well-being can have a significant impact on your ability to cast magic well and safely. If you are overworked, overtired, ill, or unhappy, it may not be the best time for you to be doing any casting work. That energy will carry through in your spell and can have an impact on your manifestation. If your spell involves helping you out of those states of mind or being, then make sure you are gentle and nurturing and that you are performing your spells at a moment of optimal health to achieve your goal.

Your personal safety is just as important as the concept of harming none. Make sure you are in the right mindset and emotional state to perform magic. Remember, what you cast can return to you threefold, so whatever your intentions are, make sure you are in a good head, heart, and body space to perform your spell work.

Grounding and Centering for Spellcasting

Success with spellcasting isn't just about safety and what tools you might use; It's also about how you prepare your mind, body, and spirit. The idea behind grounding and centering is that you ask yourself to unite with your authentic energy and power to call upon the work you want to do accurately.

Calming the mind, focusing on your intentions, and getting aligned for your magical purpose are a massive part of how to successfully cast. If your mind is wandering and thinking about what you are going to need from the grocery store, then you won't be focused on your power for manifestation. A lot of people will sometimes consider the centering process as something very akin to meditation.

In general, meditation is an all-encompassing term that essentially asks you to clear your mind and stay focused on the moment you are in. Meditation is another way to describe the centering process to help you ready your energy to make magic.

Grounding is another term to help you understand the quality of vibration—or energy—that allows you to stay within the power of Earth and her abundant fuel for magic. To ground yourself is to connect to the floor of everything, everywhere. You ground into the floor of your body and mind, and you also ground into the energy of whatever deities you are supporting.

Grounding helps us to siphon any excess energy into the ground and then pull the available power endlessly from the Earth through us. It is a way to help the direction of your energy flow so that you feel supported, balanced, and prepared for whatever spell or ritual you are about to perform. In many ways, the grounding and centering process is what directs your intuition, instinct, and power into what you are working on. It is a focus of energy on all levels.

Not everyone will ground and center before casting, and if you were to compare results of spells from someone who does and someone who doesn't, you might be surprised to find that there is more return for those who are practicing their groundedness before *and* after casting a spell.

For many who practice Wicca, the grounding process can occur with the casting of the circle, as this activity has very stabilizing, opening, and centering qualities. Before any spell, if you want to have greater success with manifestation, it is crucial to prepare your energy to work with it according to your wishes and goals.

Some people will use a circle of protection while others might use a specific meditation, incantation, or poem. You can also use crystals and stones that are specifically for the purpose of grounding, and using incense and smudging can have a very centering and grounding impact.

You will need to determine the right method for you, and if you want to have success with your spells, consider a grounding and centering ritual before you get started to make sure your energy is in right alignment with your spell's purpose.

Casting a Circle: How and Why

Casting a Circle is one of the most common aspects of practicing with Wiccan spells and all kinds of Pagan ritual and witchcraft. First, let's talk about why you want to cast a circle before you start a spell. Then, you can see exactly how it is done.

A circle in Wicca and witchcraft serves multiple purposes. It is specific energy to help you feel safe and protected, while it calls upon the elements, directions, and spirit to help you in your work. Traditionally, the circle is your gateway to magic and will always keep you in alignment with the energy of nature. Here, within the circle, you will find the support you need to accomplish your goals from all directions of the Universe.

You should always cast a kind of circle, even if it completely simple, like spinning in a circle to acknowledge energy around you that will shield you from outside forces. A circle is an energetic bubble that holds your power and your magic inside. It can be a way to keep you spiritually safe, only inviting in the energies you want to work with.

Many will use a candle, an object from nature, or an altar tool to mark each direction with one of the four primary elements. The fifth element, spirit or ether, is what is above you. In Wicca, it can pertain to the God/Goddess energy you call upon to worship in your work.

The purpose of your circle is to protect you and also to empower you while you cast. It is a connection to the divine and promotes the gateway and opening for manifestation while it holds you in the balance of all life.

Basic Circle Casting

Opening a Circle

Use creative visualization to help you picture your circle and the protective shield that will surround you and your work. You can see it like a glass orb, a tent, or a colorful light surrounding you. The size of your circle depends on the amount of space you need to work your spell.

Use a compass if you don't know what way is north.

1. From the north position, use your finger or some other kind of tool to point in front of you or to the floor at the north of the circle. You can say something like this: "As I open to the divine powers that be, I call upon the power of the North and the Earth element to protect and guide me. And so it is."

2. Now, move clockwise to the East and say something like this: "As I open to the divine powers that be, I call upon the power of the East and the Air element to protect and guide me. And so it is."

3. Continue clockwise to the South and say: "As I open to the divine powers that be, I call upon the power of the South and the Fire element to protect and guide me. And so it is."

4. Continue to the West position and say: "As I open to the divine powers that be, I call upon the power of the West and the Water element to protect and guide me. And so it is."

5. Return to the starting position of the North and hold both hands above you, either clasped together and your fingers are pointing up or using a tool of your choice. Then connect to the element of spirit and say: "I call upon the energy of the Universe and [insert preferred deities or other energies of spirit] to aid me in my magic. And so it is."

You can change the format according to your preferences and add any other information that feels the most grounding, opening, and balancing for you. Use creative visualization to picture guardian and ancestors with you, or use crystals and gemstones to create the entire circle, laying them out on the floor around you. How you choose to cast your circle must be a regular part of your preparation for a successful spellcasting.

When you are finished with your spells, you can close your circle by moving backward through the circle, counterclockwise and repeating words of gratitude to each direction and element for being with you in your practice.

The Steps of a Basic Spell

There are a few steps to help you cast spells successfully. You only need to know a few things to get you started, and all of these critical points and tips are what makes the difference between a prosperous manifestation and a flimsy spell.

1. *Set Your Intention*

   Before anything else can happen, you have to know the reason for your spell. What is the outcome or goal? What are you trying to accomplish? Be specific and clear when determining the point of your spell work so that there isn't any confusion between you and the universe.

2. *Find Your Tools and Ingredients*

With most spells, you are going to need a few things to help you manifest that abundance. It could merely be a candle and a crystal, or it could be an elaborate mixture of herbs and a more delicate process that takes a while. Whatever you need for your spell, you want to make sure you have the right tools to help you cast your intention into the energy of the Universe.

3. *Decide the Timing*

Timing can matter, as you will learn in the later chapters. Some spells need the power of the full moon, while others might need to occur at high noon under a bright summer sun. When you perform your spell, it can have an impact on the quality of the energy you are working with in conjunction with the intentions of your spell. Most spells that you find online or in books will tell you if there is a specific timing, and as you create your own, use your intuition about when a good time will be for a specific intention.

4. *Prepare the Language*

Most spells encourage and incorporate the use of particular and specific wording to help you establish your goals and intentions. Every word you speak in a spell carries great meaning and energy toward your spell becoming manifested. It is vital to prepare your choice of words ahead of time so that they are direct and in clear communication with all that is around you and working with you.

5. *Organize and Design*

With all of these components decided upon, you will then need to organize it into a usable format so that when you are performing the spell, it flows in the right direction. Decide when to light the candles, when to burn the incense, and so on. You will know precisely how it needs to flow as you are working with it.

When you are looking at the spells in this book, you will find that they incorporate all of these components to help you organize the way to cast your magic spells. These steps will help you create your spells. The more you practice the Wiccan spells you find in these pages, the easier it becomes, and the better you will be able to understand the basic steps behind every spell.

These guidelines and tips will help you in all of your spell work. Safely performing your work while maintaining a healthy attitude and groundedness will bring you a more significant return and success with all of the spells that you cast.

Going into the next chapter, you will learn more about the popular spell book for a Wiccan or Witch and why it will be so valuable to your spellcasting. Your Book of Shadows is the number one book of spells, and having your own is a part of the fun and magic of Wiccan spellcasting.

Chapter 3: Book of Shadows

A Book of Shadows has a long history in the world of witchcraft, Pagan arts, and various other forms of religion and magical devotion. It is the essence of every practitioner's work and can be seen as the lifelong journal, diary, or recipe book of all of your spells, rituals, symbols, beliefs, and preferred magical explorations.

Your Book of Shadows always comes in handy and gives you an opportunity to grow and expand with your quest for knowledge in the magical and Wiccan arts. Not every Wiccan or Witch's Book of Shadows will look the same or have the same content, and that is why it is necessary to give you some information about what it is, where it comes from, what goes inside of it, and various forms of magic that you may choose to illustrate and depict in your personal Book.

History of the Book of Shadows

The traditionally known Book of Shadows has often been called a Grimoire throughout history. In myths and legends of magic and sorcery, famous wizards were depicted as having their sacred Grimoire that is full of spells, potions, and magic, where Merlin from the Legend of King Arthur is one of the most notorious.

Several versions of Grimoire, or Book of Shadows, have been published since the dawn of popular culture's embrace of Neo-Pagan religions, especially with the advent of Wicca, which was officially founded in the mid-1950s by Gerald Gardner, who is thought to be the originator of the term "Book of Shadows."

For Gardener, his Book of Shadows was his personal diary of all of his Wiccan worship, craft, rituals, information about deities, and so forth. Over time, it was added to and became the sacred volume of knowledge for his coven, and over time, it was the most famous book of the Wiccan religion.

It has been published several times, and since Wicca's debut in the mid-twentieth century, several other versions have been published by various authors and practitioners of Wicca and other Pagan arts. In fact, you can most likely find a Grimoire or Book of Shadows at your local book shop.

From the ancient times of early witchcraft and the need to organize herbal magic and remedies to the development of the Wiccan practice by Gerald Gardener through his own personal Book, your Book of Shadows comes from a long history of magical people who knew how to detail their mysteries in one sacred text.

Why You Need a Book of Shadows

Having your own Book of Shadows is an essential step for anyone who wants to practice the magical arts. Your Book is your way to enforce your beliefs, rituals, manifestations, and experiences while you go through the journey of awakening to your power as a person.

Many people view it as a journal of magical discovery, as it is something you can add to every day to note your progress, add new spells, make changes or write new notes in the margins about spells you have already cast and their development, and so much more.

Your Book is how you can keep yourself focused and organized with all of the work you want to do through your Wiccan practice. It has a way of becoming like a friend to you. It will hold many of your secrets and truths while you discover more about making your spells come to life.

There are so many different ways that it can be utilized on your path, and as you get more acquainted with casting, you will find more and more things that you want to add to it. It has an invaluable set of information and is your ultimate resource. Many Wiccans and Witches will adopt another coven or solitary practitioner's published Grimoire to get going and have some ideas of what to put inside.

For you to get going with your own Book of Shadows, you only need a few things to get you started. You can use any kind of notebook you like or find something exceptional that you want to keep adding to. You can always cut out pages that you have written notes on and tape or glue them into your main book. It's a creative process. Have fun with it!

Table of Contents: What's Inside?

What goes in your book of Shadows is up to you and your practice. If you are looking to join a coven, your coven will have its own Book that you will likely have to copy and learn from, so you won't be creating your own. For the solitary practitioner, you will have authority over what goes in your Book, and it will always be unique to your adventures with magic.

Here are some of the things you may find in a Book of Shadows:

- Book Title and Date - when did you start your sacred text?

- Book Blessing - Say a few words on the first page, like an inscription, to bless your book, and let it know how much it will always mean to you.

- Index - give a brief overview of sections, like a table of contents, if that is how you wish to organize your book.

Some of the sections listed in your index might include the following:

- <u>Magical Rules and Principles</u> — What are your personal beliefs or the rules you choose to follow in your practice? What are your spiritual values on your path?

- <u>Goals and Intentions</u> — What are your short-term and long-term goals in your practice? Write down how you plan to succeed in your goals, what you would like to achieve, and how long you plan to give yourself.

- <u>Record of Dreams and Divinations</u> — What messages are you receiving from the spirit or your own higher self through your dreams and divination experiences? Use your intuition to record your introspections and interpretations.

- <u>Research and Study</u> — Keep a record of what you are discovering and learning along your path that feels important to your practice. Examples might be astrology, specific Gods and Goddesses, tarot, crystals, and their meanings, etc.

- <u>Spells and Incantations</u> — Keep a space with plenty of room to write and add new spells and incantations. You may review some of your spells, and add notes or ideas to improve each one based on your experiences with them.

- <u>Ceremonies and Rituals</u> — It's important to create a space where you can plan and detail your special ceremonies, celebrations, and rituals, depending on what your practice is and what you want to celebrate. Keep notes about how it went, what worked well, and how you might change it for next time.

- <u>Herbal Potions and Remedies</u> — These are personal recipes for brews, potions, and concoctions for healing and magical purposes.

You can include some, none, or all of these sections, and you can also come up with as many others as you want or need. Organizing your Book of Shadows is unique to you and your practice. See it as your creative devotion to your spiritual journey and allow it to unfold with you over time as you grow.

White, Black, and Red Magic

Some other types of information that might be included in your Book of Shadows are the kind of magic you are working with. There is a lot of controversy and debate over good and evil and white and black when it comes to magical arts. Some say that if it's black, it's evil, but that is simply not the way it works. There is also red magic, which, for some, is uncommonly heard of and is often misinterpreted and misunderstood.

This section will give you a brief knowledge about the different types of magic and what they can mean to your Book of Shadows.

White Magic

White magic has its connotations in being pure, virtuous, healing, whole, and beneficial. It has been historically considered a more appropriate form of magic to practice; there has been much persecution of another color of magic (see the next section) that gave white magic a better name.

According to historical context, white magic is seen as a healer's magic. Wise men and women who practiced magic for selfless reasons and the good of others, both physically and spiritually, were considered to be practitioners of the white magic.

Other sources have also shown that white magic is simply a part of the balance between light and dark and has its focus on the more masculine qualities of Wicca. For example, the harmony between opposing forces is one of the central beliefs of Wicca, and for those who choose to practice white magic only, or intentionally, they are guiding their source of power through the lighter energies and have a superior opening to work with that kind of magic.

If you have ever seen the popular yin-yang symbol, you will be familiar with the energetic balance between light and dark forces or the divine masculine and feminine energies in all things. White magic perceives reality through the lens of the white and the light and is associated with male energies, action, force, healing, wisdom, and manifestation for the good of all. You can also perceive white magic in the feminine form as the Maiden aspect of the Goddess who is all light and pure and comes to life at the time of year when the light is returning to the days and the dark period is coming to an end.

Depending on what you choose to practice, white magic can also be incorporated into your research of a particular deity or God/Goddess aspect. It all comes down to your faith, intuition, and beliefs and how you choose to enjoy the forces of white, or light, magic.

Black Magic

You've probably read all kinds of things online about how dark or black magic is evil, and practicing it means that you are supporting a dark art. According to the internet and other religious concepts, black magic is associated with the Devil, evil, hexes, curses, and so on and is a large part of what caused some people to be burned alive at the stakes in the centuries of witch trials and persecution.

Amazingly, this is a fear-based identification and always was, and black magic has nothing to do with "evil" or the Devil. In the last section, you began to see how white magic is part of a greater whole. In the concept and beliefs of Wicca, a great honoring and devotion to the balance of all energies in life is a benefit to embracing the world of the divine and the cycles and rhythms of nature.

Black magic is another side of "all that is" and can be regarded as the shadow realm or shadow side of your Wiccan practice. Unlike white magic, black magic embraces the less appealing forces of nature, like death and banishing, deeper emotions, and uncomfortable realities. It is an excellent source of power from the perspective of balance and is a requirement to understand Wicca in general, as well as all of the energy in all life.

Black magic can be viewed as the feminine counterpart to the balance of black and white. It is the yin of the yin-yang concept and embraces the night, the dark time of year, the Crone phase, the waters and emotions of all life, death and rebirth cycles, as well as many other forces. It is an authoritative source of energy to incorporate into any practice and should never be considered as evil. If you are in alignment with the Wiccan Rede "harm none," then you will know that whatever magic you perform must be pure of heart and intention. Therefore, black magic is used in Wicca as a balance to the light and the white and is seen as a part of a greater whole.

Black magic is about power, protection, banishing negative energies, reversing hexes, creating healthy boundaries, resilience, self-control, healing from loss and grief, inner strength, and death. It is a connection to the Crone, as well as the part of the cycle that embraces a darker night or the dark night of the soul and can be common among practitioners who worship a Crone Goddess like Hecate. It can also be viewed as masculine energy, depending on your practices and what deities you call into your circle for guidance and support.

Red Magic

There are a couple of interpretations of Red Magic that we will go over in this section. One of the more commonly known versions of red magic in culture revolves around the Hoodoo or Voodoo, which are practices brought to America from West Africa. These practices have a lot of similarities to other forms of magic ritual and spell and are also often related to some form of Bible scripture, as well as the use of potions, brews, and herbs, as with other spells. In addition, there may also be the use of more bodily fluids, such as saliva, urine, blood, semen, and menstrual blood.

Another form of Red Magic that you may have heard about from online sources is the concept of sex magic and that it is often referred to as red magic. Sex magic has nothing to do with sexuality, promiscuity, kink, or any kind of sexual expression involving arousal and the intention of spicing up your sex life.

Sex magic is a way to create and promote a more powerful manifestation. The energy of orgasm is incredibly powerful, and when you are casting a spell or performing a ritual, using the power of your sexual energies and the balance of your own masculine and feminine divinity, you can encourage and create a more powerful manifestation.

In general, it is suggested that you practice this kind of red magic on your own before you would consider including a magical partner. It isn't about sexual outcomes with another person; it is about casting magic into the Universe of all things and all energy through the use of orgasmic power.

Red magic, on both fronts (Hoodoo and Sex), has more to do with the visceral physicality of our natural power and has a sharp and distinct potency to ask for what it is you want to manifest. More research may be required to incorporate a journey through Red Magic into your Book of Shadows, and it will be well worth it to ask a lot of questions before delving into what that will look like for your practice.

Symbols, Signs, Runes, and Rituals

Within every Book of Shadows, there will be an assortment of magical symbols, signs, and runes that can be utilized through your spellcasting work and rituals to empower the energy of your spells. There are a large number of these symbols, and many of them come from a variety of cultures and religious backgrounds.

The best way to discover the magic of each symbol, sign, or rune is to find them through your research and expression of your craft. There are a variety of sources to find these symbols, and they will all serve a unique purpose to your spell work.

Examples of some symbols are:

- *The Triple Goddess* — It's waxing crescent moon on the left, a full moon in the center, and a waning crescent moon on the left (sometimes, a pentagram in the center of the full moon). It identifies the three stages of the Triple Goddess (Maiden, Mother, and Crone).

- *The Horned God* — It's a circular shape to mark a head with sideways crescent moon laying at the top of the circle on its side (sometimes a pentagram in the center of the circle). It represents the masculine aspect of God/Goddess.

- *Celtic Knot Symbols* — several variations of Celtic knots (i.e., Celtic Cross knot, Triquetra, and Odin's Cross). They are representative of various concepts like protection and calling on the God/Goddess.

- *Pentagram/Pentacle* — The pentagram is one of the most notable of Wiccan symbols. It's a five-pointed star that relates to the five elements and is a symbol of protection and ritual consecration. The pentacle is a disc that can have any of the above-mentioned symbols inscribed on it, most often the pentagram.

- *The Elements* — There are symbols for each of the four elements and the fifth Spirit, which can be engraved on anything magical in your work. They are representative of Earth, Air, Fire, Water, and Ether.

Runes are a whole other set of symbols in the form of an alphabet and have their origins in ancient Pagan religions and practices. Carved onto a piece of wood, bone, or stone, runes have an ancient symbolic meaning ascribed to each one and are used for divination and guidance in your practice.

As with the other signs and symbols listed above, runes can be written, inscribed, or carved into your ritual and spell ingredients to represent specific intentions and manifestations. These symbols are very useful as individual signs and can also be read together in a group to form a more accurate and detailed story or divination within your spells.

With all of these symbols and signs, you will also need to incorporate these magical engravings into your rituals. Your Book of Shadows will contain a variety of different ceremonies, most often things that you will repeat within a season, cycle, or time of year. The symbols you choose to include in your ritual ceremonies will depend on what you are celebrating, and you can inscribe the runes or signs into the instructions for your ritual.

All of your practices will be decorated by the Universal and spiritual message of each unique symbol or talisman of energy, and as you grow your Book of shadows, keep a separate section of these pictures and their meanings so that you can draw upon them for your spellcasting needs and magical uses. They are here to empower and invoke and will give you the right information to use when you are performing any ritual or spell incantation.

With all the details you have learned in this chapter about your personal Book of Shadows, you can now begin to craft it with the spells outlined for you in the next section. There is a variety of basic starter spells to get you started. Get yourself a big notebook and get excited to begin writing your very own Book today!

Chapter 4: Crafting Your Book of Shadows — Spells to Get You Started

This chapter is what you have been waiting for. It will give you a long list of spells to help you get started with your very own Book of Shadows. You don't have to copy them down, word for word, and you can try them out a few times before you commit to adding them to your Book.

Make necessary changes as you see fit. Don't be afraid to explore and enjoy the adventure of working your very own spells with these classic and basic examples of spells on love, wealth, health, luck, and other spells.

Love and Relationship Spells

SIMPLE LOVE SPELL

You will need the following items for this spell:

- A piece of paper, lined or not lined
- A red-colored marker, pen, or pencil
- An envelope
- Your preferred perfume
- Favorite red lipstick or another color you might prefer
- Some flower petals (pink and red; rose petals are very effective)
- Red candle and matches

1. Cast a circle.
2. With the pen and paper, write out all of the qualities you are looking for in a partner or lover. Be specific.
3. Spray your favorite perfume onto the paper when you are finished writing.
4. Fold the paper and put it in your envelope, but don't seal it yet.
5. Hold the flower petals of your choice in your receptive hand.
6. Creatively visualize your scene of happiness in love. What does it look like for you? Be specific with your vision of love. Let the reflection of this image flow into the petals in your hand.
7. Put the petals in the envelope and seal it, and with red (or another lipstick color) lipstick applied to your lips, seal the envelope with your kiss.

8. Put it on your altar and light a red candle.
9. Let the candle burn until it goes out.
10. Keep the envelope sealed, and never open it until your spell has worked.

***Special Note for Intentions: It is better not to use any characteristics or qualities of a specific person you know when writing it out on your paper. The spell doesn't work that *way*.

SEEDS OF LOVE SPELL

Consider performing this spell on a Friday. Friday is ruled by Venus, Goddess of Love and Romance. It will also work best on a waxing moon phase.

You will need the following items for this:

- An apple
- A piece of rose quartz
- Red rose (pink will work if you cannot find red)
- Green candle
- Pink candle
- Matches
- Rose incense or essential oil that you can burn

1. Cast your circle
2. While preparing your spell, think about the love you want to invite into your life.
3. Light the incense or the essential oil burner.
4. Light the red and green candles and lay the red rose in front of the burning candles.
5. Hold the rose quartz in your hand while you repeat some words to call upon the love you want to invoke and invite into your life. Sample incantation:

"Goddess of Love, Goddess of Light,
Grant me my wish on this lover's night.
I ask for sweet love, eternal and true,
With the flame of these candles,
And the scent of rose, too.
I ask for your aid and guidance to love,
Carry it with you on wings of the dove.
So mote it be!"

6. Thank the Goddess, and let the candles burn out completely. While they burn, eat the apple and save the seeds, thinking of love the whole time you eat.

7. After the ritual, put the rose, seeds from the apple, and rose quartz in a place where they can receive the energy of the moon (on a windowsill or altar space—make sure it feels sacred to your magic).

8. Wake up the next day, and plant the seeds in a pot of soil. Give them water and light to sprout and grow.

9. As you care for your seedlings, love will come into your life and begin to grow.

10. Let the rose petals dry and keep them with the rose quartz on your altar. You can put them in a small bag or sachet to remind you of your spell and carry with you.

HEALING YOUR PARTNERSHIP SPELL

You will need the following items for this:

- White candle
- Pink candle
- Matches
- Small cauldron (or fireproof dish or pot)
- Pen and paper
- Two pieces of string

1. Preparation for the spell: you can do this after you have your circle if you want your sacred space, or you can do it prior to the circle casting.

2. On one sheet of paper, write out all of the issues you may be having in your marriage or partnership. You can address your letter to the God/Goddess, another deity, or just to the great divine wisdom. Be as specific as possible. You will not need to show this to anyone else, so go nuts and pour your heart out.

3. On the second sheet of paper, go into great detail about what you want from your relationship. Go for all of the things you truly want, not what you think might work. Be clear and specific. Consider how you want your partner to treat you and talk to you, how you want your affection to be, what kind of romance you want to create, and so on.

4. Take some time to reread what you have written and then meditate on it. This would be an excellent opportunity to ground, center, and cast your circle if you haven't done so already.

5. With all of your ingredients and circle cast, light your white candle (peace and spirituality), followed by your pink candle (affection and love).

6. Put your first letter detailing your relationship issues and concerns into the cauldron, and set it aflame. Watch the flames devour the paper and meditate on the fire burning away and releasing all your relationship concerns and doubts. Say these words, along with the burning paper:

"Sacred fire, sacred light,
Carry away these energies tonight.
Let our love refresh and renew,
By your fire, making way for the new.
So mote it be!"

7. Take your second letter and reread it (out loud for a more powerful impact, but silently is okay, too). While reading, visualize the two of you, happy and harmonious.

8. Tie the two pieces of string together, each at one end, so that they make one long string. Make sure the knot is tight and secure. This knot represents your bond of love.

9. Fold the paper a few times over or roll it up and then tie the string around it. Say the following words as you do:
"Dear Goddess, Dear God,
Let me bond again with my love.
I ask for us to have harmony, love, and peace,
May your aid help the strength of our bond increase.
So mote it be!"

10. Close your circle and then bury the paper and string near a tree or other plant in your garden that represents love to you. Let Mother Earth take over and grant your love blessings!

SOULMATE SPELL

You will need the following items for this:

- Four red candles
- Two white candles
- Matches

1. For this spell, you will be using your 4 red candles to mark your circle, so as you cast, you will be placing each one of the red candles at different points, but do not light them yet. Place the candles 2-4 feet away from the center, where you will be standing or sitting.

2. If you can, sit with your body facing the north position.

3. Take several moments to center and ground yourself in your circle.

4. When you are centered and relaxed, open your eyes, and begin to call upon the elements to cast your circle. You can say whatever you usually would for each direction while lighting the candles one at a time, or use words appropriate to call a soulmate. Start at the north and move clockwise. E.g., *I call upon the north and the powers and spirit of the Earth to support me with your strength and grounding.*

5. Move to the East for Air and follow the same instructions from step 4. E.g., *I call upon the east and powers and spirit of air to free the path between me and my intention.*

6. Move to the South and continue. E.g., *I call upon the south and the powers and spirit of fire to strengthen my passion, desire, and emotion on this day.*

7. Continue in the west. E.g., *I call upon the west and the power and spirit of water to consume my intention to manifest and create.*

8. By now, all four red candles should be lit, and you can face the north position again.

9. Use a strong and powerful voice for your next incantations. You don't need to shout, but put some power behind your voice.

10. Have your two white candles/holders ready for this next step. Say the following or something like it and then light a white candle; place it in front of you, slightly to your left: *Within the balance and divine spirit of nature, I stand!*

11. You will light the second white candle and set it in front of you, slightly to the right and next to the other white candle. Before lighting and placing it, say something like this: *I am one with all things and the power and divine force of nature. I am happy to announce this night that I intend to draw my soulmate to me.*

12. Now, with both candles lit in front of you, say: *As I will it, I manifest into my life the soulmate that I desire. I am a creator and a power of light, and as I will it, so it is!*

13. Pick up the two white candles, one in each hand, and raise them to eye level, saying: *Two lights in an infinite Universe will unite at last by passion and love.*

14. Tilt the candles slightly to combine their flames into one. (If you are worried about dripping candle wax, you may consider laying out some newspaper to drip it on)

15. With the flames of the two candles combined, say: *As we come together as one flame, I bring this truth to pass and call my soulmate to me. So mote it be!*

16. With the two flames still combined, blow them out as one light and say: *I release my beautiful intention into the Universe. My purpose and creation have begun, and I will await my soulmate's love.*

17. You will now move counterclockwise through your circle to close it, blowing out each red candle as you go and stating some words of closure.

18. Turn to the west and say before you blow out the candle: *Water, my gratitude to you! Carry my purpose to the ends of the Earth with you!* (blow out the candle).

19. Turn to the south and say, "*Fire, my gratitude to you! Bring burning power and haste to this goal of love!* " (blow out the candle)

20. Turn to the east and say, "*Wind, my gratitude to you! Take my lover's intent to the corners of the world with you!*" (blow out the candle)

21. Turn to the north and say, "*Earth, my gratitude to you! Bring my love to me and ground us in fidelity!*" (blow out the candle)

22. Now, return to the north and close your eyes. Ground and center yourself and let the energy that you have created permeate your being. Give thanks and gratitude to the spirits present with you, and move forward with your day when you are ready.

GETTING OVER YOU SPELL

Perform this during a waning moon. Use it to get over a crush, an ex, or a broken heart. Uphold the Wiccan Rede of "harm none."

You will need the following items for this:

- A picture of the person you are attempting to get over (if you don't have a picture, draw one as best as you can, and cut it out and write their name on it)
- 1 piece of ginger root
- Black cloth
- Black cord or string

1. Cast your circle and call upon your spirit guides or other energies to help you with your spell.

2. Ground and center yourself inside your circle.

3. Hold the ginger root in your hand, and consider your feelings for the person and your reasons for getting over them. Let all of your feelings rise in your body, no matter what they are (anger, pain, sorrow, jealousy, longing). This is a good thing, even if it feels uncomfortable. It will help you release the feelings better to sense and know them at this moment.

4. Project your feelings into the piece of ginger, and let it absorb your feelings. Let out whatever wants to come out (crying, anger, shouting, etc.)

5. Take as much time as you need when giving your feelings to the ginger. It could take as much as ten minutes or an hour. Don't rush it. Let the feelings flow.

6. When you are ready, wrap the ginger and the picture of the person in the black cloth, and tie it shut with the black string. Secure the string with three knots and say: *I have a heart that is strong and free. I shall pine for you no more, and with this binding, so mote it be!*

7. Bury the bundle somewhere outside in the earth. As it decomposes, so will the connection to this person or whatever hold they had over your heart.

Wealth and Prosperity Spells

ABUNDANCE SPELL

Schedule this spell around a full moon.

You will need the following items for this:

- Copper bowl or silver goblet or chalice
- Three gold coins
- Fresh spring water (not tap—try to gather it from a flowing stream or spring in nature)

1. If possible, perform it close to a window so that you can receive the light of the full moon coming in the window, or complete this spell outside to get closer to the Full Moon energy.

2. Fill the copper bowl halfway with the spring water.

3. Cast a Circle.

4. Drop the gold coins in, one by one.

5. Place the bowl to allow the reflection of the moon to shine in the water inside of the bowl.

6. Focus on the reflection of the moon on the water's surface and state the following words:

I call for abundance to flow into my life.

I awaken my wealth by Full Moon's light.

My intention is prosperity

And my gratitude will last from here to eternity.

7. Close your circle.

8. Leave the bowl overnight. You can leave it under the Full Moon if you desire, or keep it on your altar or wherever the full moon's reflection can appear in the water or near the bowl.

9. In the morning, put the coins in your purse or wallet and never spend them.

WORK PROMOTION SPELL

This spell is useful if you are already putting in hard work to achieve your goals. You are not slacking off at work and are hoping for the best. It will help you move forward in your career.

You will need the following items for this:

- Beeswax candle
- A big handful of raw, rolled oats
- Bay leaves (whole and intact, fresh or dry. Make sure they aren't crumbled and in pieces)
- Clay Pot

1. Cast a circle.

2. Ground and center yourself, and think about the promotion coming up. Consider all of your recent efforts and hard work to get ahead. Feel the contentment and warmth and pride of a job well done, filling you up with light.

3. Toss the rolled oats into the clay pot.

4. Light your candle and place it near the pot.

5. Sprinkle bay leaves around the pot and candle, in a circle. (*Note: you can set this up on your altar as well).

6. State the following words: *Abundance, prosperity, wealth, recognition. I call for my career to receive this ignition.*

7. Close your eyes and visualize yourself agreeing to your promotion and how it will look for you in this new position. Nurture these feelings for several minutes.

8. Let your candle burn until it goes out. Move it to a safe place if necessary. Once the candle goes out, you can clean up your ingredients. Carry that vision of accepting the promotion with you. (*Note: you can keep everything on your altar to remind yourself of your intentions to help you keep a positive mindset about work).

MONEY FORM THE WAXING MOON SPELL

Perform this spell on a waxing moon—between the crescent to the full moon.

You will need the following items for this:

- Brown candle (the darker, the better—brown represents wealth and attracting income)
- Gold coin
- Cinnamon stick
- Orange zest
- Dried or fresh basil

1. Mix the spices and herbs and have them with you wherever you will cast your circle, along with any other items you need.

2. Cast your circle.

3. Light the candle and concentrate on the flame. As you focus on the flame of your candle, take 30 deep breaths, and visualize your prosperity and wealth entering into your life.

4. Gather the spices into your hands, and put the gold coin with them. Rub the spices and the coin between your hands and absorb the aromas.

5. State the following words three times: *Money glow, money grow, money flow!*

6. Let the candle burn down, or snuff it out if you need to.

7. Close your circle.

8. Keep the coin in your wallet. The effects should occur within a few weeks.

PROSPERITY SPELL

This is a long-lasting, treasure-chest spell to keep on your altar.

You will need the following items for this:

- A small box with a lid of your choice (make or buy it; embellish it, and make it personal and fun!)
- A magnet
- Coins
- Gemstones (money attracting)
- Crystals (money attracting)
- Beads
- Anything resembling money
- Glittery objects

Preparations for your treasure chest:

Cleanse all of the objects you want to put inside. You can do this after you have cast your circle or before that time. Smudge with sage, bathe in warm salt water, and charge in the sun or under a waxing moon. Any or all of these cleansing options will work.

1. Cast your circle.

2. Consecrate the tools that you cleansed (the objects to go inside your treasure chest). You can simply envision white light going through your hands into them, and think about how powerful they are to you. Light some candles in your circle (optional), and sit or stand at your altar with your treasure chest objects in front of you.

3. Ground, center, and meditate in front of your objects. Breathe in profoundly 7 times when you are ready to move forward with the spell.

4. Place the magnet in your box, at the center.

5. One by one, take an object to go into the box and hold it in your hand, pouring your energy and intention to it. Put praise into it as being sacred to you, full of abundance and bounty. Say these words to direct into each object you touch: *Money, Wealth, Prosperity, flow into my life, three times three!*

6. Place the object into the box and "see" prosperity flowing into your life.

7. Repeat steps 5 and 6 with every object.

8. Once all the objects and treasures are in the chest, close the box and hold your hand over it. Say the following: *Treasure box, with thanks to thee, may you be a magnet of prosperity. May wealth flow through you and into me. Let it harm none, so mote it be!*

9. Now, charge the box with energy. You can either use your own if you feel practiced with using your power, or you can set the box under the waxing moonlight and in the sunlight.

10. Once you have fully charge it with energy, place it on your altar or another special place. Don't let anyone else touch it, if possible.

11. Let it remain on your altar as an object, symbol, and magnet of prosperity.

NEW YEAR PROSPERITY SPELL

Try to coordinate this spell on a waxing moon before New Year's Eve. You may also modify this spell to be a general quarterly spell that you do every few months to maintain your intention of prosperity.

You will need the following items for this:

- Silk, satin, or velvet fabric (something "rich"), about 5 in by 5 in
- A piece of gold or green ribbon
- A tablespoon of cinnamon in a small bowl
- Sesame seeds (approx. 4)
- A coin (gold if you can find one, but any coin will work—just paint it gold)

1. Cast your circle outside in the sunlight or daylight if it is overcast. Create a workspace within your outdoor circle where you can work your sacred magic. (If it isn't possible to work outside, work in the window where light can be upon your objects and items. If daylight isn't possible, use an abundant candlelight or fireplace.)

2. Prepare your gold coin by painting it if you don't have one that is naturally gold.

3. Spread out your square of precious fabric. See it as a patch of the Earth—grassy, green, and mossy or rich-tilled soil (if brown). See it as the fertile Earth where you will plant your seeds of wealth.

4. Bring the bowl of cinnamon close enough for you to smell it and breathe it in (take caution that the powder doesn't get sucked into your nose, as it will cause irritation). Cinnamon is fire, passion, fertility, and material wealth. It will be good soil for planting seeds of abundance. Put the fabric onto the piece of cloth.

5. Empty your 4 sesame seeds into your dominant hand. Begin to think about the four seeds you will be planting for a year of financial fertility and success. E.g., investment, savings, promotion/raise, and frugality.

6. Picture in your head all of the ways you will take good care of your wealth and prosperity, such as putting a deposit in the bank, carefully calculating bills, paying off your credit card, etc. Use your creative visualization to "see" this activity and outcome.

7. Squeeze and hold the seeds in your hand while you visualize the specifics of your abundance and managing your financial fertility.

8. When you feel ready, plant the seeds in the cinnamon. Hold your hands over the pile of herbs and seeds, and make an opening for light from the sun or window to cast through your hands and onto the herbs.

9. Lay your coin on top of the cinnamon and seeds as an act of sealing your goals, aspirations, and intentions.

10. Gather the corners of the cloth, and tie it off into a pouch with the ribbon.

11. Carry the pouch with you until New Year's Eve.

12. Just before midnight on New Year's Eve, hold your pouch in your dominant hand—you will be coordinating with all of the energy that manifests across the world on New Year.

13. As the countdown approaches, hold out your receptive/magical hand (non-dominant) and hold it over your head or at heart level if that feels more comfortable, palm outward. (Don't worry about what everyone else is doing. Everyone is occupied at this moment.)

14. As the countdown starts, visualize your receptive hand like a magnet for all of the powerful energy being manifested all over the world to pull into you and empower your spell.

15. At the stroke of midnight, put your hands together to hold your charm pouch and shout, "Happy and Prosperous New Year!" Direct the energy all around you and to prosperity, through your hands and into the pouch.

16. Hang the pouch somewhere in your home or office, or wherever you keep financial statements, bills, and so forth.

17. After a couple of months, you can carry it with you in your bag or purse.

18. Recharge it at the Summer Solstice in June by burying it in the ground or by letting it sit in a full day of sun and through the night of a waxing moon.

19. Prosperous blessings!

Health and Well-Being Spells

SLEEP WELL SPELL

For a satisfying, restful sleep and pleasant dreams, this is a spell that promotes healing and rejuvenation.

You will need the following items for this:

- Sprigs of lavender, fresh or dried
- Smoky quartz ("dream stone," detoxifying, grounding)
- Piece of parchment paper
- Crisp, clean bedsheets
1. Make your bed with the clean sheets. You can light some candles to create a friendly, soothing, and warm effect in your room (optional). Make the bed, making sure the candles are

close enough to you, so you don't have to get up to blow them out. You don't have to cast a circle, but if you want to, cast a simple circle around your bed to keep you feeling safe and protected.

2. Sit on your bed in a comfortable position while holding your smoky quartz. Focus on the energy of the stone for several minutes, and let it ground you. Try to release any troubling thoughts as you meditate with the stone.

3. When you are calm, centered, and grounded, close your eyes and say the following incantation three times, holding the stone in your right hand and turning your wrist in clockwise circles: *The moon is up; the night is here, and with this piece of stone, I clear all thoughts of worry; for seamless sleep, let it carry me to dreamy waters deep.*

4. Wrap the stone and the lavender in the parchment and place next to your bed (or under your pillow, if you like).

5. Try it a few nights in a row to help you regain some comfort with your sleep needs. Practicing always makes for a better manifestation.

HEALING HAPPINESS SACRED BATH SPELL

This is a sacred ritual bath when you are stressed and feeling blue. It also works when you are in need of some tender self-love and care.

You will need the following items for this:

- A colored candle of your choice (choose something that pertains to healing your current state of mind, situation, or emotional well-being. E.g., yellow = happiness, joy, sunshine, and self-esteem; blue = tranquility, calmness, and healing; orange = joy and success)
- Other candles to surround your bath (optional)
- A cup of Epsom salt

- ¼ c of rose petals
- ¼ c jasmine flowers
- Essential oils to anoint your candle and add to your bath water (e.g., rose, neroli, or lavender)
- Lighter/matches
- Music of your choice (try whale song, nature sounds, or solfeggio frequencies to calm and relax your mind). Play your music throughout your ritual.

1. Mix your herbs and Epsom salt together in a bowl.

2. Place candles around your bath and light (don't light your colored spell candle yet).

3. Draw the bath water to a pleasant, soothing temperature.

4. Anoint your colored candle with essential oil of your choice. You can also carve symbols of healing, happiness, and joy into the way as you see fit.

5. Add the herb and salt mixture to the bath water and several drops of essential oils.

6. Climb into the bath water and relax into the aroma and warmth. Meditate for several minutes on the feeling. Visualize your energy transmuting in the water, and all negative energies are being pulled out of you. Take in the scent of the herbs and oils.

7. When you are ready, hold your colored candle in your hand and light it. Say the following incantation as you do:

Sacred water, sacred light,
Hold me close with all your might.
Fill me with your warm embrace,
And let me have this soothing place,

To release my doubts, my worries and fears,
My hurting soul, my sorrow, my tears.
As I light this candle flame,
I will let go of all my pain,
And warm my heart and soul with you,
Oh, sacred water, you'll see me through.
And so it is!"

8. Relax in the bath water for as long as you want, letting yourself sink into the healing energy.

9. When you are ready to get out, say a prayer of release to the water, which can be something like this:

With this water, I release,
That which does not serve my peace,
As you flow away from here,
Release all of my worries, doubt, and fears.
Turn it into something new,
Loving, bright, and joyful, too.
And so it is!

10. Leave the candle burning in a safe place and have a relaxing and calm evening. This would be a great time to brew up a healing cup of tea or calming potion.

HEALING CLEANSING SPELL

This is a spell to clear negative and unwanted energies from your being. You can perform this anytime you need a boost, when you feel drained, when you have low energy, or when you are tired from the outside influences of life.

You will need the following items for this:

- Sage smudge stick (Air)
- Silver candle (Fire)
- Sea salt (Earth)
- Chalice of water (Water)

1. Cast your circle.

2. Light your candle and smudge stick.

3. Waft the smoke all around you and over every energy center or chakra of your body.

4. Ground and center your energy, meditating for several minutes while the incense carries through the room.

5. With every deep breath you take, relax more into your center.

6. Visualize any negative energy flowing out of your energy centers, leaving your body and being collected and dispersed by the sage smoke in the air.

7. Hold the incense stick in your hand, and say:
   With this symbol of sacred air, I cleanse myself of what is not wanted there.

   Feel the cleansing aspects of the sage fold into you and help you release negativity.

8. Hold the candle in your hands, and say:

With this symbol of sacred fire, I burn away what I don't

desire.

Visualize fire burning away unwanted energies from your being.

9. Crumble sea salt in your fingers and rub it between your hands, saying the following:

With this symbol of sacred Earth, I let go of the old, so I can

be born again.

See the salt pulling the unwanted energies away and absorbing it.

10. Dip your hands into the chalice of water and say:

With this sacred symbol of water, I cleanse the energy that is

a bother.

See the water rinsing you of all unwanted energies.

11. Sit silently in meditation for several minutes, feeling the energy of the elements cleansing and purifying you. See your energy rebalanced and recharged.

12. Speak aloud or in your thoughts to any remaining energy that you may be holding onto. Ask the energy to leave you with direct intention. Say something like the following:

Any energy that hasn't let go, I release you now so that you

can go home.

I cannot keep you here with me, and that is why I say,

farewell unwanted energies!

Be authoritative with your voice and your energy. Be very declarative. You can change the words around to suit your needs.

13. Now that you have released all of the negative energies, you can begin this next vital step. Using creative visualization, begin to fill your body with light. Picture the places where you felt as if the energy extracted was negative, and fill these spaces with bright, colorful lights.

14. See a beam of light going through your crown, coming from the cosmos. As it beams into you, let it fill your entire being with positive life force energies.

15. Say the following as you see the light filling your body:

I am grateful to the energies of all that is; may I be filled with

the healing powers and cosmic gifts, and so it is!

16. Close your circle and feel your energy renewed.

HEALING A FRIEND FROM FAR AWAY SPELL

With permission from your friend, you can perform a distance healing spell.

You will need the following for this:

- 3 white candles
- Picture of the person you want to heal or help (if no picture is available, write their name on a piece of paper and visualize their image during your spell)
- Rose quartz, or other healing stone
- Incense (peppermint, gardenia, or eucalyptus)

**NOTE: some traditions will invoke the power of the Goddess Brigid for her healing powers. You can choose whatever embodiment of healing spirit corresponds with your practices.

1. Cast your circle.

2. Light the white candles and place them in a semi-circle in front of you on your altar or workspace.

3. Place the photo of the person you are healing inside of the semi-circle.
   Place the crystal on top of the picture.

4. Call the Goddess Brigid or another healing benefactor through some words and devotions of your choosing, depending on the deity you are calling.

5. Meditate for several moments on your intentions. Ground and center with these intentions.

6. Visualize the healing of your friend: you can sing, chant, drum, or dance—whatever feels most appropriate or intuitive.

7. Direct this meditative energy and focus into the crystal on top of the photograph. The quartz will enhance the strength of the

purpose, so really "see" the energy passing through the crystal and into the picture of your friend.

8. See the candles and their flames forming a protective ring of flame around your friend, burning away any illness, wounds, grief, etc. See the fire as a block from pain, protecting them.

9. See this healing light coating them and warming them with love, tenderness, affection, and healing power.

10. Ground yourself after this spell, and close your circle. You can leave the candles burning safely around your friend's photo with the crystal.

Wiccan Luck Spells

LUCKY OBJECT SPELL

Here are some important reminders for a Wiccan Luck Spell: 1) Harm None, or your spell will not work; 2) In addition to casting a spell or charming your talisman, you still have to put in the effort to achieve your dreams and goals while you carry it with you. A talisman, charm, or spell will help you open to the right moment for luck, but you have to do the work to be ready and open to it.

You will need the following for this:

- A unique object, like a crystal, gemstone, piece of jewelry, amulet, or another item
- Three gold coins

1. Cast a circle as you usually would.

2. On the floor, your altar space, or your work table, arrange the coins in a triangle around your talisman or object.

3. Touch each coin, one by one, and touch each coin with your dominant index finger. As you touch the coin, speak the following three times: *I ask the Earth, the Moon, and the Sun to imbue luck into my talisman. With grateful thanks and gratitude, I look for luck that is ever true. And so it is!*

4. Visualize light around your talisman as you ask for it to enhance with powers of luck.

5. *Modification: You can add candles to your spell to enhance the power and arrange them in a triangle with the coins so that your talisman is surrounded by candlelight and coin magic energy.*

6. Meditate on the feelings of luck and receiving gifts of luck from the universe.

7. Close your circle, and keep your talisman on your person at all times. Do not reveal its purpose to anyone.

BYE BYE BAD LUCK SPELL

Some say all your troubles come at once, and when they do, you can really feel it. This spell is here to help remove the energies that cause a string of bad luck or challenging incidences.

You will need the following items for this:

- Parchment paper
- Black pen
- Long, thin green candle (luck and prosperity)
- Matches
- Fireproof bowl or cauldron

1. Thoroughly clean your house to purge any unwanted energies. You may want to smudge every room as well.

2. Cast a circle where you want to work.

3. On a blank paper, write down all of the adverse incidences in detail in order of how they happened. Summarize how it made you feel and why it feels like a "bad luck" streak.

4. Light the candle, and set fire to the paper when you are ready (you may want to read it out loud to announce the energy you are trying to clear).

5. Drop the paper into the bowl or cauldron and let it burn.

6. While the paper burns, say the following in any variation: *Bad luck moments and misfortunes of the recent past, I burn and release you now; you cannot last.*

7. Let the paper burn away and scatter the ashes outside of your house, perhaps on the street to get them far away from you.

8. Close your circle and feel some newfound positive energy!

BASIC WICCAN GOOD LUCK SPELL

The power of this spell is enhanced when performed on a waxing or full moon and is best used to strengthen and empower an already existing goal or intention of success.

You will need the following for this:

- Frankincense incense
- Orange or gold candles, 3 pcs
- Pen and paper

1. Cast your circle.

2. Arrange the candles on your altar or preferred workspace in a triangle. Do not light them yet.

3. Speak the following words: *Goddess, God, Spirits, and Guides, thank you for your assistance and light. I ask you now for help with my goal, to [insert your goal or intention here]. I am looking for luck while I work to achieve, which will bring me the success that I need. And so it is!*

4. Visualize how your life would look if you had already accomplished your goals and had success. Feel how it would feel to be in this life, with that joy and prosperity.

5. Meditate for a while in this state and let yourself fall deeper and deeper into this meditation. Clear your mind and let yourself open to guidance from spirit.

6. When you go into your intuition, you will receive a message from the spirit—a symbol, a word, or an idea. Write it down on a piece of paper, whatever comes up.

7. Take the piece of paper with the image or words, and place it in the center of the triangle made of candles.

8. As you light each candle, state the following: *Sacred fire, sacred light, ignite my highest good tonight.*

9. Sit with the burning candles and the image you drew, and meditate on the luck you already have had and more coming your way, opening your heart to even more good fortune and success.

10. Express gratitude to your deities or spirit guides, and close your circle.

11. Bury your paper in the ground outside, and say the following: *Sacred earth, sacred light, seal my dream with highest good tonight.*

12. Your luck will arrive in a way that is exactly right for you. Be open to it and trust the energies that come for you.

13. Good Luck!

PASS-THE-TEST LUCK SPELL

This spell gives you good luck on exams and tests. You still have to study, but this spell will give you a boost of power and energy to help you succeed on the big day.

You will need the following items for this:

- Green candle
- An object to symbolize what the exam is testing you on (math, science, a notebook from your class, a textbook, a pop quiz, etc.)
- Lavender, Chamomile, and Rosemary, fresh or dried

1. The night before your exam is the best time to perform this spell magic.

2. You can cast the spell in a circle at your altar or wherever you want your workspace to be.

3. Light the candle with focus and intention about passing the test.

4. Scatter the herbs over your symbolic object (you can cover the object with parchment or muslin cloth if you are worried about herbs being on it)

5. Spread the herbs around with your hand. Breathe in the aromas. Visualize seeing the grade you want on your test.

6. Chant the following three times: *Good fortune, hard work, and luck be by my side; I will pass my test with pride.*

7. Blow out your candle, and get a good night's sleep!

8. Good Luck!

BUSINESS LUCK SPELL

This is best for deadlines, complicated deals, business expansion, difficult coworkers/employees, challenging business partners, and all business-related luck needs. You will need the following items for this:

- A handful of whole bay leaves, dry or fresh
- Green ribbon or string
- Three gold coins
- Piece of parchment

1. Cast a circle in your preferred workspace.

2. Make the parchment paper loose and pliable by balling it up and then flattening it back out.

3. Place the bay leaves and coins in the center of the parchment.

4. Gather the edges and pull them up together to form a pouch. Tie the edges with the string.

5. Hold the pouch in your dominant hand, and ground and center your energy.

6. Visualize the outcome you are hoping to attract with good luck. Spend several minutes with this.

7. To enhance the quality of this spell, use additional tools like crystals to add to your talisman or some candles to bring luck.

8. Keep in your work environment.

Other Spells

HOUSE PROTECTION SPELL

If your house has a negative feeling or has never really felt like yours, try this spell to help you shift your energy and protect the space from harmful or unwanted energies. It's best performed at sunrise.

You will need the following items for this:

- 4 glass jars with lids
- 1 cup of lavender (peace and purification)
- 1 cup of basil (protection and cleansing)
- 1 cup of sea salt (protection against psychic attack)
- 1 cup of rice (wards off spirits and encourages good fortune)
- Compass

1. Thoroughly clean your house.

2. Mix all of your herbs, either the night before your ritual or the morning before the sun comes up.

3. Get up before sunrise on the morning of your ritual, and fill each jar with some of the herbal mixtures. Evenly distribute between each jar.

4. Go outside, and place each jar in the corner of your yard at the point of the cardinal directions (North, East, South, and West). Use your compass to help you find the accurate placement.

5. As you place each jar, state the following: *Sacred [direction] of blessing and light, banish negative energy from my sight. Bring only light and love and truth; Goddess bless this space with the rising sun and setting moon.*

6. If you cannot place your jars outside, put them in the corners of your house that correspond with the cardinal directions.

7. Spend time meditating on your jars and their placement around your home. Enjoy a soothing cup of tea and light some incense and a candle (optional). Your jars will mark a shift of energy and protection in your home.

8. Blessings on your home!

STOP SMOKING SPELL

When you are ready to stop smoking and ditch the habit, this spell will help make it easy and painless. It's best performed at a new moon.

You will need the following items for this:

- 10-20 small pieces of paper (post-it notes work well)
- Pen
- Empty pack from cigarettes
- Black string or cord
- Fresh mint leaves, a cup or two
- Amethyst crystal

1. You can cast your circle before or after this step: write down all of the reasons you want to quit smoking for good. Write down all of the reasons you can think of why are ready to be a non-smoker. E.g., "Smoking makes me feel unwell." "Smoking is staining my teeth." "I am always out of breath and coughing."

2. Spend some time grounding and centering in your cast circle, reflecting on what you have written on the papers.

3. Pick up each piece of paper and read it aloud. As you read the reason you want to be a non-smoker, affirm your choice with a positive outcome. E.g., "Smoking makes me feel unwell" becomes "I will have so much more energy and health." Another example: "I waste so much money buying cancer sticks" becomes "I will save so much money and will be less likely to get cancer."

4. Meditate on how it would feel if you were already a non-smoker. Imagine how it feels, how you would look to yourself, how much it would change your life for the better, etc.

5. Roll up the piece of paper (or fold), and put it in the empty cigarette box.

6. Repeat this process for every paper you wrote on, putting each piece into the box until there are none left.

7. Close the box and tie the cord around it lengthwise, tying a knot three times.

8. Gather the fresh mint in your hands and rub it between your palms. Cup your hands over your palms and breathe in deeply. Let the freshness fill your body. Allow the scent to purify, cleanse, and heal your lungs and body.

9. Cup the amethyst in your hands. Imagine it pulsating with energy. Sit this way for several minutes, and feel the healing power of the crystal.

10. When you feel ready, say the following: *Sacred body of my own, I am a non-smoker; my body is my home. I love myself and all my light. Goodbye smoking from now on through the night! So mote it be!*

11. Enjoy the feeling for a few minutes before closing your circle.

12. Carry the amethyst with you regularly to help your energy. If you feel like smoking, let the power of the crystal flow through you.

**Note: You can use this spell with nicotine replacements. The object of the spell is to help you break the mental and psychological habit.

SUPPORTIVE SELF-LOVE SPELL

Loving yourself is potent magic, and this spell can help you achieve that energy within your life. This spell should be repeated often to help you exercise your ability to honor loving yourself often.

You will need the following items for this:

- Favorite incense
- Favorite color of candle
- Favorite essential oil
- Favorite aromatic herb or spice
- Favorite outfit
- Favorite flavor of tea
- Favorite crystal or gemstone
- Cauldron and charcoal disk
- Matches/lighter
1. Dress in your favorite outfit for magic.

2. Cast your circle of magic.

3. Light your incense.

4. With your essential oil, anoint your candle with your favorite scent. Carve a meaningful symbol into the wax (optional).

5. Place the candle on your altar or desired workspace after you have rubbed the oil on the outside and light it.

6. Place the charcoal disk into the cauldron, and light it until it is a glowing ember. Sprinkle your favorite herbs on top of the charcoal to burn and waft aromas into the air.

7. In front of these sacred elements, hold your favorite crystal in your hand, and let its energy fill you with happiness and love. See the energy of the stone coursing through your veins.

8. Visualize a light coming from the cosmos and beaming through your head and into your body and filling you with light. The light can be a color that makes you feel happiness, love, and joy.

9. Now, see the energy of your heart glowing like a lightbulb, getting brighter and brighter, extending throughout your body, and filling the whole circle that you have cast. Meditate with this love for yourself for several minutes.

10. When you are ready, say the following:

With all my heart and energy of light,
I ask for wisdom to love myself right.
From Mother Earth to Father Sky,
Fill my heart with your loving eye.
Help me see my true quality,
While I practice loving me.
I fill myself with loving light,
From within and from cosmic bright.
I am worthy of my love,
I give it to myself and all that is above.
Thank you to the divine in life,
For showing me how to love myself right.
So mote it be!

11. Place your favorite crystal on your altar by your candle. If you want to, you can also carry it with you in your pocket and sleep with it under your pillow.

12. Repeat this spell often or as often as you need it.

13. Add it to a sacred ritual bath.

14. After you have closed the circle, brew your favorite tea, and sit by your altar and candlelight and burn some more incense if you feel so inclined. Soak in the loving feelings you feel for yourself. And relax.

TALKING WITH YOUR SPIRIT GUIDES SPELL

This is an intuition spell to help you open your powers of intuition to receive divine guidance from spirit guides. Tapping into your innate ability to communicate with spirits will help you on your path, and this spell will help you stay awakened to those abilities.

You will need the following items for this:

- A 5 x 5 inch square of cloth, purple is best
- A cord or string (purple is preferred)
- A piece of quartz crystal
- A part of amethyst
- 5 purple spell candles (you can also use tea lights)
- Small piece of paper and a pen
- Sandalwood incense

1. Cast your circle on your desired workspace.

2. Set the five purple candles around you in a circle (they don't need to be a part of the circle you cast for protection and ceremony).

3. While lighting the candles, ask your spirit guides, divine guidance, and any other energies to help and protect you during this spellcasting.

4. If you aren't already seated in the middle of your candle circle, you can now take a seat and light the incense.

5. Take several deep breaths and relax. Hold your palms open to help you receive information from the universe. Spend several minutes in meditation, grounding and centering.

6. As you align with your higher self, allow your mind to receive a symbol that represents your higher wisdom and intuitive powers. Ask the spirit to send you this symbol, and let that intention extend out of the top of your head, through your crown, like a beam of light communicating with the spirit.

7. When you feel that your crown chakra is open, say the following words: *For clearer sight and clearer mind, a symbol of myself I will find.*

8. You can repeat this statement a few times while you focus and meditate on the energy of your higher self.

9. Once you begin to see a symbol, focus on it for a while, as long as you can. It can be absolutely anything.

10. Draw it on the small piece of paper when you are ready. This is the symbol that represents your higher wisdom.

11. Place the piece of paper, quartz, and amethyst crystals in the cloth, and tie the edges with the string.

12. As you close the pouch, you can say: *Dearest Angels, Spirits, and Guides, with gratitude, I walk with you by my side. I ask for clearer guidance from you, expanding my intuition, too. May this talisman heighten my mind and take me through to another side.*

13. Give gratitude to the spirits and energies, and close your circle.

14. Keep your talisman with you, and place it under your pillow at night. It will act as a beacon of divine communication. Use your talisman to meditate on confusing symbols, input, or messages you are receiving to get a clearer idea.

Chapter 5: Moon Magic Spells

Since the dawn of our human civilization, our lives have been governed by the power of the Sun and the moon. The moon has played such a vital and important role in myths, traditions, cultural practices and beliefs, and religious interpretations. For hundreds of thousands of years, it has been a great source of light, especially when it is full. It's also a way to help people structure and measure time.

The moon is closely connected with a variety of Goddesses and Gods all over the world and in various cultures, and throughout magic and mythology, it has been a central theme of human concerns like love, fertility, passion, death and rebirth, mystery, femininity, and afterlife matters.

Today, the moon has its same magic and power and will continue to influence people's minds, bodies, hearts, and spirits, whether or not they practice Wiccan or any other kind of moon worshipping religion or practice.

The power of the moon is considered watery, feminine, receptive, and of the Goddess. It can sometimes feel magnetic, making you feel "pulled" towards its energy. For some, it is physically powerful; for others, it may just feel like a heightened sense of awareness or perception.

Because of this connection to intuitive powers, psychic sense, and powerful magnetism to the great Goddess divine, the moon is a vital mode of perception and ritual practices in magic. When we intentionally connect with the power of the moon, we are engaging a live channel of harmony with the energy of the moon's cycles, the rhythms of nature, and the divine consciousness of all things.

The moon helps us manifest desired changes in our lives through the various cycles and the kind of energy emitted from the ever-turning moon. Lunar phases are beneficial in determining and interpreting when and how to use the moon for your spells.

Lunar Phases and When to Use Them in Spells

Witches and the moon are old hats. Witches have been dancing under moonlight since the birth of humanity, and so it goes without saying that if you are a practicing Wiccan or witch, you will find yourself in some connection or devotion to the moon and her vital energies and cycles.

Some will say that the moon is the most potent energetic force to affect your magic spells, rituals, and incantations. There are a variety of reasons people may think this way: the moon effects the tides, menstrual cycles, moods, and so forth. That is some pretty powerful pull to have such an impact as that. The entire ocean ebbs and flows because of the moon. Think about that for five minutes.

Some Wiccans and witches will not bother as much with magical timing, and everyone will see fit to develop their own unique and individual practices and techniques along the way. You may have to do some experiments to determine what is best for you. If you are interested in using the potent magic of the moon for your spells and craft, you will likely notice the impact of that magic overall on any of your spellcraft. See a quick overview of the moon phases below.

Phases of the Moon:

Phase: Dark Moon

Appearance: Invisible

Approx. Rising Time: Sunrise

Approx. Setting Time: Sunset

Phase: Waxing Crescent (New Moon)

Appearance: Slim crescent (facing right side)

Approx. Rising Time: Mid-morning

Approx. Setting Time: Mid-evening

Phase: 1st Quarter

Appearance: Half full (facing right side)

Approx. Rising Time: Around noon

Approx. Setting Time: Around midnight

Phase: Waxing Gibbous

Appearance: 3/4 full (on the right side)

Approx. Rising Time: Mid-afternoon

Approx. Setting Time: Earliest hours of the morning

Phase: Full Moon

Appearance: Round and full, complete

Approx. Rising Time: Sunset

Approx. Setting Time: Sunrise

Phase: Waning Gibbous

Appearance: 3/4 full (on the left side)

Approx. Rising Time: Early evening

Approx. Setting Time: Mid-morning

Phase: 3rd Quarter

Appearance: Half full (on the left side)

Approx. Rising Time: Midnight

Approx. Setting Time: Noon

Phase: Waning Crescent

Appearance: Slim crescent (on the left side)

Approx. Rising Time: Earliest hours of the morning

Approx. Setting Time: Mid-afternoon

Now that you have a general idea of all of the moon phase, you can see how their timing might affect different spells. The next section will discuss spells and each moon phase and how to incorporate them elegantly into your spells and rituals.

Dark Moon Magic

**Some people will call the smallest crescent waxing moon a "new moon" and the invisible moon a dark moon. You will have to determine your preference in your own practice. This book will offer that the New Moon is the very first glimpse of waxing crescent moon.

This moon is a powerful banishment moon. It is not harmful to banish unwanted energies, but just be sure that you are in a mental state of "harm none" when working with this powerful moon energy. For those who practice harmful forms of magic, this moon would be the best for curses. However, that is against the Wiccan way of magic and will not be promoted here.

Consider the dark moon an apt time to banish that which is not wanted or is ready to leave but is still clinging on. Call it the "moon of serious banishment." Examples might include banishing addictions, negative entities or spirits, serious illnesses, and diseases. This moon has serious energy to help you clear and release the more difficult situations in life like cancer, a menacing stalker, and addiction to drugs and alcohol. If you want to banish your habit of drinking too much coffee or a needy ex who won't stop calling you for late night talks, you might find a better opportunity on a waning crescent moon.

This is an excellent moon to look at your shadows, dig deeply, go beyond fear, and enter your cave of unwanted mysteries and miseries. This is a superb moon time to work with divination and powerful soul searching.

Waxing Crescent Moon Magic/New Moon

A waxing moon is a growing moon. It is going from non-visible to fattest fullness. A waxing moon has magnetic energies that help bring things out into the open. This is building magic, such as growing something in your life, setting up a foundation and adding the walls, developing and building a business, growing your self-esteem, and growing your financial success. It is a moon that can bring things to us through the magic of building and growing. Call it the "growing moon" or the "self-improvement moon."

According to some practices, a waxing moon can be considered the best time to work on matters that pertain to the self, involving new beginnings, plans, projects, and relationships. When you want to conjure or grow some new positive energies in your life, like patience, compassion, or a brighter attitude, then this is a perfect time. This is a moon of self-improvement, bigger psychic openings, artistic and creative endeavors, beauty, absorbing knowledge or new learning periods, and meditations to ignite more passion and inspiration in all of your work.

First Quarter Moon Magic

The half-moon in its waxing phase is the time of attraction. You might even choose to name this moon "the attraction moon" to help you remember its benefits and powerful magic. The previous moon, the self-improvement moon, was about going within and bringing things to the surface; the attraction moon is about pulling desired energies from outside of yourself to you.

This moon is an excellent time for spells that involve things that you want to attract into your life. Typical examples are money, social and career success, and protection. Love is probably the most popular choice, along with money and success. This is a moon to attract people into your life, especially lovers and partners, but also friends, colleagues, clients, and even a pet or an animal companion.

If something has gone missing from your life, like a precious object or a wallet, you may cast a spell at this time to help you find what you are looking for. This is also an excellent opportunity to cast magic to find the house of your dreams if you are house hunting.

Waxing Gibbous Moon Magic

The waxing gibbous moon is getting closer to the full moon, and it is an energy-boosting moon to help you give some extra push to your goals and projects that need to make it over a finish line. It is the "boosting moon." It's all about reeling and going that final distance with what you have already set into motion and have been working on. When your work might be falling apart, stalling, stagnating, or is feeling flimsy, the waxing gibbous moon will help you push forward and through.

It is a good time for renewing strength, determination, and will power in all of your ventures and efforts and will help see you all the way through. Some examples of a situation where this is applicable are giving in to temptation on your diet, burning out from working hard on a major project for work, and starting to get distracted and lazy because you are tired and lackluster. Use the "boosting moon" for all of the spells to help you renew your efforts and keep going on.

Full Moon Magic

The most powerful moment of the lunar cycle, the full moon, is the time when the Earth is between the moon and the Sun, and the rays of sunlight are bouncing off the moon's face and reflecting fully back to us. It is in total alignment. This moon is an all-purpose moon and has such powerful energies it can be used as a constructive or "building" moon or as a destructive and releasing or "letting go" moon.

This moon is for your most important and powerful spells. It has the most energy of all the moons and will give any of your rituals and spells the direct power and influence that it needs to manifest your intentions and goals. This is for the moments of significant change in your life that need the magic of the full moon to help those changes occur swiftly and smoothly.

You can plan any spell on the full moon, but consider this moon for your priority spells and incantations. What are the things that matter the most in your life, and how will you ask this moon for aid and support?

Any magic, meditations, purpose, or goals that are revolving around your openness to spirit, your psychic abilities, and development, dreams and divinations, and intuition are particularly enhanced at the time of the full moon.

Waning Gibbous Moon Magic

After the peak of the full moon, the waning begins. The waning energies of the moon are going to repel rather than attract energies, so this time will be the most important time to get rid of things, like shedding a skin.

The waning gibbous moon is a good time for minor releases and banishment spells, general cleansing rituals in your home and workspace, and even for your energies that you may be carrying over. You can cleanse personal objects, magical tools, and implements, your altar, and your car. This moon can be called the "Dusting Moon" as if you are just going around the place and dusting everything. Perhaps there is no significant buildup of unwanted energies, but it is good to do a maintenance check to keep things clear and open.

This can also be a good moon for closure with certain things, such as relationships that were not fulfilling for you or complicated business relationships that need to be let go of. This is a place for reflection and introspection. It is a nice time to take stock of how you are feeling about current matters in your life. Ask yourself some questions: what is affecting me the most in my life right now? How did my choices bring me to this place, and am I satisfied with those choices? What adjustments, if any, do I need to make moving forward?

Third Quarter Moon Magic

Call it the Waning Half Moon or the "Remover of Obstacles Moon." This moon can be beneficial with leaping over hurdles that present themselves on your path. Obstacles always appear at some point on our journey, and this moon can help you achieve an opening with your spell work to make sure that you don't stumble over the roadblock ahead. It is bursting away from anything that would set you off track or slow down your progress.

Many people will use a third-quarter moon to help deal with temptations. After all, temptations can be a massive obstacle in achieving your goals. Working with this moon during your spell work would help banish the roadblock of temptation, whether it is on your diet or exercise routine or involving study or promotion. Use the "Remover of Obstacles Moon" to help you stay on your path.

Another way to use this moon's energy for a spell is when faced with transition periods. Whether they are purposeful or something that you have no control over, working a spell to aid with transitions at this time will have an even more powerful impact on your path.

Waning Crescent Moon Magic

The waning crescent moon is helpful in cleansing and clearing negativity from all parts of your life. This is a stronger banishing time, as it gets closer to the strongest banishing moon again—Dark Moon. Whatever has been plaguing you that is annoying, concerning, or frustrating, (unless they are so serious that they need the Dark Moon), the "Banishing Moon" will help you.

This moon will clear the decks of anything that needs to get going. It has more potency than the previous moon for this kind of work, so if you find that you need even more power for letting go of something, the Waning Crescent moon is an excellent time to cut cords, tie off loose ends, and bring hopeless cases to a close. This is also applicable when what you want is more than just dusting off but not quite banishing something seriously from the dark moon. It is a swift and benign ending with a Banishing Moon.

Best Ways to Use Moon Phase Magic

So, what happens when your magical needs don't always correspond with the best moon timing? This has certainly been known to happen, and you may not want to be waiting for the ideal timing to get going on your practice of a specific spell. So, how do you work around all of that?

This is when you can get creative and think outside of the box. An example might be if you are trying to lose weight. You can use each moon phase differently to help you with your goals. A Waxing Crescent moon will be ideal for helping you grow your will power and your energy to stick to your weight loss goals, while a Waxing gibbous moon will help you have those little triumphs over cravings of tempting foods. In a waning moon, you can cast magic to destroy or banish tempting foods that you know will be bad for your progress. You get the picture.

Always consider what you are trying to accomplish, and then consider what the current moon phase can do to help you with that accomplishment. You may need to get your goal outlined clearly ahead of time and look at the moon phase calendar ahead. Your whole goal could be achieved in a deliberate casting that covers the entire lunar cycle. I guarantee that no matter what intention you are casting for, any of the moon phases will have strong, elemental power to contribute in some way. All you have to do is get creative with how you work through a moon phase.

Let's use love spells as an example. Your overall goal could be to bring a soulmate into your life. You can use a Waxing moon time to call your soulmate to you, and variations of that waxing moon can be utilized to help you grow love within yourself to draw them closer and to empower the love that you will feel when you come together. You can also use the power of a Waning moon to help you let go of and banish any old cynicism or bitterness you may be feeling in your heart from older love partnerships. You can cast magic to release your wounds and heartaches and help you open more fully to love.

You don't have to use an entire lunar cycle to cast multiple spells for one goal. You can simply time a one-off, specific spell throughout the cycle and fit it in where it feels appropriate. If you are eager to perform a spell, and it isn't the right moon time for it, consider how you can dynamically utilize the current moon power to help you achieve your goals. There is always a creative way around it.

Wiccans will also use planetary signs and signals, such as astrology, days of the week, and so forth, rather than just the moon's phase. You may find that utilizing the astrology of whatever sign the moon is passing through to help you out. Days of the week all have specific energies and are ruled by different planets, and you can use this kind of energy as well if the moon isn't right when you need it to be in a cycle for your spells. Not everything will line up neatly and perfectly every time, and so it is up to you and your practice to find the timing that will work best for you and your casting.

Fortunately, magic is not an exact science; it's more like creative art, like fine cooking, and so it will take some playful experimentation and practice while you get acquainted with the moon and her powerful resources better.

Solar and Lunar Eclipses

Wicca will always have some kind of connection to the moons and the seasons, and a part of that ritual reality is there will often be a regular state of eclipse. You may think that this is too advanced, but eclipses are just enhanced moon/sun energies that need some special understanding to properly use them for your spells. Eclipses are a unique moment, and you can enjoy feeling their power through your rituals and spellcasting for an even more powerful and beneficial moon and sun experience.

Eclipses in General:

During an eclipse, time seems to stand still or hold on for a moment before continuing forward, business as usual. It has a charge of intensity that can be felt by everyone and when you are able to connect with one and coordinate your magical practices around it, you will surely feel the intensity of this power. It is like a time between worlds and will hold your spell closely and reflect it back to you in a potently magical way.

A Solar Eclipse

Just like the moon, the sun waxes and wanes; however, it will do this over an entire year, instead of a 29-day cycle, like the moon. The shortest day of the year and the longest night is the Winter Solstice, and the sun is only visible for a few hours. This would be considered the fully waned moon. After this, the sun waxes as we move toward the Spring Equinox, and the days become longer and brighter with the Sun's energy. By spring, days and nights are equal in length. By the time of the Summer Solstice, the sun stays visible for the most extended period (like a full moon phase) before it starts to wane into the fall and by the Autumnal Equinox, where days and nights are equal again, edging to the darkest time of the Sun, the Winter Solstice.

So, with that knowledge, you can now look at the solar eclipse and how the solar energy of an entire year can be packed into just a few minutes of eclipse energy. Some have called a solar eclipse a "micro year" because of how the energy from a full year of the sun's waxing and waning can be felt in such a short moment. The sun is whole and then partially or completely hidden by the shadow of the moon before becoming visible once again. In those moments when the sun is covered, the energy of a whole year's sun cycles is condensed, and it feels as if time has stopped.

The Moon's presence in this phenomenon is of vital importance as well. It is her shadow falling against the Earth's surface, appearing between the Earth and the Sun and bringing together and unifying the solar and lunar energies in one moment. It is a sense of wholeness and completion that occurs and can be so viscerally felt at this time more than others.

Solar eclipses can only occur in daytime and on a new moon. This energy is a time for planting new seeds, ideas, and projects. Just consider how much more potent your magic will be with the full power of the sun backing up the full potential of a new moon! It Doesn't need to be visible to you for you to work your magic. In many cases, a full solar eclipse is visible at certain times of the year to specific continents. All you need to do is know when they are coming to prepare accordingly. You can still harness that power without being on the continent where they will be most visible.

When working with the energies of a solar eclipse for your magical purposes, consider what kind of moon you are working with, as well as the season of the year you are in. Is the sun waxing or waning? What are the lunar influences? What time of year are you working with? Cater your spells directly to these influences, and watch your magic, spells, and rituals become empowered with this strength and energy!

A Lunar Eclipse

The moon has a monthly cycle, rather than a yearly one (approximately 29.530587 days). This is when the moon waxes and wanes and then starts all over again. The moon is completely dark and invisible just as it is becoming new again. A crescent moon then appears to begin the waxing journey, heading to fullness. After the fullest moon, it begins to wane back down into a crescent until it reaches total darkness.

With a solar eclipse, you feel the "micro year," and with a lunar eclipse, you feel a "micro month." During a lunar eclipse, the moon is full and then is partially or fully hidden before becoming visible again. In just a few, short minutes, the energy similar to an entire moon cycle can occur (only with a total lunar eclipse will this happen).

It is the Earths shadow that falls across the moon, making us more aware of her presence and her relationship to the moon's energies. The Earth appears between the moon and the sun and the three of them in perfect alignment at this moment create a strong and potent lunar and earthly force. Both the Earth and the Moon are considered the feminine energy and so at this time, focusing on the Goddess is particularly helpful and beneficial, if it is part of your practice and desired in your work.

Lunar eclipses can only occur on the night of a full moon, so you will be working with that powerful full moon energy in your spells and rituals. This is a perfect time for letting things go, and you will be able to do that much more powerfully with this eclipse influence.

As with a solar eclipse, the lunar eclipse doesn't need to be visible for you to utilize the power of this time. You won't be able to enjoy every eclipse with your eyes unless you have the ability to be a regular world traveler! You can just schedule accordingly by looking for the timing of the eclipse to help you with your spells.

For your spellcasting work around a lunar eclipse, consider working on your psychic abilities and openness to spirit. It is a good time for working on clearing blocks and energies that are stuck. Reflect on how the moon's energy is full and what season you are working in. What kind of moon time is it during the year? What seeds were planted before it became full? How long have you been working toward something powerful, and have this moment to release it fully and give birth to it?

Consider all of the essences and energies of a lunar eclipse before you work with it. Check your moon phase calendar to find the specific dates and seasons for them and enjoy working with these extra powerful moments in time!

Moon Circle

All over the world, people gather to celebrate the moon. Whether they are Wiccan or Pagan, the moon has always been a draw for people to come together and celebrate. All over the world, they cast their magical circles and join hands to enter the space between worlds. Moon circles are always happening, most often at the full moon, and other circles convene at the time of the New Moon as well.

Most will always conjure magic at the full moon time, when the sun and moon are in complete opposition to each other, bringing us into closer balance with ourselves and each other. All over the world, on the night of a full moon, people are celebrating with candles, incense, food, and spell work. That is such a powerful energy to consider. If we are all working together on the same night for these moments, it makes the energy of all things much more powerful. It's no wonder the full moon has such a strong, long, and potent history.

A circle can be a couple of people or a large group in a room or sacred space, or they can be outdoors in the open under her powerful fullness and magic presence. However, as many people are involved in a circle, the energy is sparked between human life forces and the energies of everything all around. It will always feel more powerful on the full moon when you consider just how many people all over the world are sitting together with their fires, candles, tarot decks, and friendship, hailing the life force behind this luminous power.

Moon circles are a time for people to come together and reveal what has come to fruition. Whatever kind of circle you are in, if you have a moon circle, you will likely talk about what seeds you have planted back at the new moon, two weeks ago, and how that has come to fruition. The full moon circle is your collective harvest time.

Moon circles are great places to determine what worked and what didn't. It is the community where you can talk about your connection to her divine source and express what you have reaped from planting your intentions in the soil of your life. What was asked for? What came back to us? It is a time and a place of self-discovery as well as community discovery.

Moon circles are a place to dance and sing, sway and laugh, cry, and absolve our worries and fears. The moon lights the path for everyone involved to help you resolve any pressing matters with the love and connection of those who are there in balance with you. It is a place to release new intentions and manifestations into the world and to have others bear witness to our life progress.

You may not have access to a moon circle at this time, but they are not hard to find, and you can even join one online and be a part of a collective of people all over the globe who come together to share and celebrate. You can even start your own moon circle and see who might want to join you and become a part of the journey of the moon's cycles. It can be a fun practice to involve friends, family, or new acquaintances to help you and others explore the growth and expansion that comes from working with moon energy.

Bring your candles and your crystals. Bring some soothing tea and wine. Bring some honey oatcakes. Whatever the occasion calls for, a Moon Circle is a vibrant, bright, and illuminated time for you to get closer to others through the magical power of the moon.

Moon Magic and Healing Spells

With all of this new information about the moon phases and how to bring them into your spell work, check out these moon magic spells for your Book of Shadows, and have fun organizing your magic around the magic of the glorious moon.

NEW MOON SPELL

A New Moon Spell can be performed on the day of the moon or three days after. This is a time of new beginnings, opportunities, love, and health, as well as many other options.

This spell will help you form a bond and relationship with the moon's energy by inviting her back into her growth phase.

You will need the following items for this:

- Smudge stick
- White candle
- Black cloth
- Silver/white cloth (optional)
- Moonstones/crystals (optional)
- Blessing oil/essential oil
- Mirror (handheld)
- Pen
- 3 Sheets of paper
- Cauldron or fire safe dish

1. Decorate your altar with moon colors—silvers and whites. This can include cloth and fabrics, objects and candles, or crystals.

2. Smudge the area of your altar and where you will be working.

3. Cast your circle.

4. Wrap your white "moon" candle in the black cloth and place it on your altar.

5. Smudge the candle in the cloth and meditate on the darkness of the moon and her return to light.

6. Try to locate the moon, either through a window or outside. When you can spot it, take your black cloth-wrapped candle and hold it up to the moon, and say the following:

Welcome back, moon who grows!

I am happy to see you again, and what you know.

Another cycle, passed and gone,

Now we are moving forward and along.

And we will find you growing strong.

And so it is!

7. Unwrap the candle from the cloth, and place in a holder on your altar. Light it while you say the following:

    Today is new, with the moon on her way,
    With every tide, she grows bigger each day.
    I am grateful for her return.
    As I praise her, let this candle burn.

8. Face the east, where the sun rises, and hold the mirror up so that you can look over your shoulder to where the moon will be (again, you can perform this ritual outside, if you are in a windowless room). Say the following:

9.

    New Moon, bring me your guidance and wisdom.
    Show me with protection, my vision.
    You help me every step of the way,
    I am thankful for your guidance every day.
    With my thanks and blessings,
    To you, New Moon.
    So it is!

10. Place your mirror next to the candle on the altar.

11. Spend the next several minutes in reflection and gratitude for the growing moon. On the first sheet of paper, you can write down everything you are thankful for. Once you have written all of your expressions of gratitude, put the page on fire with your moon candle and let it burn in your cauldron.

12. On the next piece of paper, make notes about what you have NOT been doing right lately, such as mistakes, errors, poor judgment, choices with negative consequences, things that may have hurt you or others, and so on. Forgive yourself, and release these negative energies by burning the paper with the flame of the moon candle, placing it in the cauldron to burn out.

13. On the last sheet of paper, make a list of all the things you would like to have in your life—your goals, intentions, desires, and dreams. Be specific. Leave nothing out. Do not burn this list. Keep it until the next new moon.

14. Warm up your blessing oil or essential oil over the flame for a few moments and then anoint your forehead, at your third eye, to open yourself to the blessing of the new moon. When you are ready, you may blow out the candle and close your circle to end the spell.

FULL MOON WISHING SPELL

This all-purpose, full moon wishing spell will help you capture the energy of the full moon for whatever your needs may be or to help you bring something unexpected into your life.

You will need the following for this:

- A clear, glass jar (pint size or larger)
- Pure, clean water
- A bell
- Silver coin
- White/silver candle

**You will want to cast this spell where you can have a clear view of the moon. That could be through a window near your altar or workspace or outside.

1. Wherever you are working, cast your circle.

2. Fill your jar with water, and light the candle near where your spell will be performed.

3. Sit under the moon, and absorb her light and energy for several minutes.

4. Drop the coin into the jar of water. Allow the water to settle until it has relaxed from the ripples of the coin drop and is smooth again. You want to have the reflection of the moon on the water's surface and shining down on the coin if possible.

5. Gaze at both the refection and the coin together and use your bell. Ring the bell three times while looking at the reflection.

6. Speak your wish or intention aloud (you can also ask the moon to bring you general good fortune as well).

7. Close your circle.

8. Bring your equipment back inside (if you are outside), and leave your coin in your water jar on your altar until the next full moon or until your wish has come true.

WAXING MOON COURAGE SPELL

Add some courage to your plans with this waxing moon spell.

You will need the following items for this:
- White candle
- Red candle
- 1 or 2 sprigs of holly or honeysuckle
- Oil burner
- Lavender essential oil
- Black pepper (freshly ground is preferred but not required)

1. Cast your circle

2. Burn the lavender essential oil in your oil burner.

3. As the fumes begin to enter the air, you can add the pepper grinds onto the burner.

4. Light the white candle on your altar. Stand or kneel if you want, and ask for courage for your specific goals and intentions and whatever challenges lie ahead as you stare into the flame.

5. Use your creative visualization for several minutes to view your triumph. See the specifics of your success.

6. After you have spent time with this meditation, you can now light the red candle.

7. Stand in front of your altar, in front of your candles, and say:

Courage and strength, I shall possess,
That all my fears become less and less.
On winning ahead, on to the other side,
On victory's road, I will ride, ride, ride!
And so it is!

8. If it is safe to do so, let your spell candles burn out, or you can blow them out.

9. Close your circle.

WAXING MOON SUCCESS SPELL

You will need the following items for this:

- Yellow candle
- Something to carve the candle with (like a pin or sharp-pointed object)

1. Cast your circle.

2. Carve a symbol of success into your candle wax (money signs, rune symbols, anything that represents success to you).

3. Light your candle and focus on the flame.

4. Use your creative visualization to visualize your success beyond your wildest dreams. Get creative and specific. See yourself in a life of success.

5. Sit and watch the flame flicker and dance for as long as you need while you meditate.

6. Let your candle burn out and close your circle. Be sure to supervise your candle so that it stays safe.

7. Once the candle has burned out and the wax has cooled, keep your wax in a container or bag on your altar.

BANISHING SPELL FOR THE WANING MOON

You will need the following items for this:
- Pen
- Paper
- Cauldron or fore safe bowl

1. Cast your circle.

2. On the paper, write down everything you want to banish from your life. Be clear and specific, and remember: harm none.

3. Once you have finished your list, read through it and out loud if you want to make it very clear and obvious. Keep focused on your intention to banish these elements from your life.

4. Light the paper on fire, and drop it into your cauldron, allowing it to burn all the way out. As it burns, see all of the things on your list leaving your life and being extinguished.

5. Now, imagine what your life will be like without all of those elements in your life (you may start planting those new seeds at the new moon and waxing crescent phase ahead).

6. Close your circle.

7. Take the ashes outside and bury them in the ground under the moon.

THE POWER OF ACCEPTANCE SPELL: WANING MOON

You will need the following items for this:
- White candle
- Paper
- Pen

1. Cast your circle.

2. Take some time to ground and center yourself and reflect for a little while on what you need acceptance with.

3. On the piece of paper, write down all of the things about your self or life that you have difficulty accepting.

4. Then, write down all of the changes and challenges that you know you need to face to accept and come into terms with these things.

5. Light your candle and focus on the flame.

6. See yourself letting go of all of these traits, issues, or circumstances, and accept the new life you want to set into motion. Use your creative visualization skills to picture this

happening. See doors opening for everything you want to go on, accepting them along the way.

7. See yourself in your third eye, feeling peace and fulfillment.

8. Watch the candle flame as long as you need to.

9. Let the candle continue to burn safely until it goes out. Close your circle.

10. Keep the cooled remains of the wax on your altar until the acceptance has proven itself to you.

Many have suggested that candle magic is one of the oldest forms of magic in our human culture and evolution. It may or may not be correct, but within the candle is the power and ancient resource of fire, which was how we evolved in specific ways and, over time, how we chose to worship in certain ways, too.

Pagan religions of old not only used candles for their rituals and worship but also torches, bonfires, and flaming symbols in devotion to their deities. It was the only source of light at night until the advent of electricity, other than the moon, and so it is easy to notice why this sacred element was so honored and revered in magical ways.

Even after the invention of electricity and modern lighting, the fire continues to be a powerful force used in many religions and cultures for more than just heat, light, and a way to cook food. Candles are regularly used in various cultural traditions and practices and can be found in a majority of households for a variety of reasons. Consider the blowing out of the candles on a birthday cake and the lighting of candles at a holiday dinner with family.

Candles conjure a pleasant, warm, and magical atmosphere, and it is no wonder why they are still used in so many spells and magical rituals today. They are also the element of the South, and when you cast your circle, having at least one candle burning to represent this energy is ideal. It some of the most accessible and beautiful magic you can use, and this chapter will help you know more about what candle magic can look like.

How Magic Candles Works

Candles are a great source of magic for a beginner, as well as a seasoned practitioner, because of how they help you to focus and direct your magical intentions and purposes. It is a great way to assist you in strengthening your divination, visualization, and communication skills with yourself and with the divine spiritual energies called in to aid and guide you.

A candle is a beacon, announcing to the Universe that someone is calling for energies to unite and make new energy out of it. The power of all thoughts can be imbued into a candle's flame and magic, and that is what the basis of magic really is—turning thoughts and energies into realities.

Magic is the art of sending a particular thought, goal, or intention into the spiritual plane to have it take shape and manifest in the physical world. Candles are messengers who help you achieve this magical goal. They are also channels or mediums to convey your messages or intentions and goals to those divine energies called upon to help you and guide you.

The candle burns through the wick, the wax, and the air all around and slowly disappears, carrying your message from the earth plane to the ethereal plane, striking a chord of energetic intention into the fibers and vibrations of the whole universe. To see your intention burning away through the magic of candles is truly a helpful way for you to put your purposes further out into the world. It is a symbol of the physical manifestation of your purpose into a message for the divine.

To go a step further, the candle is thought by some Wiccans to be the perfect balance of all four elements. The wick that passes through the center of the candle and leaves the bottom, like a root plunging into the soil, is the element of Earth. It is present to keep the candle burning, without which it could not burn all the way down to the bottom. The wax of the candle is seen as the water element. As it transforms from a solid form into a melted and watery form and then eventually evaporating as gas, it has all of the qualities of water's many shape-shifting forms, and it's what gets carried away to spirit.

Without oxygen around the candle, the flame could not burn. The element of Air, present all around you, is what calls the candle flame into being and keeps it burning. If you eliminate the air around it, with a candle snuffer or lid to a candle jar, you extinguish the light and the flame. And last, but most appropriately, the fire element is represented by the burning flame at the top of the candle, which rests close to the wax as it melts away and burns the wick as it continues to burn.

It is valuable to consider the magic of the whole candle and how it can establish the presence of all four elements, carrying your message away to the fifth (spirit). When you use candle magic, you are harnessing the power of the elements and how they contribute to every act of magic you are performing in your practice.

Color Magic in Candles

In addition to their elemental magical properties, candles come in a considerable variety of colors, and like with most things in this world, there is special magic behind every color that you use in your spells and rituals. Color magic helps us further direct our intentions and purposes by more clearly stating and representing what we choose to manifest.

Throughout the centuries and our history as a people, colors have carried specific meanings across cultures and have a universal identity and characteristic associated with each one. When you see the color red, you might instantly think of love, passion, desire, blood, and heat. When you see the color green, you might think of money, luck, four leaf clover, and Mother Earth. Colors pull our energies in specific directions because of their symbolic associations.

Utilizing color magic with your candles helps to reinforce particular goals and intentions that are being set. You may see in your research that these candles will be referred to as "spell candles," but any colorful candle you find can be charged and consecrated for magical uses.

Magical Properties of Color

The list below will offer you some of the magical properties associated with each color. You may find other sources in your research that provide additional insight into various ways that color can have symbolism and meaning. Use your intuition when working within your practice, and let it guide you to the right color for your candle magic spells.

Red — Love, romance, passion, courage, intense emotion, willpower, strength, physical energy and vitality, health, root chakra, and fire

Orange — Power, energy, vitality, attraction, stimulation, adaptability (especially with sudden change), and sacral chakra

Yellow — Communication, confidence, study, divination, intellect, inspiration, knowledge, and solar plexus chakra

Green — Prosperity, wealth, growth, fertility, balance, health, luck, abundance, growth, renewal, heart chakra, Mother Earth, and Mother Moon of Triple Goddess

Blue — Healing, psychic ability, understanding, peace, wisdom, protection, patience, truth, understanding, harmony in the home, and throat chakra

Violet — Devotion, wisdom, spirituality, peace, enhancement of nurturing capability or quality, balancing sensitivities, divination, and third eye/brow chakra

White — Clarity, cleansing, spiritual growth, understanding, peace, innocence, illumination, establishing order, purity, crown chakra, and Maiden of the Triple Moon

Black — Force, stability, protection, transformation, enlightenment, dignity, banishing and releasing negative energies, Crone of the Triple Moon

Silver — Spiritual development, psychic ability, wisdom, intelligence, memory, meditation, warding off negative vibrations, psychic development, and divine feminine/female Goddess

Gold — Success, good fortune, ambition, self-realization, intuition, divination, inner-strength, health, finances, and divine masculine/male God

Brown — Balance, concentration, endurance, solidity, strength, grounding, concentration, material gain, companion animals, home, Earth, and balance

Grey — Contemplation, neutrality, stability, complex decisions, compromise, binding negative influences, complex decisions, and balance

Indigo — Clarity of purpose, spiritual healing, self-mastery, emotion, insight, fluidity, expressiveness, meditation, crown chakra

Pink — partnerships, friendship, affection, companionship, spiritual healing, child magic, and spiritual awakening

Adding Herbs, Oils, and Symbols to Your Candle Magic

Color is vital, and sometimes you won't have colorful candles for every spell, and that's okay. There are other ways to enhance the magic of your candle spells with herbs, oils, and symbols. Anointing your candle with sacred oil is a common practice and simply involves rubbing the scented and consecrated oil all over the wax of the candle before burning it. This can be done on its own, or you can add herbs to the process by rolling the oiled candle through a selection of dried herbs that will correlate with the magic of your spells.

These two simple acts enhance the power of your candle spell significantly and can help you open up even further to divine guidance and sacred manifestation.

As you learned in the chapters about the Book of Shadows, there are a variety of symbols, runes, and sigils that carry significant meaning and that can be used in all of your magical practices to empower your spells. With candle magic, you can carve the symbols directly into the wax to further carry your message to the spirit plane.

Your symbols should be specific to your goals and intentions, and you may need to do some research to decide carefully on which symbols are required for which spell. Trust your intuition, and let it guide you. You can carve the symbols before anointing them with oil and herbs, or after. You can also choose to use the symbols alone without any other ingredients. It is up to you, your spells, and your magical purposes.

Reading the Candle Flame: Divine Communication

There are many ways to read the magic of your spell through the flame of the candle. After the spell words and incantations are spoken and the candle has been lit, you can watch the flame to receive messages about the potential success of your manifestation. There are some who will view the results in the following way, but you may need to use your intuition in these matters, or research other sources:

<u>High and Strong Flame</u> = Manifestation is proceeding quickly.

<u>Low and Weak Flame</u> =T is not much spiritual energy invested in your intentions.

<u>Wick With Black/Thick Smoke</u> = Active opposition to your work (possibly coming from ill-meaning persons, or your unconscious mind is working against your intentions).

<u>Dancing Flame</u> = It has high energy for your spell but also very chaotic.

<u>Flickering Flame</u> = Spirits are present; prayers are being acknowledged.

<u>Popping/Sputtering Flame</u> = It signifies communication/interference with outside forces; something could be working against you; you may need to add more concentration and energy to your spell.

<u>Goes Out Flame</u> = A flame that just goes out indicates that your work is finished, and a stronger opposing force has ended the work.

<u>Candle Won't Light</u> = The spell cannot help you with the results you are seeking.

<u>Candle Won't Go Out</u> = You are not done working, and you need to spend more time with your spell.

There are many more interpretations to consider with candle magic that you can incorporate into your research and Book of Shadows, including reading the smoke and its colors and how the wax melts or drips or doesn't drip at all. Always tap into your intuition for guidance on these matters to help you align with your uses in your practice.

Once your candle has burned down, you can find fun in interpreting the melted wax, like reading tea leaves in a cup. The name for this technique is "ceromancy" and will require some practice on your part. It has a lot to do with seeing beyond the reality of what is in front of you and using your power of divination and clairvoyance. You can work on identifying shapes, patterns, symbols, images, and so forth, and try to determine what the "mood" of the candle spell might be or what is the final message from spirit.

Try not to overthink it, or you might skew and muddle the energy of your spells. Give some practice to it when you aren't doing important spell work, and have fun with it!

Practicing Safety with Candle Magic

Let's be straight and honest: fire is dangerous and can take down a whole house and the surrounding areas with one flame. It is significantly important that you practice fire safety whenever you are using candle magic or any kind of burning ritual in your spellcasting process.

Many candle spells ask that you leave the candle burning until it goes all the way out. If you are trying to conjure certain magic, this is a crucial part of your spell and needs to be considered. All you have to do is make sure that your candle is safe. Don't leave your house while it is burning, or check on it periodically while it burns.

You can also find certain kinds of containers, like flat-bottomed cylindrical vases made of glass, to put your candle in to burn. In this kind of container, the flame is contained, and even if gets bumped or knocked over inside the glass, it will be safe.

Additionally, the oils can be flammable if not worked with properly, and the wax and flame can burn your skin, so take necessary precautions while developing your candle magic skills, and make sure you are practicing safe magic.

Candle Magic Spells

RED CANDLE LOVE SPELL

You will need the following items for this:

- Red candle (try one first and then later if you want to work a more powerful spell; add more candles)
- Lighter or matches
- Rose essential oil

1. Cast your circle at dusk.

2. Anoint your candle with the rose oil. You can also carve a symbol into the wax that represents love or the kind of love you are calling into your life. (optional)

3. Light your candle and watch the flame for several minutes, or as long as it feels right. Meditate on the flame, and feel the love you desire growing inside of you. Allow that feeling to fill the space all around you.

4. After you have centered in this state for a while, say the following words, twelve times:

   I ask the forces of Nature and Spirits all around,
   I ask the Angles watching over me to hold me on the ground,
   Help this love grow stronger and stronger within,
   Bring this love to me from someone somewhere,
   So that love I can truly win.

5. Let the candle burn out if it is safe, and close your circle. *Try utilizing the power of a waxing moon to help achieve more powerful energy.*

HEALING CANDLE MAGIC SPELL

Disclaimer: Use healing spells, like this candle magic healing spell, in conjunction with conventional medicine, or medical treatment.

You will need the following items for this:

- Blue candle
- Green candle
- Sage bundle (smudge stick)
- Honey (preferably local)
- Salt
- Lander oil
- Spring water
- Mint
- Flower petals (white colored)
- Bowl
- Piece of paper and pen

Use this spell for yourself, or for a person in need of healing magic.

1. Cast your circle.

2. First, carve a symbol of healing into the blue candle (healing color properties) and light it. Watch the flame for several minutes, meditating on healing energies and your intentions of healing.

3. On the piece of paper, write down all of the healing wishes and feelings you want to manifest (for yourself or someone else). Be specific. If it is for a particular medical condition, ailment, or sickness, describe what it is and what you want to happen in a healing way.

4. Next, carve a symbol on the green candle that represents you (or the other person). Hold the candle in your hand, and hold it out in front of you while you cast a mental image of the healing

intention or the person's face or body. You may want to see yourself or the other person having already been healed. See in your mind's eye how they will look and feel after they are recovered.

5. Ask for the powerful divine energies to help you support this healing process.

6. Light your sage bundle and smudge your paper of healing intentions, the bowl and the candle representing the person being healed. Let the smoke cleanse and purify these ingredients of your spell.

7. Put the paper in the bottom of the bowl.

8. Rub the honey on the top half of the green candle, representing the person, starting at the middle and working up to the top.

9. Rub lavender oil on the bottom half of the candle.

10. Set the candle down on top of the paper in the bowl.

11. Put a ring of salt around the candle and sprinkle some mint and sage.

12. Add some spring water to the bowl and sprinkle the flower petals on top of the water.

13. Now, light the candle and see the person, or yourself, surrounded by healing, white light. Focus on the candle flame, and say the following words:

> *White light, candle bright,*
> *healing love, healing light,*
> *Let this energy suffice,*
> *To help with healing overnight.*
> *Bring all presence to healing and becoming whole,*
> *Let this light bring full healing to the soul.*
> *Let [me/person's name] recover fully,*

From this challenge and difficulty.
Open up to healing grace,
From the divine, in every space.
I open up to all that is,
Healing light and love, give us this.
And so it is!

14. Allow the candles to burn out on their own if it is safe to do so, and close the circle.

15. Once the candles have entirely burned out, bury the remaining ingredients in the soil outside.

DREAM JOB CANDLE SPELL

You will need the following items for this:

- One candle, color of your choice
- Green candle (luck)
- Piece of paper
- Pen
- Cauldron or fire-safe dish

**Face the direction of the south for this spell and incantation. Perform in the daylight hours, when the sun is highest in the sky.

1. Cast your circle, and face the south to perform the spell.

2. On the piece of paper, write out all of the details of your dream job. Be specific and include job title, salary, the city you will live in, benefits, and career goals.

3. Light the first candle, and say the following words:

With this candle burning bright,
I summon the dream job I will have by light.

4. Now, light the green candle, and say the following words:

With this candle burning bright,
I ask for luck to see me right.
My dream job waits for me to find,
All the luck I need to climb!
And so it is!

5. Now, take some time to meditate on your dream job. Take deep breaths, close your eyes, and see it in your mind's eye. Take several minutes to picture this in your head. Open your eyes, and focus on the candle flames for several minutes and continue to focus on that picture.

6. Now, read your paper aloud to yourself or quietly if preferred.

7. Light the corners of the paper on fire with both candle flames and drop it into your cauldron to burn and come to life!

8. Say the following words while you watch it burn:

Fire burning brightly now,
Cast my dream job into the light around.
Bring forward into my life,
With burning passion, brightest light.
So mote it be!

9. You can use this time as well to thank any deities for guidance along the path to help you succeed with your goals and purpose.

10. Allow both candles to fully burn out if it is safe to do so, and close your circle.

11. Keep any leftover candle wax to keep you focused on manifesting your dream job!

TRIPLE CANDLE LOVE SPELL

The power of three enhances and elevates any spell. Waxing moon phases are helpful for this spell.

You will need the following items for this:

- 3 red taper candles + holder/dish to hold all three together
- Red yarn, string, or ribbon
- Rose oil
- Yarrow oil
- Lavender oil
- A sharp tool to carve symbols into the wax

1. Cast your circle.

2. In each of the candles, inscribe a heart with a pentacle inside of it.

3. Now, anoint each candle with one of the oils so that each candle has a separate oil on it.

4. Bundle the candles together with yarn so that the symbols are all facing each other and touching.

5. Tie the string in a bow, and set them in a dish or holder that will keep them together.

6. Light all three of the candles as you say the following words, or something similar:

Life, Love, Heart,
I am ready for love to start.
I ask from above,
The gift that is love,

Oh, spirit, with all of my heart!
As below, so above!
And so it is!

7. Let them burn a third of the way down. Snuff them out and reserve them for the next night.

8. Repeat the ritual, burning down another third. Then, perform one last time on the third night until they go all the way out.

9. Watch for signs of a new romance.

FLAME OF FINANCIAL GAIN

You will need the following items for this:

- Green candle
- Gold candle
- A sharp tool to inscribe in the wax
- Patchouli incense
- Pine incense
- Many acorns (smooth stones can be a replacement to represent earth and abundance of the Earth)
- Piece of paper
- Pen

1. Cast your circle.

2. Carve the rune symbol **Fehu** on each candle, toward the base.

3. Place them in candle holders and put the patchouli incense next to, or in front of, the gold candle and the pine incense next to the green candle or in front of it.

4. Light the incense and get it smoking, and light the candles.

5. Draw another **Fehu** symbol on the paper, and put the acorns on top of it.

6. Leave the acorns (or stones) on top of the paper on your altar until extra abundance comes your way.

7. Let the candles burn down if it is safe to do so, and close your circle.

BURN OUT THE NEGATIVE

When you need to clear bad energy, low feelings, emotions, or anything negative around the house, use this spell. It's best used on a waning moon.

You will need the following items for this:

- Black candle
- Sandalwood oil
- Mint, basil, and white sage (dried)
- Bowl
- Baking sheet/parchment paper

1. Cast your circle.

2. Crush up your herbs together in a bowl so that they are in small flakes and pieces. You will be rolling your candle in these herbs.

3. Spread the herbs out evenly on the parchment-covered baking sheet (you can use your paper or a flat surface if you don't have the other items).

4. Rub sandalwood oil on your black candle.

5. Roll your oiled candle over the herbs, and cover it with the herb mixture. The oil should help it stick.

6. Set the candle in a holder and light it. It may spark a bit because of the oil, so take some precautions.

7. As you light the candle, say the following words, or something similar:

> *Negative energy, I banish you and send you far from me.*
> *Bad attitude, poor spirit, lack of faith,*
> *I say farewell to you on this day.*
> *Divine wisdom, divine light,*
> *Please bring me happiness and joy tonight.*
> *I welcome peace of mind and an open heart.*
> *Goodbye bad energy, I'll have a happier start.*

8. Repeat the words three times and meditate on your energy being cleared. Spend time in front of the candle flame until you feel ready to close your circle and move forward.

9. Let the candle burn all the way down if it is safe to do so.

Chapter 7: Crystal Magic Spells

Crystals are amazing conduits of energy and can be regularly used in any of your magic spells. Like a candle, crystals are excellent channels to add even more specific energy and magic to any of your incantations and magical purposes. As you have read throughout the book, there are several spells already that contain a crystal or gemstone that can bring you additional energy and success.

Crystals collect and receive energy and hold onto it. They will carry any information you wish to implant into them for a long period. They can also collect energies that you don't want them to have, so it is common practice to cleanse and purify your crystals between spells or if they are used often for specific reasons.

Purification and cleansing can occur in a cast circle or at any other time that feels appropriate. Warm salt water, sunlight, and smoke from and smudge stick are all ways to cleanse your stones and crystals of unwanted, old, or stagnate energies. Furthermore, once they are purified, you can then imbue them with whatever magical intentions you want them to collect and hold. Some Wiccans and Witches will refer to this step as "consecration."

All stones and crystals already have unique qualities and properties that will reflect certain energy into your spell. Some are more appropriate energies for healing and health, while others about psychic power and divination. There are stones for love and stones for protection and grounding.

The list of possible crystals is long and will require additional research on your journey, so you can find all the stones that resonate most with your practice. The next section will give you a list of some of the more commonly used and essential stones.

Common Crystals for Magic Spells

Agate: restores energy and healing, enhances creativity, enhances intellectual work, acts as grounding stone, works as protection spells for children, highly protective

Amber: *promotes* calming energy and impact in spells and for the person wearing or holding it, draws out negativity, releases physical pain, acts as good luck charms, brings positive energy.

Amethyst: aids with releasing addictions, calms and soothes ailments, relaxes and calms, enhances the psychic ability, helps control harmful behaviors, promotes psychic awareness, scrying

Bloodstone: abundance, fertility, physical health and healing, relief from grief or loss

Citrine: cleanses negative energy, provides focus and mental stimulation, aids work and employment, boosts career, promotes honesty and communication, improves self-confidence and empowerment

Emerald: enhances creativity and imagination, magic spells for love, fertility, domestic affairs, prosperity, luck and fortune

Hematite: protection, grounding, a staple of the altar for its protective and grounding qualities, useful in a wide variety of spells, and balancing of the body, mind, spirit

Jade: dream interpretation, confidence, self-sufficiency, grounding, calm, serenity, peace of mind, body balancing

Jasper: red jasper for protection; yellow jasper to clear the mind and communication; brown jasper for concentration and grounding

Labradorite: dream recall, increases intuition, aids psychic development, helps resolve subconscious issues, associates with all chakras, provides wisdom and clarity, stimulates imagination, develops enthusiasm, heals personal addictions and dependencies, attracts success

Lapis Lazuli: openness, insight, truth, inner power, spiritual universal truth, interpretation of intuitive thought, psychic ability, soul guide magic

Malachite: emotional courage and support during times of spiritual growth, helpful during significant life changes

Moldavite: transformation, spiritual awakening, dream states, communication with the cosmos, spiritual protector, spiritual evolution, cleansing, communication with spirit guides, enhances psychic abilities

Moonstone: feminine energies, calmness, awareness, confidence, moon energies, soothing and relaxing, openness to ascension

Obsidian: grounding and protection, centering, healing, and clarity

Onyx: assists with making right decisions, encourages happiness, good fortune, dispels negative energies

Quartz: many varieties

- *Clear quartz:* clears the mind, amplifies the qualities of other crystals and gemstones close to it, logic, healing, creates a safe space for meditations, connection to the divine

- *Rose Quartz:* "mother stone," heart stone, love and happiness, protection for children and loved ones, opens imagination and creativity

- *Blue Quartz:* concentration and communication, the "student's stone"

Selenite: connection to spirit, a conduit between physical and spiritual realm, simultaneously cleanses and recharges, intuition, higher self, spirit guides, honesty and purity, heightened personal vibration

Shungite: healing, protection, purification, psychic protection, grounding

Sodalite: Cooperation, communication, knowledge, intelligence, rational mind, education and learning, wisdom, study, logic and intellect, inner calm, clears mental noise, self-awareness, self-improvement

Tiger's Eye: courage, willpower, loyalty, truth, luck, protection, truth-seeking, perception, cuts through illusions, brings to light manipulative or dishonest intentions

Spend time getting acquainted with these stones and hundreds of others to bring into your regular spell work. They will enhance the energy of your magic, as well as the magic of your power and personal energy!

Crystal Magic Spells

COMMUNICATION IN RELATIONSHIPS SPELL

You will need the following for this:

- A piece of Lapis Lazuli (openness, insight, truth, inner power, universal spiritual truth, interpretation of intuitive thought)
- A part of Rose Quartz (heart stone, love, happiness)
- A piece of Sodalite (cooperation, communication, wisdom)
- A portion of blue cloth (sized to wear as an amulet or medicine bag)
- Cord (long enough to be a necklace)
- Small piece of paper and a pen
- One head of dried lavender
- Blue candle
- White candle

1. Cast your circle.

2. On the small piece of paper, write the following words: *I am committed to clear and open communication. I am open to all sides of the conversation and can listen as well as I can speak. My loved ones have something to say as much as I do, and we can share as we talk to each other.*

3. Light the white candle on your altar and state the following words: *With this candle, I do light; bringing spirit, I do invite to help me open my voice of knowing, to speak with open heart and mind ongoing.*

4. Light the blue candle and state the following: *With this candle, I do swear to use my voice with love and care, for those, I am with in sacred bond so that we may speak our true voice songs.*

5. Set the blue square of cloth out between the candles.

6. Place the paper on the cloth between the candles on the altar, and lay your stones on top of the paper.

7. Place your hands over the stones and visualize yourself having clear, honest conversations with those you love. See the calmness and creativity between you. See yourself speaking your mind freely and lovingly. Charge the stones with the energy of clear communication. Spend as long as you need to in this visualization.

8. Place the piece of lavender on top of the stones, and gather the corners of the cloth together to make a bag or pouch.

9. Tie it with a long cord and then tie it around your neck so that it hangs over your heart.

10. Blow out the candles, and close your circle.

11. You can wear this medicine bag whenever you need a clear voice and communication within your partnerships.

HEALING CRYSTALS SPELL

You will need the following for this:

- A piece of Shungite (healing, purification, grounding)
- A piece of bloodstone (physical health and healing, abundance)
- A part of amethyst (relaxing, calming, helps with harmful behaviors)
- Healing herbal tea to drink after

1. Cast your circle and sit in the center in a comfortable position.

2. Ask the divine to hold you close while you open to the healing wisdom of the universe (you may choose a particular deity to help you).

3. Hold the Shungite in your hand, and see a beam of light coming through your head from the cosmos, pouring into you from above and filling your whole body with loving, healing light.

4. See this light pouring from your hand into the Shungite, and ask for the divine to charge the stone with healing power and magic for you. You can create words to say to help you deliver the message clearly.

5. Set the Shungite down, and repeat the following activity with the other two stones: bloodstone and amethyst.

6. Once all three stones have been charged with healing light, hold all three of them in your hand, and state the following:

These three stones, a powerful force,
Will keep me healed and on the right course.
Loving my wholeness, body, heart, and mind,
With these three stones, I will heal in time.

7. You can keep the stones in your pocket, or carry them in your purse. You can also make them into an amulet or sacred medicine bag to wear around your neck.
8. Close your circle, and brew a cup of healing tea. Hold your stones or wear them, and as you sip your tea, visualize your healing and how you will feel when you are healed again.

DREAMS AND VISIONS SPELL

You will need the following for this:

- Purple candle
- A piece of Labradorite (dream recall, psychic development, subconscious mind)
- A piece of Moldavite (dream states, spiritual evolution, communication with spirit)
- A piece of Selenite (connection to spirit, intuition)

1. Cast your circle.

2. As you light the purple candle, communicate with your spirit guides, and ask them for what you want to discover in your dream state. Be honest and transparent, and let them know that you wish to receive a message and help with interpretation.

3. Place the stones in front of the candle on the altar, and speak the following:

Sacred stones of dreamer's sight,
Let my intuition open up tonight.
May you bring me powerful knowing,
And by this candle, receive its glowing.
Great Goddess, God, and Mother divine,
Let my dreams give me the answers and signs.
And so it is!

4. Allow the candle to burn all the way out on your altar. You can close your circle and go about your day.

5. When the candle is out, collect the crystals and put them under your pillow while you sleep. You may want to keep a dream journal or paper and pen by your bed so that you can write down any messages that come to you first thing in the morning.

PERSONAL PROTECTION SPELL

You will need the following for this:

- These stones of protection: Hematite, Obsidian, Onyx, Shungite
- Black candle
- Sage smudge stick

1. Cast your circle.

2. Light the black candle of protection on your altar.

3. Light the sage and waft the smoke around your whole body and your altar.

4. Place the stones in front of the candle, and waft the sage over them.

5. Ask the energies and spirits to aid you in your spell, and say the following words:

> *By the magic of the stones,*
> *Let them keep safe my whole home.*
> *Wanting that which keeps me safe,*
> *Let them protect me both night and day.*
> *Let them keep harmful energies at bay,*
> *Wanting only to be kept safe.*
> *And so it is!*

6. Thank the energies and spirits present with you, and spend some moments grounding and centering in front of your candle and sage.

7. Hold the stones in your hand, and allow them to fill you with the energy of protection.

8. Let the candle burn, or snuff it out.

9. Close your circle.

10. Carry your stones with you, or keep them on your altar at all times.

Conclusion

What an incredible journey it has been! The *Wiccan Spell Book* is your wonderful beginning to get you started with a wide variety of spells, how to practice them, and how to make your very own Book of Shadows. This book has certainly been fun to write and share with you and as you further explore magic. Remember that it has everything to do with clear intentions and energies to help you manifest your results and experience success with spellcasting.

You have learned about the basics of Wiccan spells and several guidelines to successful spellcasting, including grounding and centering, safety, and casting a circle. You have also spent time learning about the value and importance of a Book of Shadows, how to make one, what goes inside, and why it can be one of your most-prized magical tools.

We also took a more in-depth look at the Moon and how her phases and energies can have a compelling impact on the spells you choose to cast. Timing isn't always everything; however, working with the moon's energy can make all the difference in the magic that you are casting. Additionally, you were able to glean some knowledge and understanding about the magical uses of candles and crystals and how they can channel even more powerful energy into your spell work. Candles and crystals, combined with lunar phases and other tools, including your dominant purpose, are all you need to manifest some powerful magic.

The *Wiccan Spell Book* is also full of a wide assortment of spells for you to start using today! Most of them have straightforward ingredients, and all of the instructions are right there and ready for you to use. Start incorporating your favorites into your everyday practice, and decide which ones you might like to put in your personal Book of Shadows. The spellcasting fun begins whenever you are ready to start, and this book has given you all of the skills and steps that you need to get started!

As you move forward on your spellcasting journey, remember to explore and find the things that resonate most with you. Wicca is a creative experience; feel free to expand and modify any of these spells to be more aligned with your personal magic. Have fun digging more deeply and searching for more knowledge of your practice. Use these spells as a template to create your own, and build a Book of Shadows through your intuitive knowing.

It has been such a pleasure sharing this magic with you, and if you have found this book useful and helpful in any way, a review on Amazon.com is always appreciated. So mote it be, and Blessings to thee!

Wicca Herbal Magic:

A Practical Beginner's Herbal Guide for Wiccans and Modern Witches, Includes the Must-Have Natural Herbs for Baths, Oils, Teas, and Spells

By Gaia J. Mellor

Introduction

Welcome to Wicca Herbal Magic! You are about to embark on a journey through the world of herbs and the magic of what they can do through their use in spells, remedies, potions and charms, teas, baths, oils, and incenses. This book is a perfect resource for the beginning Wiccan, looking for an in-depth and informative approach to learning about the magical uses of herbs.

Herbalism has a long history and has existed in many different cultures across the planet. There are a ton of ways you can use these beneficial and delightful plants, and this book is organized to help you learn how they can help you achieve greater manifestation, healing, wholeness, prosperity, and love through their powerful magical properties.

This book is a fun way to discover the secrets and arts behind the world of plant medicine and magic. You will learn about the ancient art of herbalism and how herbs have been used medicinally and for spells and rituals throughout the centuries. There is an excellent chapter that provides a long and in-depth list of some of the most magical herbs to help you get acquainted with how to build your herbal cabinet.

You will enjoy learning about the management of herbs, including where to buy them, how to acquire them from nature, or wildcrafting, drying and storing them, as well as how to prepare them for magical purposes.

After you have learned all of the basics of how herbal magic can come into your practice, there are a great many delightful recipes and instructions for making magical teas, how to bring herbs into the ritual bath, the use of magical oils and how to make them for spell work, designing and constructing magical charms, such as sachets, pillows, poppets and pouches, and more!

In addition, you will gain an understanding of incenses and how they work, what they can bring to your spell work and rituals, and some great ideas for certain aromas to bring about love, meditation, and divination, as well as, a blessing incense for your home: a great thing to have around at all times for any Witch.

Finally, the end of this in-depth guide to herbal magic will provide you with Tables of Correspondence that are an excellent quick reference guide to a full list of herbs, essential oils and incenses, so that you always have access to what you are looking for.

This book is a joyful and fun approach to becoming more acquainted with herbs and how they can expand your Wicca, or magical practice, exponentially.

The chapters in this book are designed to help any beginner feel confident and excited to take pleasure in the magic of these powerful plants and have a great time exploring all of the unique ways that they can come into your life and help you manifest, purity, abundance, joy, peace, psychic connection, love, protection and more!

Get started with your herbal knowledge now, and witness how your magic becomes even more powerful and exciting! So, mote it be!

Chapter 1: The Ancient Art of Herbalism

The world of plant magic dates back many thousands of years and has evolved with us over time. Our earliest ancestors were discovering what these plants, berries, barks, and flowers could do before there were science and technology to test their qualities and purposes. We learned about their magic through a deep and profound connection to them as energies of life that lived in tandem with us.

What many Witches, healers, shamans, and others have learned steadily over time, is that each specific plant has a very specific quality and intention and that we all have access to this magic should we choose to adopt this ancient knowledge. Plants won't keep a secret from you; they want you to discover what they offer so that you can live in harmony and balance with all the life that surrounds you.

Our journey through time has been alongside the power of plant magic and medicine it was the earliest tribes, farmers, healers and "doctors" that were able to supply the people of the village or the town with their knowledge of these powerful herbs.

What our ancestors learned was that there are a lot of ways to utilize plant medicine and magic and that there can be fatally wrong ways to use certain plants, or parts of plants, as a remedy or healing agent. Trial and error have been long-standing factors in evolution and when you study herbal lore, this is certainly prominent.

Many early "herbalists" or healers (Witches as they were often called) were able to detect and understand even more in-depth knowledge about what the plants could offer and made use of these vibrant energies in their spells, incantations, rituals, healing potions, broths, brews and so forth.

Many religions today still use certain herbs for their rituals, as they were borrowed from some of the earlier Pagan, or Earth-worshipping religions, in Western Europe. In the East, other cultural groups were also using what was natively grown in the area to aid in health and healing, as well as, to honor their gods and beliefs through rituals with herbs and incenses.

It was as long as 5,000 years ago that herbal uses were actually beginning to be written down and inscribed on clay tablets by the ancient Sumerian culture. These tablets listed over 300 different kinds of herbs and their medicinal uses. In China, around the same time, documentation of herbal remedies was also taking place and would become the basis for the Chinese Medicine practices that are still prominent in today's modern culture.

In the Americas, Native people were working and living closely with the land and had a more strong spiritual connection to the herbs, plants, flowers, and trees that they coexisted with. They had members of their tribes who were the healers (what modern-day people call a "Shaman") who were incredibly well acquainted with all of the uses and benefits of these herbs for medicinal purposes and were also well acquainted with the spirit of the plant. To them, it wasn't only about what medicine it would bring to the physical health of a person, but also how it had a magical impact on that person's spirit.

In Europe, Pagans were healing and working with herbs for long periods of time before the religion was destroyed by Christianity and yet the Church had no notions of how to heal with herbs and attempted to save lives through exorcisms and faith in God, rather than through the use of plant medicine and magic.

Some monasteries and cloisters adopted this knowledge as a way to benefit a broader group of souls and so there certainly were monks and nuns who practiced the herbal arts in these times, and considered these tools a gift from God, rather than the work of the Devil, as so many Witches were accused of over the ages.

A lot of the real dealings with herbalism and witchcraft caused a traumatic rift in our ability to treat ourselves with this beautiful knowledge of how herbs can heal and bring about powerful change and great balance. Many women, or men who practiced these sacred and powerful healing arts, were scrutinized for their "craft" and many died because of their skills and knowledge. It is a terrible fate for anyone to give the heling touch and then find out that they must die for it, however, when you consider the history of herbalism, some sacrifices were certainly made along the way.

Fortunately, the knowledge of herbs can never be lost. They have been here for longer than we have and have always had a powerful way of communicating with us, letting us know who they are and what they do for us. Consider that people understood the properties and qualities of herbs and how they benefit health and balance with all life, across the planet on separate continents at the same time. As a civilization, human beings have all been working with plants throughout history, bonding with their magic and power in a variety of unique and exciting ways.

Beginning to learn about herbs with your own excitement and pursuit of healing and magical knowledge is an essential step in your own personal discovery as a Wiccan or a Witch, as it will connect you to the ancient power and magic of all those who came before you and practiced the very same wisdom.

This journey through *Wicca Herbal Magic* is only the beginning of what you can begin to understand and notice about our living, breathing, growing friends. The same herbs grown in the gardens of yore can be grown in your very own backyard.

This ancient art has always been with us and has a long-standing honesty that will always keep us in a deeper connection to the power of the divine in all things and to the power of nature and how she works to help us on our paths. Moving forward into the next chapter, you can go a little bit deeper and learn more about the connection between Shamanism and herbalism and how they use certain drugs or medicines in spiritual rituals and practices, as well as understanding how plants correspond to more than just healing remedies and physical well-being.

Chapter 2: The Use of Herbs in Medicine and Magic

Wicca and Herbalism

The art and craft of Wicca have only been around since the mid-20th century, but the concepts and practices are as old as human interest in the powers that be. Not all Wiccans use herbs in practices, but a majority of them do because of the close ties and links to the divine creation of the gifts of remedy from nature and Mother Earth.

The principles of herbalism have been around for centuries, as you read in the previous chapter, and as Wicca made its debut in the 1950s, so too did the connection between Wicca and herbalism and how many practitioners were engaging in the medicinal and magical properties of herbs for a variety of spells, rituals and incantations.

Even the founder of Wicca, Gerald Gardner, depicted many uses for specific herbs in his notorious "Book of Shadows", the tome that became the blueprint for Wiccan books of magic and ritual for decades to come.

Herbalism is not confined to Wiccan craft and culture and has existed since before Pagan religion, even in a coarser form that was less easily understood by the concept and study of science. The Pagan cultural religions that Wicca is based on, however, also highly prized the connection between our bodies and the elements and frequently utilized herbs for healing purposes and practices, as well as for divinations and ritual ceremonies.

The invention of herbalism came from the ancient practice of understanding the offerings of plants and their medicines (see Chapter 1: The Ancient Art of Herbalism) and how to use them effectively. As time wore on, and new practices emerged, a more well-defined connection to their uses was more greatly available to the public in written formats and recipes for use.

Modern Wiccans have much of their practices revolving around the use of herbs, plants and there are a significant number of spells and beliefs surrounding each one, when they should be utilized in conjunction with the Wheel of the Year, and how they affect your magical practice, as well as your health.

Wiccans will devote entire rituals, just to the harvest of certain foods and herbs and many of the festivals that are celebrated throughout the year feature and prize the herbs that are in abundance. The correlation between Wicca and nature is strong and so as the year progresses through all of its stages, cycles, and rhythms, Wiccans will spend quality time in observance of the season's bounty.

It is highly typical for specific herbal rituals to occur under the Solstices and Equinoxes, frequently being a moment of collection, storage and preparation to use those herbs for their most vital and powerful properties for the year to come.

Wicca and herbalism relate powerfully and will continue to do so as long as Wicca is practiced across cultures. Herbs and the gifts of Mother Nature are the bread and butter of Wiccan art and craft and should be studied in depth by any practitioner of Wicca to feel that closeness and devotion to herbal magic and medicine. The next section will explore another quality of herbalism that comes from the profound connection between the shamans of the world and how they use plants and herbs for healing, much like a Wiccan would use herbs for magic, ritual, and blessing of health.

Within the constructs of our various cultures and civilizations, the use of herbs in both medicine and magic has always been present. The sacred wisdom inherent in these little plants has been taught to us through the ages by the plants themselves. They teach us to bring understanding to healing our whole system: body, mind, and spirit.

All cultures have had some way of working with the native plant and flower species of their landscapes, which has caused a wider and broader view of how the whole planet is full of medicines that not every culture has had access to, or learned the wisdom of, through healing practice.

Ancient cultures were less likely to travel long distances and across seas, and so the knowledge of various exotic plants was not known to everyone until a lot later in our human history. In today's world, we are much more capable of finding these resources through online research and books, as well as by taking a trip to some of the far-off places where Shamans and Medicine Men and Women still practice the ancient cultural healing arts of their tribes and communities.

For what it's worth, medicine has always been considered a magical performance: combining certain ingredients and applications to a sickness, or emotional state, to bring about and manifest a change. If you think about it, that is precisely what casting a spell does. When you apply specific focus, intention, herbs, and other ingredients, and the right timing to a situation, you empower the energy of things all around you to follow suit. Medicine and magic are basically part of the same family of wisdom and this book will treat them as such.

As you go deeper in your own studies of herbal magic and medicine, consider how they work hand-in-hand and that the medicinal quality of an herb or plant, may give you the perspective you need to understand how to use it in Wiccan spells and rituals. It is entirely possible also that your intuition will guide you in exactly the right way you need to go to establish a magical connection to these plants. Several people have even reported being able to fully hear and receive the energetic message of what the plant wants to express to you. If you are a wide-open channel for spirit, the plants might very well start talking to you, so be open to anything when you are working with plant magic.

Some of the people who have been known to speak with plants are Shamans. In the next section, you will get a more significant understanding of how different kinds of Shamans work with plant medicine and magic to connect to spirit and heal through the divine, followed by a section on plant correspondences.

Shamanism and Herbalism

Shamanism is a broad term to describe a lot of different names for this one thing. In every culture, the language of the tribe has its own name for what a Shaman is and what they do, however, Shamanism is considered the oldest spiritual practice known to humans, dating back archeologically as far as 70,000 years.

A Shaman will create transpersonal connections with all of the sacred realms and will facilitate this experience for others so that people can have their own holy quest to deepen their inner knowing and personal truth. It has no connection to religion and has a much greater opening and opportunity for one to be closely connected to nature in all things. In a way, we are experiencing spiritual healthcare when we work with Shamans or shamanic practices.

Essentially, within the concept of what Shamanism teaches or supports, is that at any given point on your journey through life, you will experience disharmony within yourself. This disharmony is what can cause serious illness, disease, emotional disturbances, and so on. If left unresolved, these energetic imbalances will create or manifest all of these issues that cannot always be cured by Western medicine or technology.

A Shaman is not a preacher or a guru; they are here to guide on the path of spiritual awakening and healing to help you resolve the discord within you, on all levels, not just the physical. When they are healing someone, they will make a journey to the astral plane in order to commune with the benevolent spirits who are here to aid and guide us forward. The astral plane is a parallel reality to our own that consists of all of the animal, nature, plant, and other spirit forms that will respond to the Shaman who is a conduit of this communication.

There was a time when more people were awakened, or at least aware of the natural world and considered the natural world to be a conscious force, just as alive and aware as we are. Shamans gained higher ground with these elements and were therefore treated with more respect and honored as a wiser channel of spiritual knowing, leading to their work as the village, or tribe's, "healer".

Shamanism is undoubtedly a potent example of the connection between medicine and magic. These realities are exposed and expressed through the Shamanic journey and open the earth plane to the senses and relationship to the plant and natural world. One term for it might be called "Plant Spirit Shamanism", but you could also refer to it as Shamanic Herbalism. To treat a plant or natural essence as though it had thoughts and feelings is a part of the magic of medicine.

There have been many "folk healers" throughout history, crossing continents, from the Amazonian Curanderos, the to the Pagan Witch folk of Europe, and into today's modern herbalists and flower essence healers. Throughout history and into the present, the traditional rituals and healing methods that have come with the plant medicine and magic understand the following: the origins of disease come from disharmony, discord, and imbalance in our emotional/ spiritual bodies that manifest in the physical and that herbs and plants are powerful and effective in healing these disturbances.

This is, in essence, what Shamanism practices: the healing of the spirit body to heal the Earth body through the use of various medicinal herbs, flowers, roots, leaves, and barks. There are so many ways to learn Wicca Herbal Magic from these concepts, drawn from the beautiful power of the Shaman's approach to healing and the combination of medicine and magic. Here are some great ways to bring more of these ideas into your own modern practice. Work with plants and herbs as a Shaman might with these critical practices:

1. Spend Time in Nature to Meet the Plant Allies:

   Take a trip into the woods or the wilderness and don't try to look for what it is you need to find. Let it call to you. Be guided by the plant and allow yourself to spend quality time with it. Listen to what it tells you and why it is calling to you now.

   Any time you go out in nature, let your intuition guide you to what the plant spirits want to show you. They listen to you and your spirit, too, and can show you the magic and healing powers that they carry if you are open to it.

2. Make an Offering in Return for the Knowledge of the Plant Spirit:

   Communicating with the plant that calls to you is crucial. When you show the plant your intention, then it can understand how to communicate with you the best. Energy and purpose are what guide your journey.

   Making an offering to your plant allies shows them that you are willing to give something in return for what they can offer you on the mind, body, and spirit planes. Some will leave tobacco buried in the Earth around the plant, while others might sprinkle new seeds to grow new life. Either way, an offering states that you honor the gift given from the plant spirit to help you learn and understand who it is and what it can do.

3. Shamanic Plant Gazing:

   The idea behind "gazing" is that you look beyond the physical attributes of the plane to merge your consciousness with the energies, qualities, and healing intentions of the plant. This is a way to cross over into a higher dimension and collaborate with the spiritual plane of the plant to create an attitude of mindfulness, meditation, and recognition of how the plant operates beyond the physical aspect.

This is where the magic of plants comes from and how they impact the soul, not just the body. When you "gaze" you let go of your mental assumptions about what the plant is and how it works so that you can manifest the open energy to truly hear what it has to offer.

These are just a few of the ways you can begin to have a more magical connection and approach to practicing with herbs, through the concepts of Shamanism. Other ways that Shamans will use herbs and plants is to cause an intense experience of total mind awakening through the power of certain psychedelic medicines that cause visions, sounds, and other energetic experiences, to help you find more profound truth and knowing. Peyote and Ayahuasca ceremonies are some of the more notorious experiences that people are locating in today's world to help them discover more on their truth path through the sacred healing power of plant medicine and magic.

These kinds of ceremonies and rituals require a lot more preparation and experience and so if you are interested in working with a Shaman specifically for this kind of healing, you will need to decide on the right path for you.

Within this truth and reality described by the Shaman's journey, there are a variety of other ways that plants are connected to our lives and the energies of all things. In the next section, you will look more deeply into the properties of plant correspondence and how it relates to herbal magic and medicine.

The Power and Principle of Plant Correspondence

The power and principles of plant correspondences are exactly what they might seem like: a correspondence to another part of nature to establish a link, bond, or natural identity or signature that describes or illustrates the character and qualities of a given plant.

A correspondence in plant magic and medicine has everything to do with how we can attribute certain qualities from one thing in nature to another. Take the sun, for example: the sun is warming, hot, powerful, light, brings joy, helps things grow, and is associated with creative power and masculine energies. When you are practicing Wicca or other Pagan religions, you can easily make these correlations based on your worship and devotion to nature and her rhythms and cycles, as well as other divine forces associated with solar energies.

A plant can have a strong correspondence with this solar energy and will reveal some of its own unique characteristics through its association with the sun. Since the sun has everything to do with energy, vitality, health, manifestation and creative power, it is then considered in correspondence with herbs that produce a similar result, or have a similar energetic quality or "spiritual expression".

It is shown that plants that resemble the sun tend to have the same effects or qualities, whether it is through the color and shape, or an act of opening and closing its petals or leaves based on the hour of the day. You can then go on to consider the physical impacts of herbs and what correlation, or correspondence, they may have with a sun-like energy. Herbs that make one feel warm and relaxed, or bring heartier blood flow, could be considered in correspondence with the sun. Herbs like St. John's Wort, Clove, Citrus, Centaury, Chamomile, and Calendula are all in correspondence with the sun.

So, what does this all even mean? The principles of plant correspondence have to do with the elemental, planetary, and natural connections between all of the shared qualities and properties that they all simultaneously contain. Throughout history, herbalists and shamans have correlated the balance between all forces of nature and how we and they all share a common bond or thread of commonality. This is correspondence. Let's consider the next 6 celestial orbs in our solar system and determine some of the inherent qualities that can be found between the planets and plants.

The **Moon** is representative of emotions, dreams, divination, illusions, astral travel, the subconscious, and psychic enhancement. In the plant kingdom, correspondence with the moon will include plants that are high in water content, or happen to thrive and grow near water, medicinally sedative, moisturizing, sleep inducing, cooling, painkilling and hormone balancing, as well as being associated with the female reproductive system. Examples of these herbs are not limited to the following: poppy, lavender, lily, morning glory, jasmine, mugwort, and sandalwood.

Mercury is associated with memory, intellect, messengers, travelling between worlds, communication, spiritual guidance, trickery, invisibility, and deception. Much of what Mercury represents has to do with the mind, or rather the brain, and the central nervous system.

Anything effecting speech, thoughts, lungs and the nervous system will be in correspondence with Mercury. Plants that are stimulating to the mind, or are fast growing, winding and creeping, and with a subtle or quickly fading scent are considered to be a mercurial plant. Corresponding plants with mercury are said to act as a catalyst with other plant energies and forces and some examples of plants in correspondence with this planet are eucalyptus, licorice, cardamom, mint, skullcap, lemongrass, and juniper.

The planet **Venus** is our celestial lady of love and is associated with all of the following concepts: beauty, nature, harmony, sexuality, fertility, abundance, power of attraction, talent and ability, and the power of aphrodisiacs. It is noted that because of her opposition to Mars, she works against his influence. Plants in correspondence with the planet Venus are luscious flowering plants that tend to have big, soft, furry leaves and are often used in tonics and astringents to help with the beautification of the body.

Venus rules the kidneys and liver in the body and so any herbs that are in correspondence with Venus energy will likely have an impact on these organ systems. Examples of plant correspondences with Venus are rose, passion flower, violet, lemon verbena, vervain, apple, burdock, and thyme.

Mars, the planet of war and the mythological husband to the Goddess Venus, is all about the masculine forces of power, aggression, fire, active energy, protection and quickness. It has an overall energy of vitality, will, and physical strength. These plant correspondences are prickly, spicy and/or thorny.

They tend to be very energizing, heating and stimulating and correspond with purifying the blood as well as sexual potency, and are also thought to be helpful in repairing injuries and healing disorders of the immune system. Examples of these plant correspondences are chili peppers, nettles, red sandalwood, ginger, and galangal root, to name a few.

Jupiter, the planet luck, is about expansion, fortune, personal power, and super-consciousness. It tends to be in opposition to the planet Saturn and works in the realms of laws, religion, and faith, but is not limited to these energies and is more of a force of luck and prosperity. Plants that are in a correspondence with Jupiter are relaxing, calm and expanding.

They are warming and calming without sedating the body. Jupiter corresponds with the digestive system, arteries, and metabolism. Some of the corresponding plants are pine, oak, fennel, cedar, sage, agrimony, as well as some foods like olives, figs, nuts, and fruits.

The planet **Saturn** has a heavier energy. It has to do with karma, protection, binding, banishing and restricting negative energy. Saturn works strongly with the energies of authority, discipline and restrictions that are imposed by others and it is also the planet associated with the energy of witchcraft. Saturn corresponds with the bones of the body, including the teeth and the energies of constricting, drying and cooling are often related to the plant correspondences of this planet. Plants that are invasive, poisonous, slow-growing, or shade loving are likely in communication with Saturn. Some examples of these plant correspondences are comfrey, horsetail, belladonna, cannabis, henbane, cypress, henbane, and myrrh.

Looking at all of the planets, what did you notice? 1) All of the planets correspond with a human, anatomical system or quality 2) Plants and herbs correspond to certain planetary conditions or energies 3) plants and herbs correspond with specific energies of the human body to perform healing or balancing of an individual system.

Breaking it down, it is really all about the fact that everything is connected and that anything in nature has a correspondence with anything else in explanation through the energetic imprint, appearance, quality, and characteristic of that matter. Let's consider the elements as another type of correspondence with plants so you can understand the power and fundamental principles.

As you may already know from your own Wiccan or other practice, the element of **Earth** is all about the following qualities: material energies and wealth, grounding, structure, growth, manifestation, building, prosperity, birth and death. Earth energy is very strong and deep and has hidden depths. Correspondences in the plant world with this element are those that can slow the body down, moist and fertile, and even sedating, as this is very grounding. Examples of these plant correspondences are mosses, lichens, ivy, oak, patchouli, sage, and nuts.

Air is the element of movement, communication, language, ideas, thoughts, wisdom, expansion, beliefs, spiritual knowledge as well as other forms of knowledge, and learning. In magical practices and divination magic, airy essences like smoke, feathers, fragrances, and hanging charms and amulets are associated with air. Dream catchers, wind chimes, and hanging charms are all air-like energies. In plant correspondence, this would relate to those herbs and elements that blow their seeds on the wind, tall grasses that sway in the breeze, feathery leaves, and plants and herbs that have a crisp and clean fragrance. Some of these plants are dill, dandelion, yarrow, sweetgrass, lavender, and peppermint.

The element of **Fire** is passion, transformation, purification, vitality, destruction, willpower, spiritual force, protection, courage, vitality, and hope. In magical work, it has a connection with burning and smoldering, candle magic, and evocation. Any plant that has a spicy or stimulating power will be of fire. Sometimes stinging and thorny, fire plant correspondences are used when the body feels chilled, stagnant, heavy and lacking in motivation. Examples of these plants are pepper, ginger, chilies, nettle, angelica, and cinnamon.

Water is the element of emotion, dreams, the subconscious mind, purification and cleansing, psychic awareness, and alchemical transformation. Magically, this element is connected to mirror magic, potion and brew making, love spells, sacred baths and rituals, and crystal scrying. The plant correspondences of water are soothing, receptive, and water-loving, offering a balance and calmness to the emotions as well as the cycles of sleep. Some examples are willow, lotus, coltsfoot, lady's mantle, lobelia, and spearmint.

With the planets and the elements as examples, you can begin to understand that there are always these connections in nature and that as you discover how to form a bond and relationship to plant and herb magic and medicine, you will be in frequent connection to these types of correspondences. They are always speaking of their link to all that is around them and when you are getting to know the magical properties and qualities of each unique herb or medicine, you are going to notice these very human and interplanetary qualities popping up with the way they appear to you and how they affect your body, mind, and spirit.

Combined with the way of the Shaman in working with plant medicine and magic, these correspondences will help you walk the path of truly understanding the gift of each unique plant and herb.

Chapter 3: The Most Important Magical Herbs

This chapter will work through a large variety of the most important herbs that you may use for medical and magical herbal explorations. You are in for a treat because as the chapter unfolds you will become acquainted with the unique characteristics of each plant and how they can help you in the physical, emotional and spiritual realms.

As with anything that you might be ingesting or applying to your body, take precautions and do some additional research. What you learn in this book is certainly not a way to replace professional medical care if you need it, but can be an excellent resource for both medicine and magic for your whole life-care practice.

As you read through this list of essential herbs, consider all of the ones you may have used in your cooking and food dishes. So many of them are commonly used to flavor food, and many people today don't view these magical plants as remedies with magical properties. It is sure to change your perspective on your culinary cabinet in your kitchen.

Each herb will list the magical properties followed by the medicinal ones. As you become more acquainted with each one, see if you can then go find them in nature, in the store, or in your local apothecary and get an even more in-depth understanding of them. Let them tell you who they are and form a new relationship to each one of these delightful, earthly gifts.

Angelica

Magical: Very powerful herb used for protection against negative energies, while also attracting positive ones; protects against negative energy; incense for healing and exorcism; add to the bath to promote healing, remove negative energies; can be scattered around certain places for protection and purification; promotes temperance; sprinkled in the shoes, it is said to help prevent weakness and tiredness; sprinkle around outside of house for protection; brings lost love back home to you.

Medicinal: useful parts are considered to be the roots, stems, and seeds; aids indigestion and flatulence; coughs and colds; roots are used to make a decoction (slowly boiled reduction) to use for salves and ointments to treat skin irritations and ailments; medically, roots and stems are what is used primarily.

Basil

Magical: the Greek word of origin, "basilikos" means "royal"; used for spells and rituals of wealth and protection, as well as love; helps to dispel confusion, fear, and/or weakness; protects against hostile spirits; can bring luck when you sprinkle in spells, or use in charms and amulets; attracts money and success (Greek "royal") and can be worn to attract prosperity and financial gain.

Medicinal: use of the leaves and flowers as a tea can help to calm the nerves, settle the tummy, help in the overall health of the bladder, and ease cramps; useful as an insect repellent and to draw out the bite of a sting as a topical application. Delicious as a culinary herb.

Bay Laurel (Bay Leaf)

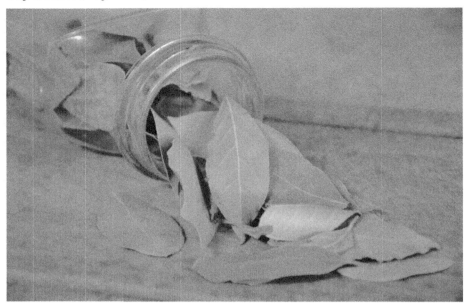

**Bay Leaf and Bay Laurel are the same thing and are regularly assumed to be different.

Magical: protection and purification; good fortune and success; house blessings and business blessings; strength and healing; clearing confusion; enhancing psychic powers; attracts love and romance; helpful in dream pillows for prophetic dream enhancement; used in many spells for prosperity and financial abundance; can be carried to aid in personal and psychic protection.

Medicinal: known to help with digestion and is used to flavor many soups and dishes; has been studied for its effect in fighting and preventing certain cancers; used in some cosmetic and beauty products.

Burdock

Magical: a cleansing magic; cleanses negative emotions and emotional energies; use in incenses of protection or protection spells.

Medicinal: root, leaf, and seed are known for their medicinal properties; useful to increase the flow of urine (diuretic); can kill germs; reduces fevers; blood purifier; useful as a skin treatment for wrinkles, excessively dry skin, acne, eczema, psoriasis.

Caraway

Magical: memory, passion, protection, love, and health; often used to help in love spells to prevent your love from straying; considered an ideal herb for cleansing and charging magical tools; carried to improve the memory, put in pillows for dreams and dream recall; useful in children's magic to help keep them protected and free of illness.

Medicinal: seeds are used to stimulate digestions, help to improve the appetite, prevent flatulence, or ease it when uncomfortable and regularly occurring; used to flavor certain dishes; helps to heal and prevent stomach issues in children and is commonly used as a flavoring in bread and sweet treats.

Celandine

Magical: helps to promote joy and victory, helps to cure or relieve depressed emotions and energies; helps with legal matters or courtroom battles; when worn it acts as protective energy and helps promote or increase self-confidence in the face of challenges and adversity; for ritual work to release unwanted energies.

Medicinal: Use with caution because it can be upsetting when overused. Most commonly used is Greater Celandine and it has been known to treat specific issues of the digestive systems, such as gastroenteritis, IBS, upset stomach, constipation, stomach cancer and polyps in the intestines, appetite loss, liver, and gallbladder issues; also has uses in detoxification, couch, asthma, chest pain, fluid retention, high blood pressure, gout, and some heart conditions; as a skin treatment, useful for warts, rashes, and eczema when used topically; fresh root can be chewed to relieve toothache.

Chamomile

Magical: reduces stress, calms and heals; promotes love and affection; aids with relaxation and helps promote a restful sleep; added to sachets and charms to promote success, healing, love and prosperity; burned as an incense to encourage money flow and wealth; protective and banishing of negative hexes or spells when sprinkled around the home; burned as an incense to help relieve stress and promote healthy rest and sleep; washing hands in chamomile water before gambling can increase your luck; keep chamomile with lottery tickets to increase luck; use for love spells.

Medicinal: use the flowers to aid and soothe digestion; can help with fever reduction; anti-inflammatory properties; sedative to help with any kind of nervous disorder and issues with sleep and anxiety; helps to relive diarrhea and stomach issues in both adults and children; useful as an insect repellent when applied as a topical infusion; most often used as a tea infusion when used medicinally.

Cinnamon

Magical: used for prosperity, strength, power, protection, healing, success, love and luck; incense or in a charm to raise any spiritual vibrations; a popular herb that helps to draw money and wealth and abundance spells and rituals; helps to stimulate psychic powers; brings passion when worn as an amulet.

Medicinal: Cinnamon is a dried bark skin from a tree and can be used as the dried skin, or dried powder in spells or in medicines; astringent uses; digestive aid when added to tea infusions; indigestion, flatulence, dysentery, and diarrhea are all stomach and intestinal issues that cinnamon can aid; useful in helping with menstrual cramps.

Cinquefoil

Magical: health, wisdom, money, love, power is represented by each of the 5 points on the leaf; known to stimulate memory, self-confidence and eloquent speech; often used for blessing of the home and/or business; dreams; divinations of intended soulmates; commonly used in spells and rituals for romance and love; used as an infusion to wash hands and forehead to remove any hexes or negative energies imposed by others; helpful in protective charms and spells when hung around the home in sachets, or places where you sleep and dream.

Medicinal: the root and the plant are an antispasmodic, antiseptic and can help reduce fevers; treats diarrhea when drunk as a tea; gargled for sore and irritated throats; external lotion and astringent; concentrated decoction will help relieve a toothache.

Cloves

Magical: useful in magic of protection; helps to banish unwanted energies; gaining what you are looking for or what is being sought; burned as an incense, clove can help to stop gossip and cleanse, or purify, any area to raise the quality of energy and spiritual vibrations; kinship in social settings and gatherings; when worn in an amulet or charm it will bring mental clarity, and protection as well as an open "sight"; incense to draw internal or external riches; carried on the person to help attract the opposite sex; cleanses the auras; aids as a comfort during loss and bereavement.

Medicinal: cancer prevention; very high in antioxidants; kills bacteria; is known to improve liver health; helps to regulate healthy blood sugar levels and is thusly considered in many diabetic treatments; reduces stomach ulcers.

Comfrey

Magical: an herb of Saturn and all Saturnian energies; useful for working with spells and rituals to promote stability, endurance and security; money work; safe travels; matters of real estate and property; ownership; carried in your suitcase it can help prevent theft and/or loss; worn in charms and amulets to promote safe travels and protection; the root can be used in incense and is used to burn for money spells.

Medicinal: flowers and leaves are used in a variety of ways; can slow bleeding and eases burns on the skin; made into a poultice, or a tea, it can relieve rashes, sores, cuts, insect bites and other skin irritations; major ingredients for a soothing sunburn lotion; known as "knit bone", it has the power to promote connective tissue growth and bone and cartilage health; heals bruises by breaking down red blood cells; external agent to help heal varicose veins and ulcers of the skin; has been used to treat colitis and gastric ulcers; has been useful in some respiratory concerns and disorders.

<u>Note of Caution</u>: it is thought that overuse of this herb can have a negative impact on your liver and should be used mostly topically,

although research is still being done to prove this accusation. When used internally, moderate frequency and do not over ingest.

Coriander

Magical: protection, health and love; brings peace and security to the home when tied and hung around the house with ribbon; love charms; healing a broken heart; promoter of peace, especially among those who have difficulty getting along; seeds can be thrown, instead of rice, at rituals of love and ceremonies of matrimony; seeds can be added to love sachets and pillows, or powdered seeds can be added to wine to create a lust potion; wards of migraines and headaches when worn on the body (seeds).

Medicinal: digestive issues in general- upset stomach, appetite loss, bowel spasms, diarrhea, hernia, gas, and flatulence of the intestines; used to treat measles, worms; joint pain; toothache; and hemorrhoids; can be used to treat infections from bacteria that have been caused by a fungus.

Dandelion

Magical: Dandelion Leaf: defeating negative energies, healing, summoning spiritual energies, purification; wish magic; favorable winds; the root is useful for divination, calling spirit and helping wishes to come true; draws good luck to you and your home.

Medicinal: all parts of the plant can be used for medicinal treatments; the ground and roasted root is commonly used as a coffee substitute; flowers are regularly made into a sweet and floral wine; useful as a cleansing tonic, diuretic; enhances bile production in the liver; leaves eaten in salads can help with cases of hypertension; helpful with gout and rheumatism as well as other inflammatory issues; useful for stomach ailments; the milky white stem fluid rubbed on warts will help them to diminish.

Dill

Magical: love, luck, lust, protection and money; helpful for protection against darker energies and for blessing homes and households; promotes a healthy understanding and relationship between superstition and magical reality; seeds for money spells; dill scent is an aphrodisiac and enhances lust; useful in ritual baths- putting seeds in a herbal bath mixture before a date will make you irresistible.

Medicinal: dill can have a benefit medicinally in the treatment of common colds, coughs, fever, and bronchitis; other uses are for infections, hemorrhoids, nerve pain, muscle spasms, genital ulcers and conditions, menstruation and menstrual cramps, issues of sleep; can be used to aid in inflammatory problems in the mouth and throat; often used as a culinary herb to flavor foods.

Elder

Magical: protection, sleep, healing, enchantments and releasing unwanted ones; wisdom, home, and business blessings; powerful for the use of dream and vision work when put into pillows and sachets; when worn, can help prevent or protect against negativity, attacks (emotional and psychic), and adulterous temptations; used in spells and rituals to assist in the death and dying process to help loved ones commit to traveling to the Otherworld.

Medicinal: flowers and berries are used in decoctions, tonics, and teas to enforce and promote immunity and overall health; defense against illness and helpful with sore throats and chest illness; the berries contain high amounts of vitamin C; often used for skin treatments and health care of skin conditions when made into a tonic or essence; induces sweating; a cold infusion is useful in eyewashes, especially to aid with conditions like conjunctivitis or allergic irritations; infusion made for sore throats and as a gargle; common ingredient for couch syrups.

Elecampane

Magical: banishes violent, unwanted or angry vibrations and energies; connected to elf magic and tarot work; incense of purification; love attraction when used in spells; baby blessings: useful in sachets to be hung around the house, or sprinkled around the home for blessings and protection; made together with mistletoe and vervain and finely ground together, it is a potent love powder.

Medicinal: the root is used to make medicines; for lung issues and diseases such as, asthma, whooping cough and bronchitis; can be used to help prevent coughing, especially in cases of tuberculosis; expectorant to help remove and cough out phlegm; also works with stomach and digestive functions, treating diarrhea and nausea, killing off intestinal worms, such as hookworm, threadworm, whipworm, and roundworm; also used to promote sweating.

Evening Primrose

Magical: attracting love and romance; promotes a connection to the faerie realms and faerie magic; useful in sacred baths and rituals to improve desirability, beauty, and love energies.

Medicinal: useful for skin disorders like eczema, acne and psoriasis; for weak bones, multiple sclerosis, rheumatoid arthritis; high cholesterol, heart disease, immune-deficiency disorders, alcoholism, Alzheimer's, schizophrenia, and leg pain resulting from blocked blood flow through the vessels; chronic fatigue syndrome; asthma, hyperactivity and attention deficit disorders; gastrointestinal issues, like IBS, colitis and ulcers; nerve damage from diabetes; women's health in cases of pregnancy and pre-eclampsia, starting and shortening labor and preventing late labor; useful for PMS, endometriosis, menopause and breast pain.

Fig

Magical: fertility, love, sex, romance, divination; safe return from travels when a fig branch is hung at the altar; fig leaves are useful for asking questions- a slow drying leaf can indicate appositive answer, and a quick drying leaf can be a negative answer.

Medicinal: the fruit of the fig is a useful laxative to help relieve issues of constipation; fig leaves are affective medicines to aid with skin conditions like psoriasis, eczema, and vitiligo; diabetes and high cholesterol; milk sap from the tree has been used to apply directly to the skin for treatment of warts and skin tumors.

Garlic

Magical: protection, healing, exorcisms, repelling vampires of all kinds, purifying spaces, objects and energies; invokes Hecate, the Crone Goddess; useful as a protective guard against negative spiritual energies, magic and the envy of other people; hung around the house it will keep your willpower strong and your family energy fruitful, happy and promote togetherness; said to help ward off "bad weather" (energetic weather); thought to absorb diseases when fresh cut pieces are rubbed on ailing body parts and then thrown into running water.

Medicinal: garlic cloves are used to help with immunity, colds, earaches, and sore throats; helps to prevent illness when used regularly as a preventive care remedy; lowers blood pressure and blood cholesterol; cancer treatment as well as prevention; antifungal properties; when mixed with vinegar, is a powerful disinfectant for wounds (place crushed or chopped cloves in vinegar for ten days and distill- use on wounds, warts, tooth and mouth pain, and rheumatism); anti-inflammatory and anti-parasitic.

Ginger

Magical: new experiences; promotes adventure; enhances and promotes sexuality, sensuality, self-confidence, prosperity and success; adds speed and strength to any spell or concoction it is involved in; promotes good health, healing and protection when added to a sachet or medicine bag to be worn; used in consecration rituals for tools like athames, or blades, the energize the tool; a root of ginger that has a shape and appearance of a human body is a prized and useful magical tool and token.

Medicinal: ginger root is an incredible herb for nausea and indigestion, as well as other stomach and digestive issues; excellent to promote healing and immunity and can be taken at the onset of colds or throughout to enhance and speed up the healing process; excellent for migraines and headaches; useful in small amounts in the bath tub to soak the aching joints and muscles in the fiery water; pain relief; detoxifies meats in marinades and when cooking; stimulating and warming; good for blood circulation.

Hawthorn

<u>Magical</u>: magic of the faeries; chastity, fertility, rebirth, fishing magic; work, career and employment success, and promotion; in the bedroom it will help to energetically promote celibacy and chastity; sacred to the faerie realms; used regularly in marriage ceremonies to increase and promote fertility; when worn or carried it will help promote happiness and is said to protect against lightening; repels evil spirits and ghosts when hung around the house; making a Hawthorn infusion to wash the floors of the home will keep away negative energies and spirits.

Medicinal: this tree is considered the "heart tree" because of its use in cardiovascular health and healing; promotes health blood circulation; berries are used to reduce high blood pressure and help to clear the hardened arteries that cause high blood pressure; flowers are useful for strengthening the heart and keeping it healthy as it ages; treatments for angina, spasms in the arteries and nerves, irregular heartbeat; can be made into teas and tinctures.

Hibiscus

Magical: useful for attracting love and romance; divination and dreams; added to charms and sachets, or burned as an incense, it will attract love into your life.

Medicinal: helpful in conditions of high cholesterol, high blood pressure; increases the production of breast milk in nursing mothers; upset stomach and gastrointestinal issues; reduction of fevers; infections.

Honeysuckle

Magical: quick abundance, success, and money; sharpening of the intuition, persuasive abilities, self-confidence; used in money attraction spells, like wrapping a ring of honeysuckle around green candles; crushed flowers rubbed into the forehead, or third eye, will help you enhance your psychic powers.

Medicinal: used for intestinal and digestive disorders, such as inflammation, pain and swelling of the intestines, dysentery, and other issues; useful in respiratory, especially upper respiratory infections such as colds, pneumonia, swine flu and common flu; viral and bacterial infections; brain swelling; boils and sores on the skin; fever reduction; some urinary tract disorders; headaches and migraines; rheumatoid arthritis; diabetes and related issues; helps to promote sweating and can also be used as a laxative to counteract ingested poisons; can be applied to the skin for itching problems from bites or dryness, inflammation and to killing of germs.

Juniper

Magical: promotes good health and banishes energies that would dissuade health and healing; attracts good energy and love energy; when carried by men in pouches and medicine bags it can increase their potency; a string of juniper berries worn will attract love; incense burned to promote magical protection; a sprig of juniper placed in the home or near the entrance of the house will help keep your home safe from theft; juniper oil for spells to attract prosperity and financial abundance.

Medicinal: the berry is used for making medicines, and can be made into extracts and essential oils. Essential oil distilled form the bark doesn't have the same properties and medicinal functions; digestive system issues are treated with juniper, like flatulence, upset tummy, bloating, heartburn, appetite loss, intestinal worms and infections, intestinal gas; useful for urinary issues like infections of the urinary tract, kidney issues and bladder stones; can be used to treat some cancers, diabetic issues and snake bites;

Lavender

Magical: used for peace, sleep, protection, healing, purification, and love; helps with healing depression; chastity when combined with rosemary; as an incense, the burning herb will help promote more profound, restful sleep and will bring harmony, peace and calm to the home; for love spells, rituals and charms, especially for attracting men.

Medicinal: dried flowers are used for medical purposes; sedative; headache relief sleep inducer; on the skin in oil form it can have a healing effect on burns, cuts, and bites that need enhanced healing; made into a tea or a tonic, lavender will help heal colds and chills from the flu; anti-depressant and antibiotic; detoxification; helps to promote and stimulate immunity; useful when made into an oil to treat psoriasis and eczema.

Lemon Balm

Magical: spiritual and psychic enhancement and development, healing, success, love; often used in love spells and attraction charms; very useful in healing and health rituals and spells, especially for those suffering from mental and nervous issues or disorders; promotes joy and happiness while balancing all systems; heals the chakras.

Medicinal: helpful with digestive system disorders including vomiting, nausea, bloating, intestinal gas, upset stomach, and colic; helps reduce pain in various issues like toothaches, headaches and menstrual cramps; very helpful in mental disorders like melancholia, depression, mental fatigue, and hysteria or mania; considered to have a calming effect and is used to promote relaxation, restfulness and healthy sleep; insect bites, sores, and tumors; relieves swollen airways and passages; helpful with high blood pressure; used as an aromatherapy to treat Alzheimer's and ADHD.

Marjoram

Magical: dispels negative energies, purifies and cleanses; helps promote prophetic or revealing dreams when placed underneath the pillow; protection for the home; added to spells and food dishes to enhance love or romantic energies; attracts wealth and prosperity; protective charms and enchantments; helps to resolve grief and sadness when applied to sacred baths for a week straight.

Medicinal: helps promote healing and health revolving around common colds, coughs, runny nose and sinus infections, as well as various digestive issues, like flatulence, upset stomach, and IBS; applied externally to hemorrhoids for healing.

Mint

Magical: vitality, energy, healing, communication; home protection spells; drawing new customers and return customers to your business; put dried mint leaves in a poppet or sachet for promoting health and healing; rub on your money, or place inside of your wallet to carry regularly to draw new wealth, money and prosperity into your life; bring bundles to your altar to help you open to receiving positive spiritual assistance and guidance.

Medicinal: only the leaves are used; digestion, flatulence, successful and healthy bowel movements; flu and cold symptoms; helps to ease hiccups; made as a steam inhalation, promotes open airways and clear sinuses, clearing the lungs and nasal cavities; useful for healing the lungs with asthma and colds; can sometimes be used instead of aspirin to relieve headaches and PMS by drinking tea infusions, or by rubbing the fresh herbs on your forehead while you lie down and relax; acts as an anti-bacterial agent, antispasmodic, and antiparasitic; helps to stimulate gallbladder and live functions; is topically very cooling and soothing and can be useful in cooling one down when overheated and can promote healthy blood flow when applied as an oil or lotion to the skin.

Mugwort

Magical: lust, fertility, divination, prophecy, psychic awareness, astral projection and travel; helpful for communication with the divine; used for scrying and consecration of divination tools; burn as an incense or add to dream pillows to enhance psychic and lucid dream states; useful to cleanse and purify crystals and magic mirrors;

Medicinal: promotes delayed menstrual blood flow; used to help regulate menstrual cycles, irregular periods, and menstrual problems (not suggested or recommended if you are pregnant or trying to become pregnant); promotes and stimulates digestion; root tonics are known to boost energy; constipation, intestinal worms, diarrhea, persistent vomiting, and some other digestive issues; stimulates gastric juices and bile flow; liver tonic; promotes healthy blood and fluid circulation; sedative; can be used to treat epilepsy in children; combined with other herbs, the root has been known to heal or aid mental and emotional disorders like chronic fatigue and depression, hypochondria; irritability, insomnia, anxiety, and hysteria.

Mullein

Magical: helpful for protection against curses, nightmares, dark magic or sorcery; place in a magic pillow to help ward of negative dreams and nightmares; can help instill courage while helping to encourage and attract love and romance with a partner; can be worn as a guard against animals and animal spirits in unfamiliar territories and areas; incense to break habits and banish unwanted energies.

Medicinal: leaves and flowers are used to aid with respiratory and lung issues like asthma, bronchitis, whooping cough, hoarseness, croup, congestion of phlegm; infusion of nettle flowers for insomnia and sleep disorders; make a mullein maceration oil to drop into the ears to help with earaches; same oil is suitable for rubbing on the joints that are arthritic; anti-inflammatory and diuretic for the urinary tract; prickles on the leaves need to be strained off after boiling for tea as they can irritate the throat.

Nettle

Magical: dispels fear, darkness, and insecurity; strengthens willpower and helps with handling unexpected emergencies; wards of evil and negativity when sprinkled in desired areas; useful in charms and poppets to offer protection against negative forces; use in spells for personal growth to remove envy, petty jealousy, gossip and difficult situations with other people.

Medicinal: the root can be used for urinary issues, such as an enlarged prostate, and regulation of nighttime urination, kidney stones; UTI, painful urination, to frequent, or infrequent urination, and when taken with large amounts of water to help flush the urinary tract system it is called "irrigation therapy"; root can also help with joint issues and ailments, like osteoarthritis;

leaves are used for helping relieve symptoms of allergies like hay fever; can be used in some situations involving blood, like internal bleeding, nosebleeds, blood in the stool; promotes healthy blood circulation, anemia, enlarged spleen issues; diabetes, endocrine dysfunctions and disorders; blood purifier; lung issues, like asthma and congestion; overall general health and healing tonic to promote a whole balanced system.

Nutmeg

Magical: luck, prosperity, attraction spells, especially attracting money, breaking hexes; use in sachets, pillows and charms for money magic and bringing financial abundance and flow into your life; excellent for good luck charms, and also to enhancing the intellect; anoint green candles with nutmeg for money and prosperity spells.

Medicinal: nausea, diarrhea, stomach spasms, flatulence; kidney disease; cancer treatments and some preventive properties; insomnia; menstrual flow, such as increasing (can promote miscarriage); useful as a general health tonic; topically acts as a pain killer, such as pain caused by arthritic or achy joints; good for toothcare and mouth sores.

Pennyroyal

Magical: promotes peace and tranquility; helps with avoiding sea sickness and encourages endurance and strength; business success; banishes negative thoughts against you as a house blessing and negative energy banishing herb; carry to help you handle negative vibrations and energies; anoint a candle with pennyroyal before and/or during uncomfortable situations or meetings.

Medicinal: topically it can be used to keep insects at bay, as a stringent to kill germs and help heal some skin diseases and conditions; flea-killing bath for pets; gout; venomous bug bites; mouth sores; stimulant to counteract feelings of weakness; has been used as a diuretic, causes sweating, and helps with muscle spasming; regulation of menstrual periods, or to cause miscarriage (not safe during pregnancy); can be used for respiratory issues caused by colds, flu and pneumonia; stomach pains and gas; liver and gallbladder disorders or imbalances.

Rose

Magical: domestic peace and happiness, lasting love and friendship, close friends and allies, divine and spiritual love, twin souls; as incense it promotes comfort, healing, generosity, nurturing, love and joy; sexual love and promotion of lustful energies.

Medicinal: leaves, glowers, and hips can be used for medicinal purposes; rose hips are a powerful source of Vitamin C; leaves are a useful and strong laxative and can help as a topical agent to heal wounds on the skin; often used in skin care products, especially the hips and flowers; aromatherapy to promote serenity and relaxation; anti-inflammatory properties, topically or internally; cardiac health; antispasmodic.

Rosemary

Magical: love and lust spells, memory, healing, and good health, purification and banishing negative energy; prevents nightmares and promotes pleasant dreams; burned as an incense for purifying and cleansing; useful when worn during study, education, learning, or needing a lot of focus; to help complete tasks; clear thinking and clear intuition; washing hands in an infusion of rosemary is beneficial for healing spells and rituals; bath magic as purification; faerie magic.

Medicinal: digestive system health, like heartburn, appetite loss and intestinal gas; liver and gallbladder issues; gout and inflammatory joint problems, like arthritis; high AND low blood pressure issues; headaches and migraines; helps to reduce memory loss that comes with the ageing process; promotes alertness and alleviates mental fatigue; beneficial in cases of opioid withdrawals; helps to heal kidney disease caused by diabetes; protection from sunburns; has been thought to help promote intense menstrual flow that can lead to a miscarriage; applied topically to the skin to help treat baldness; other topical uses for various skin conditions include eczema, muscle pain, sciatica, wound healing, insect repellent; gum disease and tooth aches.

Sage

Magical: grief, loss, self-purification, mental and cognitive abilities, wisdom, healing; as an incense, purifies and cleanses prior to ritual and removes negative energies; known to promote mind, body, spirit connection and longevity; useful in healing spells and rituals or to be worn by someone in need of healing energies; used for writing wishes on the leaves and placed under the pillow for three nights to help dreams and desires come true- leaves are best buried in the ground after the three nights.

Medicinal: leaves and flowers are beneficial for healing sore throats, tonsillitis, and laryngitis; helps with overall digestive health; an excellent cold, fever and flu tea; mouthwash for infections and soreness; antiseptic and antibacterial; helps to fortify the nervous system; for women's health it has the ability to aid with painful periods, and drying up breast milk while a mother is trying to ween, also used for menopausal health, especially for hot flashes; used in many topical skin treatments; smoked when dry it can give relief to asthma.

St. John's Wort

Magical: for prophetic and romantic dreams, protection against darker and more negative energies, uplifting energies; used in protective spells by burning as incense; banishing and protection blessings for the household and physical body; strengthens courage when worn, as well as enhancing convictions; useful for crystal care and divinatory work.

Medicinal: it has been suggested that St. John's Wort can have serious interactions with other drugs, such as prescription medications, and consultation with a doctor may be necessary before you integrate this herb with other medicines; used to help with depression or states of melancholy as an herb that is uplifting and promotes more feelings of joy and empowerment; relieves issues of lack of energy, tiredness, nervousness, poor appetite, and problems with restful sleep; used for moderate levels of depression; also useful during menopause or at the onset of menopausal symptoms.

Thyme

Magical: affection, loyalty, attraction, good opinions of other people; used to help with grief and to offer energies of courage and strength during difficult times, especially when worn on the person; for banishing negativity and home blessings and protection, hang or burn thyme; attracts good health and vitality; cleansing and powerful sacred baths, useful before working with candle magic; restful sleep and lack of nightmares when added to dream pillows and sachets; helps attract regular and constant money flow when used in bath rituals; good luck, kept in a jar in the office or at the home.

Medicinal: sore throat, whooping cough, bronchitis, general respiratory issues; stomach and digestive system issues; bedwetting in children; skin conditions and disorders when taken internally and applied externally; promotes urine flow (diuretic); cleanses the bladder; stimulates appetite; can be applied externally to the throat, as well as gargled, to help with hoarseness, sore mouth, bad breath, and other mouth and throat conditions; thyme oil is good for mouthwashes as a germ killer, and can be used on the skin as well; fights bacterial and fungal infection; used to treat baldness.

Valerian

Magical: harmony, love, dreams, reconciliation, romance, bonding, sleep magic, divination; add to pillows and sachets to promote love and protection, as well as healthy and restful sleep; energies to help settle and argument between couples; purification of sacred spaces; protection ritual baths; burn as an incense to help relationships that are ailing have reconciliation, as long as it is okay with both partners; worn to calm emotional states and energies.

Medicinal: sleep disorders, insomnia especially; anxiety, psychological stress.

Witch Hazel

Magical: reduction of passions, chastity, protection, grief over lost love, can be used in spells to ward off evil.

Medicinal: taken internally it helps with coughing up or vomiting blood, tuberculosis, fevers, colds; tumors and cancer; mucus colitis; diarrhea; often and more commonly applied topically for itching, swelling inflammation, eye issues and skin injuries, varicose veins, insect bites, minor bruises and contusions, hemorrhoids, acne, and sensitive scalp; the leaf and bark extract is used in common facial care applications as an astringent to tighten skin on the face; used to help slow or stop bleeding; minor pain relief.

Yarrow

Magical: draws and encourages love and romance, used in weddings often, healing, wards of fear and insecurity, promotes confidence and psychic awareness and opening; marriage charms and spells; for weddings to ensure a fruitful and long marriage; inside of a flannel sachet or pillow add a piece of paper with all of your fears and cares to help you overcome them.

Medicinal: yarrow flowers and leaves will intensify the healing power of other herbs when combined together; eliminates toxins from the body; externally helps to stop blood flow, while internally helps to promote healthy circulation and blood flow; topical poultice or other application is good for infections and swelling, arthritis, joint complaints, aches and pains in the muscles and tissues; one of the most useful herbs for fevers; helps to clear a blood clot and helpful with internal and external bleeding; anti-inflammatory; considered the herb for the blood.

This entire chapter is only the beginning of what you can learn about all of these sacred herbs of magic and healing. There are a thousand more ways to understand their uses and properties and as you approach your herbal magic and medicine, you will discover how each plant feels, looks, tastes, and so forth, in your journey with plant magic. Here you have learned how they can affect your body, mind and spirit and it is up to you to learn more and more about each one's significance in your life.

Think of it as a new way for you to embrace healing your whole system from the Earth to Heavens and ask each plant, as you get to know them, what other things they have to share with you.

So much of your Wicca herbal journey is about intuition and practice. Always use caution when ingesting any herb and make sure you fully understand how to use any of them before practicing a magical health regimen. You will find all you want to know when you are introduced to each plant and can hold it in your hand, smell it, consider its properties, and find out more about how it wants YOU to utilize it in your magical practices.

Have fun with these herbs and begin to build your garden or home medicine cabinet so that you can meet all of the plant allies available to show you the way through your own inner garden, as well as the garden of the Great Mother Spirit.

Chapter 4: Herb Management

When you are ready to begin collecting, storing and utilizing herbs, you will need to be prepared to take care of them and tend to them in your life as you build your magical and medicinal cabinet. It is an exciting process and will help you form a stronger bond and relationship to every plant that you acquire.

This chapter will focus on the best methods for buying, collecting, growing, storing and preparing your herbs for magical and medicinal purposes. All you need to get you started is an idea of what herbs you would like to connect with first, whether it is for spells and rituals or for medicinal potions and brews. Once you know what herbs you want to acquire, you can begin the journey of determining how you will go about getting them, where to get them from, and the best ways to take care of them in your home apothecary and altar space.

Where to Buy Herbs

Herbs can be found in a variety of places and one of the most common places to find them in our modern culture is in the local shops and apothecaries. You may not have one close to you in your home town, in which case you will have to order them online, which can be a long process that requires some thought and research.

First of all, not all herbs grow naturally and natively where you live, and so there may be some that you wouldn't necessarily be able to plant in your garden. These kinds of herbs are usually best purchased in a shop that you can visit so that you can make your selection on site. Seeing, smelling, and engaging with the herbs first is a powerful part of the herbal magic practice, and when you are able to connect with the herb in person you can establish your relationship with it immediately, and decide whether it is a good enough quality product for your uses and needs.

Shops and purveyors of loose herbs and blends are the best choice for you to obtain the herbs that you cannot find out in the wild or grown in your backyard garden. You can speak to the people in the stores to find out more information about where their products come from and how they are harvested. Some shops uphold very strict sustainable practices and have a more respectful and balanced approach to obtaining their products. Some other business might be less interested in the impact of high levels of production and manufacturing and might be contributing to some environmental decline. Asking the shop about their processes is a great choice to help you learn about where your herbs come from before you take them home to use them for magic.

Other options are to buy some herbs from your local supermarket, as you will be able to find some of them fresh and packaged in the produce department and others will be dried in the cooking herbs and spices aisle. It is harder to know where these herbs might be coming from and so you may need to align with doing some deeper research about the products and companies you are buying your herbs from.

In some cases, you can find some excellent online retailers who promote sustainable harvests and take great care of their products. When you buy herbs online, make sure you are getting them from a good source. Keep in mind that you are dealing with herbs that have gone through a great deal of processing and packaging and have passed through many hands.

You may have to do some rituals of cleansing and purifying your herbs when you get them in the mail, before you use them in any spells, and even in healing concoctions. Buying herbs is sometimes the only choice you have and that is absolutely okay. Not all of us have garden spaces at our homes, or easy access to the wilderness to collect them from their natural habitats. Buying herbs might take a little bit of research, but you will likely be able to find more exotic choices this way to round out your cabinet of herbs. See if you can find some local shops in your area to visit and start asking some questions about their products. They may even have a good suggestion of online companies to buy from whose practices are in line with your preferences.

Wildcrafting

Wildcrafting is another way of saying "going out into nature and collecting herbs from their natural habitats". This activity is a truly magical process and will give you a much deeper and closer connection to the power of plant magic and medicine. You will have to learn a lot as you go and it is always helpful to have a field guide handy to help you identify plants at first. Once you get better at it, you will feel capable at going into the wild without your field guide and hand and can simply know what plants you are dealing with and find them based on what you know about how and where they grow the best and in what season.

Wildcrafting is a beautiful activity and art to learn for your magical pursuits and you only need a few tools and some plant knowledge to enjoy the experience. As it happens, wildcrafting is the best way to acquire herbs for medicinal and magical purposes. The plants themselves are in their highest vibration because they are growing naturally in the wild and have the most intense energy, over something that you buy in a shop or online that has had a significant amount of processing. When you gather and collect plants and herbs from nature, you are communicating with the divinity of the Earth Mother and are better able to enjoy the bounty of her gifts.

Really all you need to wild craft is the following:

- A sharp blade or cutting tool (preferably cleansed and consecrated for magical work)

- A bag to carry herbs home

- A small shovel (a spoon can work, consecrated for ritual)

- An offering to leave for the plant spirits (wildflower seeds, tobacco, other nature elements like stones or crystals)

With these simple tools, you can ask the plants if they are alright with being taken, ask them the best way to extract what you need, and leave an offering of gratitude for what they offer to you. In many cases, you won't need to uproot the whole plant, but in some, it is the root that you will need to take with you for healing purposes. Planting seeds in exchange for uprooting something is a good offering.

When you have all that you need, finding the right place to go wildcrafting can be of significant importance. Find land that is safe to work on and that isn't someone's private property. Also, it needs to be a place where it is okay for you to wander off the trail and dig into the woods. Some forests and protected trails might not allow for such adventures. You may also find what you are looking for by strolling through your neighborhood, and as long as your neighbors don't find, you can forage and harvest around your own neck of the woods.

The season of the year will have importance to your wildcrafting excursions as well, and you will need to make sure you have dressed appropriately so that you don't get too hot, or too cold. Be prepared for whatever whether you will be walking into. You may also want to bring a snack, some water, and some of your other magical tools to help you perform more rituals in your explorations and wildcrafting experiences.

It is a good idea to bring some empty containers along in case you come across a natural spring or waterfall and want to collect some sacred water along the way. Whenever you do take something, be sure to talk to the spiritual energies of the plant first, and ask permission. Wait for acceptance and provide some kind of an offering in return.

If you recall from chapter 2, the section about herbs and shamanism talked about how to plant gaze and communicate with the spirit of the plants. The process of wildcrafting follows the same kind of concept and it will be up to you, your intuition, and your spiritual guidance to find the right methods for working with this sacred energy. Plant magic is powerful and potent and when you are on their land and in their territory, you will understand just how intense it can be.

Wildcrafting asks you to be respectful and engage with all of the plants based on their own unique identities. It is a sacred magic to honor the lifeforms that you will take with you to heal you and help manifest abundance and magic in your life. If you want to have a deeper connection to working with the spirit energies of plants, wildcrafting is a powerful way to do so.

Start small and just go out into your favorite outdoor area with the appropriate equipment. Relax and concentrate on this space. Just listen for a while. As you begin to walk around, observe the area around you and witness every plant, bug, a wisp of air and drop of water. Wait for the plant to call to you and when it does, begin the conversation with that plant. You may already know what it is and if you can identify it, you will know what it can help you with. Ask it for more information anyway. Listen for it to tell you what it needs to offer you and if it is okay to take it.

The art of wildcrafting comes with practice but is simple and intuitive. All it requires is your openness and ability to listen to the energies all around you. You can build your home apothecary with wildcrafted herbs, plants and flowers, and what you cannot find in the wild, you can purchase at the shops, or grow in your home garden.

Magic in the Garden

Another wonderful way to bring herbs into your life is to grow them yourself! Magical gardening is a wonderful experience and can help you design and landscape the perfect medicinal and magical garden for your practice and purposes. You can carefully select what herbs you want to grow and become more closely acquainted with them. As you explore your own garden of herbal riches, they will continue to teach you about how they go through their cycles, seasons, deaths and rebirths.

You can easily harvest from your garden and adopting the same kinds of spiritual harvesting practices that you would use in wildcrafting is highly recommended. Gardening is a sacred ritual between human and plant and in today's society, there are a lot of tips, ideas, instructions, pointers and rules to make a garden perfect and special.

For your magical garden, you will need to take a less strict approach and allow the plants to have some say in the matter. Plants are just as intelligent as you are and know what they want. As you prepare to grow your own powerful garden, decide how you want to implement that work into your Wiccan or magical practices and provide the plants and seeds with an opportunity to "talk" to you about how they want to live in your world.

Use your gut to understand the responses. A lot of gardeners only look at books and tutorials, but gardening is a correspondence for people and plants to find harmony and balance together. Attend to it like you would a dear friend or close loved one, and it will always provide you with abundance.

Many magical gardeners will use the concepts of astrology, including the sun and moon cycles to prepare and plant their gardens. You can even plan your plantings and cuttings around specific moons to enhance their sacred qualities. The use of astrological omens and influences can help you to better partner with the herbs and the plant correspondences that you learned about in Chapter 2. Astrology is its own powerful and intense science and magical property and will require some additional study for gardening purposes, but you can be sure that certain celestial forces can be impactful in your garden, not to mention that all plants have a correspondence with one or more planets in our solar system.

Using your Wiccan calendar to help you practice gardening is an excellent approach and will help you work within the Wheel of the Year, the cycles of the Sun and Moon and the energies of the God/ Goddess while you plant, tend and harvest your magical herbs.

In addition to wildcrafting and purchasing herbs in the store, magical gardening is an excellent resource for having all of the herbs and plant medicines you may need during each season of the year. Consider that you may need to use all three resources to have a full apothecary and magical herbal cabinet in your home.

Explore the options and if you have space and the time, working in your own backyard garden with the elements, seasons, moons and sun, will bring you so much closer to healing magic and medicine.

Drying and Storing Herbs

When you have brought your herbs home from the wilderness or clipped them from your garden, you will need to begin the process of preparing them for use. There are times when you may also be buying fresh herbs form the store to bring home and dry, and they would go through the same process as they would from the garden or the woods.

Some herbs, flowers, and plants will need to be used in fresh form, depending on your spell, ritual, or medicinal preparation, but in a lot of cases, you will need to effectively dry and store your herbs for later and ongoing uses. It is a simple process and only requires a few tools and some containers to get you started.

All of the herbs that you are going to be drying need a space that is cool, and free of damp air. Some spaces might be too busy with foot traffic (getting bumped all the time while drying is not good for the magic and medicine of the herb) while other places can be too moist and will cause mold in your herbs which will destroy the benefits.

Finding the right location for your herbs to dry is the first step. Some people may also consider using electric dehydrators, used for dehydrating fruits and foods for preservation. This is okay to use if you have no other choice, but when working with magical medicine, it is best to avoid technology in the processing of the plants.

Drying Racks for Hanging

A simple drying rack is an excellent option. All you need is some kind of a beam that hangs from the ceiling in your chosen drying space. It can be just one beam to start, or it can be several that would need to be several inches to a foot apart so that the herbs have space while they are drying. Many people will use a thick, wooden dowel rod that has ties on both ends that can attach to hooks in the ceiling and will hang down to a reachable height.

For drying herbs form a hanging rack, you will also need some kind of string. Kitchen twine is easy and affordable and comes in large spools to keep on hand for all of your herb drying purposes. You can use this same twine to wrap smudge sticks for sacred ceremonial incense, with some of the herbs you have collected.

When you cut herbs, you will want to bundle them together and tie them like a fresh flower bouquet. It is important to keep herb and plant varieties separated as they may take different amounts of time to dry, and so it is best to keep like with like.

Once you have the herbs ties together in a bundle, you can hang them by another stretch of the kitchen twine and tie it to the wooden rod or rack, so that the flowers and leaves are hanging upside down and pointing towards the floor.

Drying times really vary from plant to plant and will need monitoring everyday so you can be sure to store them at the right time. Too long, and they might lose some of their magical and medicinal potency; too short and they may still be retaining a lot of fluid and will end up molding in a closed container or jar. It all depends on the thickness of the stem, the fluffiness of the flowers, and the pudginess of the leaves.

The best way to check is by feeling them and sniffing them. When you touch them, if they still feel a little limp and watery, then they need more time. If they crumble at your touch, they may have been drying for too long. Find the "Goldilocks" amount of dry as part of your personal relationship with the plant. It may take some trial and error, but it is well and good to use over-dried herbs in your rituals and spells anyway. They are still powerful and magical, no matter what.

Laying Drying Racks

Another drying preparation involves a drying rack that lays flat and acts as a screen to promote air flow to both the bottom and top of the plant materials. Think of it as a window screen (and you could even use a window screen for your drying rack) laying over an open barrel. The underside of the screen has airflow since it is sitting on top of an opening in a large barrel and so the plants can receive a more balanced drying out.

You can also prop up, or stack the screen on some cinder blocks on top of a table or a workspace, as long as it is in an area that won't be disturbed. A laying drying rack is most useful for things like rose hips and flower heads. If you only need the top of the plant, the flowering portion, and you don't need stems, leaves, and roots, then a laying rack is a better choice, since these items cannot easily be tied up in a bundle.

You can also use this preparation for roots to dry out. Roots take a lot longer to dry because they are thicker and full of more water. Some people will place washed and scrubbed roots into a very low heat oven to help extract the fluids more quickly. You can experiment with this, but you want to be careful not to cook the herbs. They may do better to dry out naturally on their own over a longer stretch of time on a laying drying rack.

Jars and Bottles

Storing your herbs is partially about preference but there are some key factors to consider:

- Sterilize and clean containers before putting anything new inside (you can sterilize with boiling hot water after washing with soap.

- Make sure there is a sterile and clean lid to keep air out of the jar or container

- Label and date your herbs

There are so many different kinds of containers that can prove useful for storing herbs. Some of the cheapest and easiest to use are mason jars. They are made of glass, can be purchased cheaply in bulk and come with metal lids that are easy to clean and sterilize. Some people may want to use plastic Tupperware, but this is strongly advised against. For your sacred plant materials, it is best to use containers that are not made of synthetic, chemical based ingredients.

Once your herbs are ready to be contained, you can put them in a clean, dry jar with a lid and make a note on a label or a piece of tape, what it is and when you jarred it. You can even write a more detailed note on the jar to show you what the herb is used for or what plans or spells you might have for it in the future.

You can also bottle some potions, decoctions, syrups, and brews in a similar fashion after you have prepared the herbs in these ways. Use glass bottles with either corks or screw caps and be sure they are also sterilized before you store anything magical or medicinal inside.

Some things will deteriorate over time and that is why labelling your potions and herbs with a date will be helpful. The process is really easy and fun and once you do it a few times, it will be a piece of cake, like boiling the kettle and brewing a hot cup of tea.

Charging Herbs for Magical Use

One thing that may be important, depending on your practice, is charging your stored and ready herbs for magical purposes. So, what does it mean to "charge" your herbs? This term describes the energetic ritual of imbuing your herbs with your sacred intentions. In the same way you might cast a spell by using candle or crystal magic, your charge the energy of those items with your purpose.

Charging herbs is basically a way of showing it how you are hoping to utilize its power for certain and specific purposes. You can charge your herbs throughout the drying and storing process, or you can do it at the time of the spell or medicinal incantation.

A basic charging ritual can sometimes involve casting a circle of magical protection, which is recommended but not required. All you have to do is simply create a sacred space somehow, either with your own energy and power of intention, or other magical tools, like candle light and incense.

If you want to cast a circle to charge your herbs, all you need to do is call out to each direction as you face it and ask for protection and guidance throughout your magical work. You may already be familiar with this process and have your own unique circle casting process that you can use for charging your herbs. If you don't, check out my other books: *Wicca for Beginners: A Witchcraft Guide for Every Wiccan Aspirant, Made Easy for the Solitary Practitioner and Wiccan Spell Book: A*

You can use your own powerful energy as you hover your hands over the herbs and ask them to be filled with the light of creation and divinity for the purpose of [insert purpose here] and allow the herbs to absorb those intentions.

Many Wiccans and Witches will use crystals, incense and candle magic to consecrate, or charge, their herbs for whatever the purposes may be, so depending on what your intentions are, you can be more or less elaborate with your charging experiences.

Charging herbs is really a way for you to connect with their power and magic while you energetically express to them, and the Universe, what you will be using them for. It is a powerful collaboration that helps you and the herb, as well as the surrounding energies, agree on your purposes for manifestation, or healing magic.

You don't have to charge every herb that you use and you can practice with your intuition to decide what work you need to do with each herbal experience.

Now that you have a bigger plan for how to collect, store and consecrate your herbs, what's next!? Excitingly, the next steps are to use your herbs for all of your magical and medicinal purposes, which let's face it, is really some of the most fun when you are practicing magic. In the next chapter, you will find out about magical teas, how to brew them and some beautiful recipes to help you with your magical way.

Chapter 5: Making Magical Teas

Tea is an ancient remedy and has crossed many continents and cultures. You could even say that tea has played a significant role in our human evolution, politics, financial abundance and wars over spices and herbs. Tea has a long history and belongs with the magical tales of old for how it came into being. The first teas were just herbs dropped into hot water and as people learned and studied more about their plant allies, they watched, felt, smelled and observed the overall impact of certain healing and herbal teas on their health, healing and overall balance.

Tea has always existed in many cultures; however, it was in certain cultures that the tea was more prized and sought after by merchants and traders to bring back to other countries for commodity and sale. The famous Boston Tea party is an example of how tea was impacting taxes, tariffs and various business operations, and how it could be used to foil certain political and business representations.

What we know about tea today is that it is a cross-cultural beverage that helps us heal, wake-up, feel calm and soothed, and bring more satisfaction into our everyday lives. As you work with herbal magic, you will have a greater appreciation and understanding of how magical one cup of tea really is, and how much potent power and life force it contains within it. Looking at magic and how to use it well when you are working with herbs, you will find tea to be one of your number one healing potions for magic and medicinal use.

Brewing Healing Teas

To brew a healing tea is to brew a serious cup of magic. It doesn't take much to make one cup and the benefits as you drink and enjoy are worth all of the effort of finding the right herbs for your needs and creating the ritual of making such a loving gift for yourself, or someone else.

Brewing any old cup of tea is easy, right? You boil the kettle, drop in your tea bag, wait for the whistle and then pour. A majority of teas need about 8-10 minutes to steep and get the proper infusion of flavors into the water. Some herbs, if over-brewed, will taste too strong and bitter, while others need a much longer time to extract all of the flavors, aromas and magical compounds.

When you see the word "infusion" in any of your readings about medicinal herbal concoctions, your reading about tea. Infusion is a more technical term to describe what a tea actually is; it is simply saying that the herbs infuse into the liquid to deliver a potent energy and healing magic when sipped and enjoyed.

It all depends on the herbs you need for your purposes and what you want from them, in order to determine the blend you want to use. There are so many variations of teas blends and mixtures, and once you have a grasp on what herbs you like to use the most and how they taste on their own and coupled together, then you can start inventing your own magical infusions.

There really is no trick to it and it can be one of the simplest and easiest ways to get medicine and magic into your body. To brew a healing tea, you only need the following tools:

- Something to boil water in (kettle or pot)
- Tea pot or mug (depends on the quantity you want to brew)

- Various herbs and flowers
- Tea strainer

All of these tools are probably in your kitchen, even some of the herbs. You will steadily acquire more of the herbs you want and need, and for the most part, you only need one herb at a time to start, in case you want to explore each herb individually and truly learn and understand their properties, flavors, aromas, and side effects.

Pour the boiling water over the herbs in the pot, or if you are using a strainer that fits inside of your mug, you will pour the water over the herbs resting in the strainer. Avoid tea balls as they seem to make it harder for the boiling water to make it all the way through the ball, as it is too compact. After the preferred steeping time, you can strain the herbs and enjoy the tea.

If you desire to take your tea brewing to a more magical level, you can actually charge, or consecrate, your herbs first in a ritual with a circle cast and some incense and candle magic. You can also use your altar to brew your sacred tea and make it a much more ritualistic experience and approach to really bring that energy into the cup you are making for yourself in your healing magic work.

Always ask your intuition for what is best, and let the answers come to you naturally. You will know right away if your healing brew is meant for spell work, or if it is a simple affair to help your cough, cold and sore throat.

Either way, your cup will contain powerful magic and healing properties to be enjoyed and to help empower your mind body and spirit along the way.

Another thing to consider is the infusion made from roots, which tends to be a little different as a process. Because roots are so much thicker, it takes longer to extract their benefits, magic and healing potential; and so, with roots, you need to simmer them, rather than steep them. To make a root infusion you will need the following items:

- Pot
- Tea pot or mug (depends on the quantity you want to brew)
- Roots (measured by recipe or intuitively measured)

- Tea strainer

With the roots, add them to the pot and allow the water to come to a full boil. Once they are boiling, turn it all the way down to a very low simmer and leave them like this for about 10-15 minutes. Once they have simmered, you can strain the liquid from the roots into a tea pot or mug and enjoy. You can reuse the roots for a second infusion but should discard them after the second use.

Another great ingredient to add to your teas is an essential oil. Essential oils, as you will learn more about in Chapter 7, are highly concentrated herbal essences that will add power and flavor to your teas when you add a few magical drops. You can determine what essential oil will be best based on their properties and your healing needs.

Enjoying a healing tea is a large part of enjoying the magical properties of herbs and how they are the greatest medicine of all. As you look ahead through this chapter you will find some wonderful examples of some possible healing and magical teas to enjoy. Find some of your favorites and begin your journey with magical infusions and healing brews!

Many of the following teas are measured to brew just one cup, so if you want to brew a whole pot or more, adjust your recipes accordingly. One cup is about 8-12 oz of water to herb content.

Luck and Prosperity Teas

General Luck

This General Luck Tea is a warming, all-purpose healing tea to bring you luck in any way you need it. Combining a variety of herbs, bark, and seeds to give you a dominant flavor, this tea is healing and will align you with that lucky power you need. While you are drinking it, meditate on what kind of luck you need so that your infusing the energy with that purpose of manifestation.

Ingredients:

- Cinnamon stick (curled bark)
- 1/8 teaspoon Cloves
- 1/8 teaspoon Nutmeg
- 1 Tablespoon Honeysuckle
- Honey to taste (optional)

Mix together and steep for ten minutes. Put the cinnamon stick in the tea pot or mug while steeping. Enjoy next to your altar with a candle of luck lit.

Quick Luck

For luck in the moment or on the spot, try brewing this tea right before a job interview or important meeting to bring you the luck you need.

Ingredients:

- Several strips of orange peel
- 2 Tbsps. rose hips
- 1 Tbsp chamomile

Mix together and let steep for 10-12 minutes, strain out ingredients and enjoy! You can light a luck candle next to your tea while it steeps to infuse more luck energy into it.

Purification and Protection Teas

Protection Tea:

There are a lot of different reasons that we want to protect ourselves. This tea is useful in tandem with a protection ritual to help you with all of your needs.

Ingredients:

- 1 Tablespoon burdock root

- 1/2 teaspoon comfrey
- 3 teaspoon elder flower
- 1/2 teaspoon valerian

Simmer the burdock root in water for 15 minutes. While it simmers combine the other ingredients. Bring the burdock simmer back to a boil and then add the burdock tea to the other ingredients and steep for another 8-10 minutes. During this process, you can light a candle of protection in your workspace and also smudge all of the ingredients with white sage before brewing. Add to a ritual or spell of protection to consume inside your circle of magic.

Purification Tea:

Ingredients:

- 2 teaspoons coriander
- 2 teaspoons fennel
- 1 garlic clove, chopped or crushed
- 1 piece of ginger root, grated
- Lemon juice

Combine ingredients together and pour boiling water over them. Allow for the tea to steep for 8-12 minutes. Include honey if desired. Drink this tea in the sunlight or moonlight in order to aid your purification process.

Protection & Cleansing Tea

- 1 teaspoon bergamot
- 1 squeeze of lemon

- 2 teaspoon Dandelion
- 2 teaspoon Nettle

Combine ingredients and steep for 10 minutes. Add the squeeze of lemon before drinking. Use in your protection and cleansing rituals, or just after you have completed one and closed your circle. You could also use this tea brew to cleanse some of your ritual tools from your altar space.

Emotional Healing Teas

Stress Tea

At the end of a long and challenging day, or during times of ongoing stress and difficulty, this tea will be an emotional life-saver.

Ingredients:

- 1 Tbsp chamomile
- 2 teaspoon elder flower
- 2 teaspoon hops
- 2 teaspoon valerian root
- 2 teaspoon lavender

Combine ingredients and steep for 10 minutes. Enjoy in a relaxing, ritual bath with soothing and calming essential oils, or in a dimly lit room with lavender or sage incense. Try using only candle light while you imbibe this soothing concoction.

Frustration Tea

When you need to calm down your energies if you are feeling easily agitated or frustrated, this soothing and magical tea will do just the trick.

Ingredients:

- 2 teaspoons chamomile
- 1 teaspoon hyssop
- 3 teaspoon raspberry leaf
- Orange zest

Combine the chamomile, hyssop and raspberry leaf. Use the orange peel or zest to rub around the inside of the mug and around the top lip as well. Add boiling water to the herbs and allow them to steep for 8-10 minutes. Sip and enjoy in your favorite setting where you won't be disturbed.

Emotional Health and Well-Being Tea

This tea is good for the mind, body, and spirit and will give you an overall sense of calm and well-being. It is packed with flavor and many healing properties to provide you great balance.

Ingredients:

- 1/2 tsp elder flower
- 1 tsp fennel
- 2 tsp hops
- 2 tsp mint
- 3 tsp rose hips

Combine ingredients and steep for 10 minutes. Enjoy while writing in your journal and let whatever wants to pour out of your pen fly onto the paper. Give all of your current emotions to the page and sip away at this delicious tea.

Divination and Psychic Awareness Teas

Divination Tea

When you want to do some scrying and divination in your magic spells and rituals, brew a cup of this divination tea before you get started to help you open up to the energies and spirits for your divination practices.

Ingredients:

- 1 Tbsp mugwort
- 2 tsp lemon balm
- 1 Tbsp rose hips
- Pinch of lavender

Combine ingredients and steep for 10-12 minutes. Enjoy while sitting with some mugwort incense burning nearby while you prepare for your experience.

Clairvoyance Tea

This tea is designed to be used for ongoing psychic awareness and clairvoyance evolution to help you stay attuned and to practice being an open channel for your abilities to flow through you.

Ingredients:

- 2 teaspoon mugwort
- 2 teaspoon thyme
- 2 teaspoon rosemary
- 1 teaspoon mint

Combine ingredients and steep for around 9-10 minutes before drinking. Prepare a space beforehand where you can sit and reflect. Light some candles and some incense, or cast a ritual circle for this. Practice your psychic awareness while sipping your tea and meditating in silence in this space. Can be repeated daily for best results.

Chapter 6: The Magical Bath

The magic of water is sacred and has been used for ritual bathing for centuries. We all know that lovely feeling at the end of a long, hard day on your feet, sinking into the lusciously hot water to rest our weary bones. The power of a bath comes from so many factors and elements and the reality is that we should all indulge in the magic of what a hot-warm bath can do for the mind, body, and spirit.

Within the realms of Wiccan magic and other Pagan or magical practice, the ritual bath can become something that realizes your intentions and manifestations for a specific goal or spell. The work you do as a Witch in the waters of life is what helps you to form a greater connection to your own power and element of magical experience.

The Magical bath is almost as easy as brewing a cup of tea, and it basically is just that: a giant brew of healing herbs for you to dip your whole being into! The infusion of herbs that you choose to put in your ritual, or spell bath, is what will cover your entire being in the glowing energy of the powerful herbs that you will work with to help you transport your spirit into the other dimensions of life.

Some baths are for healing and nurturing, while others are for empowering and self-confidence. Some baths are intended to be for purification, banishing and cleansing, while others are designed and concocted to attract love and romance. Whatever your magical intentions and purposes are, the herbs you choose to use will play a significant role in the power of your bath experience and what you are hoping to take away from it.

As you have learned from your reading so far, herbs are dynamic forces that contain a great deal of potent magic and medicine. When you brew them into a tea to drink, you imbibe the very essence and nature of what they are and what they will offer your energy. In the bath, the principles work the same, and you will take the energy in through the skin, the scent, through the appearance of their magic essences coloring your water, and by the very act of submerging your whole self into this magical potion.

Think of a ritual bath as brewing a giant potion. The bathtub is your cauldron and the herbs are the sacred ingredients that will connect you to your higher purpose through the conduit of water. It is a most magical moment that you can experience in your personal practice and you can use the cosmic bath support in addition to any other spell, ritual, or kind of magic. Bring candles, crystals, and incense into the experience to help support your magic, and enjoy the abundance of what a magical bath ritual can do for your mind, body, and magical spirit!

Choosing Herbs for the Ritual Bath

There are many herbs to choose from when you are getting ready to conjure up a magic bath, and some will work better than others. There are a few key things to consider when you are preparing your herbs and elements for your giant brew:

Intention

The first important step to any spell is knowing your intention. Every ritual or spell has a magical purpose and whatever that purpose may be will impact the choice of ingredients that you will use to make your brew and cast your spells. Your intention might simply be that you want to promote relaxation or release the harmful or unwanted energies in your body, and that is perfectly realistic for any bath time, magical or not. You might also have a specific desire that you need to focus on in order to bring more financial abundance into your life and so you will have more manifestation work to do while you relax in the warm waters infused with prosperity herbs.

Your purpose for the bath is what will inform you of what to carry into the bathtub and that isn't limited to herbs alone. You may want to lace your bath with some powerful crystals and gemstones to raise the vibration and frequency of the water, specific to your needs for the spell. Crystals are an excellent addition to help empower your work. A candle or two, anointed and consecrated to burn throughout your bath will improve your focus and manifestation and the color, or the sigil that you carve into it will need to be carefully chosen for your purposes. If your purpose is to just relax, then you may be a lot less concerned with the color of the candle, of course.

Whatever your intentions are for the bath, deciding before you hop in the tub is an essential part of the preparation that will help you determine the right herbs and magical tools to bring with you.

Application

Herbs in the bathtub can get awfully messy, and so it is crucial to decide the best way to apply the herbs to the ritual. You may have only one or two different kinds of flower petals that you want to add to the water, in which case, you can just scoop them out of the water before you drain the tub. Using a strainer, like the kind you use for your pasta noodles, is an easy way to do this step.

If your herbs are finer and crumblier, then you will need to consider applying them to the bath with a large, cloth tea bag. A muslin bag, in a larger size than your average sized tea bag, can be purchased or hand made for your bath needs. It is so easy to make a small pouch with this easy to handle cloth, and it is very affordable. You can reuse them many times as well, so you can make three or four and rotate them after uses, or you can make all 4 of them into tea bags for one bath. It really is just a great big cup of tea, when you get right down to it, so think of how you would make a cup that size: how many herbs do you need and in what quantity? How many tea bags do you want to make for one bath? It is a simple and easy method that will have a quick and easy clean up.

Between the loose floating flower heads and petals, and the large, homemade tea bags, you can discover the best choices for your magical bath pleasure, and make the right brew, just for you.

Effects

Finally, understanding the impact of these herbs with the combination of hot water is an important consideration and will impact how much of certain kinds of herbs you will choose to use. Some herbs are so stimulating, they can make it feel like your skin is on fire! Too much ginger or pine in the water might make it too tingly for you to enjoy, and so you will have to decide on a smaller amount of the spicier herbs that work in conjunction with some of your other ingredients.

Likewise, some essential oils that you may want to add drops of to your bath can have similar power and effect. Essential oils are highly concentrated herbal extracts and so you really only need a couple of drops to enjoy them in the bath. If you use too much of some of the more stimulating essences, they can literally burn your skin and leave small welts, so be mindful of how many drops of specific essences you are adding to the water. One right way to add these oils is to mix them with the loose herbs in advance of putting them in the water. You can add the drops to the flower petals or herb mixture in a mixing bowl, just prior to adding it to the bath, to prevent the small, oily droplets from burning your skin. Again, it depends on the essential oil you choose and not all of them will have this effect on you.

Hot water is already very stimulating and will cause an increase in your heart rate. This is an excellent opportunity to enhance sweating, which is an incredibly cleansing and purifying activity. You may need to reflect on the temperature of the water you are using with certain ingredients. The effect of "hotter", spicier herbs with hot water, might feel too stimulating and you will need to spend less time in the bath. If you are on any medications that might have negative side-effects under these conditions, you will need to reflect on that, as well, before choosing your herbs.

Overall, you are in charge of the bath experience and what you put into it is what you get out of it. Listen to your intuition and good judgement and look at the following magic bath recipes to give you an idea about how to get into the right bath brew for you!

Regenerating Bath and Baths Salts

Bath salt as an addition to your spiritual bath experience deserves its own section. Salt in the tub is an ancient tradition that dates back to when human beings bathed in the sea for its regenerative and healing powers. It has been discovered that salt baths are incredibly purifying, help induce sweating, cleanse the auras, charge the water with high vibrational energy, and add an earth element to your ritual experience.

The power of salt in water is incredibly healing and should be considered when you are making your sacred bath brews. The number one explanation for why you should add salt to your bath is that it is a healing agent that will enhance the power of any magic you are trying

329

to accomplish. You don't have to use salt every time, but there are some great ways to incorporate it into your rituals.

There are two ways you can bring salt into your water:

Added Straight

You don't have to get fancy with it; you can just scoop a cup of Epsom or sea salt into your bath for a powerful effect. This is a very purifying ingredient and, in some cases, it may be all you want or need to use.

Mixed with Herbs and Oils

You can also make the salt a major ingredient in your herbal mixture by adding it to all of the flower petals, essential oils and other loose herbs you want to use. Her is a sample recipe to give you an idea of how to make an Herbal Salt Bath:

Ingredients:

- 1 cup of Epsom, or sea salt
- 1 cup of fresh rose petals
- 2 Tbsp chopped, fresh rosemary
- 10 drops of rose essential oil
- 5 drops of lavender essential oil

In a mixing bowl, add all ingredients and stir. Allow to rest and cure for up to 8 hours before use to allow the salt to absorb the oils and aromas. Add to your hot bath and stir the around in the water to help the salt dissolve. As it dissolves, it will release all of the aromas and essential oils into the water. Enjoy!

As you can see, it is easy as mixing any other herbal mixture. Here is another recipe for a Salt Bath recipe to help you feel refreshed and rejuvenated:

Regenerating Magic Sea Salt Bath

Ingredients:

- 1 cup of sea salt
- ½ cup Chamomile flowers
- ½ cup Anjelica flowers
- ¼ cup Rose Hips
- 1 small lemon, sliced into thin pieces
- 10 drops of Ylang Ylang Essential Oil

Mix loose herbs and essential oil together in a bowl and let cure and rest for a few hours. Add to bath at the time of ritual and stir into the water to allow the salt to dissolve. Lay the lemon slices in the water and allow to float with the other herbs in the bath. Relax and enjoy. Burn your favorite regenerating or purifying incense while you bathe. Add some candle light and bring one of your favorite crystals into the water with you. Let it sit over your heart chakra while you relax. Strain herbs from the bath before draining.

Good Vibrations Baths

Raising your energetic vibration is one of the many great ways to use a ritual bath. The activity of relaxing with herbs, aromatherapy, candlelight, and soft music will transport your energy into a higher frequency, leaving you feeling right as rain and ready for more. Try these recipes for good vibrations in the bathtub!

High Vibes Ritual Bath

This bath will help you slough off any unwanted energies and raise your vibrations back to where it should be. Useful with added meditations and rituals or spells to shift out of negativity. Incorporate and rejuvenating tea after your bath.

Ingredients:

- 2 Tbsp Calendula

- 2 Tbsp Hibiscus
- 1 Tbsp Lemongrass
- 10 drops Rose Essential Oil/ or ½ cup Rose Petals
- 1 Tbsp Thyme
- A piece of quartz crystal
- A piece of green aventurine
- A piece of rose quartz

Mix the loose herbs in a bowl, including the rose essential oil (if you are choosing that over rose petals). Once the herbs are mixed, place the crystals and gemstones into the herb mixture. Allow the mixture to sit and cure for a few hours. When you are ready for your bath, remove the crystals to add to your bath water, and spoon the mixture into one or more muslin bags and seal shut. Add to bath and let steep for a few minutes before climbing in. Burn your favorite uplifting incense while you bath and/ or incorporate a yellow candle of joy! Let your vibrations rise as you settle and release any tensions that are holding you back. Enjoy!

Picking Up Good Vibrations

You may already be feeling high on life and are just wanting a boost of some like-minded and spirited energies. This bath will hold you open, relaxed, and ready to receive light and abundance from all around you.

Ingredients

- 1 Tbsp Lemon Balm
- 2 Tbsp Chamomile
- 2 Tbsp Holy Basil
- 2 Tbsp Lavender
- 1 Tbsp Rosemary
- ½ cup Epsom salt
- Soothing music (example Solfeggio frequencies, or meditation sounds)

- Mugwort incense
- Silver Candle

Mix the herbs together in a bowl. Put mixture into muslin bath bags and tie shut. Add the salt to the bath. And stir to dissolve. Add tea bags. Light the silver candle to help you open up to the spirit and the feminine goddess. Light the mugwort incense to help you pick up on higher, lighter vibrations form spirit. Add your body to the bath brew and relax to the soothing sounds you have chosen meditate with. Enjoy!

Cleansing Baths

Cleansing baths are opening, refreshing, and connecting and will help you feel renewed for whatever life has to offer you. Enjoying a cleansing bath is simple and easy and is the perfect time to meditate on healing your whole being.

Sweet and Tender Cleansing Bath

These cleansing herbs will help you feel refreshed and relaxed. Energetic cleansing, as well as natural cleansing, is something pleasing about this sweet and tender bath. You will step out of the tub with a cleansed aura and sense of being.

Ingredients:

- 3 Tbsp Sage
- 3 Tbsp Sweetgrass
- 2 Tbsp Hyssop
- 1 Tbsp Peppermint
- 3 Tbsp Lavender
- ½ cup Sea salt

Mix the herbs together with the sea salt in a mixing bowl and let rest for a few hours before your bath. Try to leave the herbs as whole as possible so that they are easy to scoop out after your ritual. If you measure them and they don't fit into a measuring spoon because of this, don't worry! Use your intuition and judgement to gauge quantities. Add to a hot bath and stir to help the salt dissolve. Relax with some sage incense burning before and after your cleansing bath.

Spicy Cleanser

This warming and slightly spicy bath tea will help you unravel and unwind after a day of being out in the world. Sometimes we need to wash off the day and this bath is a great way to do it.

Ingredients:

- 2 Tbsp Cinnamon
- 2 Tbsp Cloves
- 1 cup of loose Chamomile flower heads
- Sandalwood Essential Oil
- A piece of Citrine

Mix the cinnamon, cloves, and sandalwood together in a bowl (you can use powdered ingredients, or whole cloves and cinnamon bark- it is up to you). Add the mixture to a muslin bath bag and tie off. Draw the hot bath water and add your tea bag, along with the chamomile flowers which will float in the water. Rest in the bath and place the citrine over your third eye while you visualize your whole energy being cleansed by the water and the bath. Let the power of the bath tea warm you up and soothe your spirit while you purify your soul.

Ritual Purification Baths

A ritual purification bath is something that you can do to help you better align with your focus for spell work or to honor your practice of Wicca, Witchcraft, or other practices. The bath is a ritual and will help you engage with the right energies and essences that you need for preparation in other rites and for your devotion to the divine. You may choose to use these sacred bath experiences to purify your energy to align more clearly to your devotional work with the Goddess/God energies, sun and moon, or specific holiday celebration form the Wheel of the year.

You may choose to modify the herbs and essences based on your own unique practices, and these recipes are just an idea to help you see what herbs can be most beneficial for purification experiences.

Before the Ritual Bath Preparation

No matter what kind of magic you are preparing to accomplish, this ritual bath is intended to help you purify before you commence with casting your circle and calling upon the divine spirits to aid you in your work. It is designed to help you clear out all unnecessary energies to prepare you for your magical work ahead. You can create this bath experience just before any altar work, spell casting, rituals, or celebrations, to put you in a higher alignment with your purpose and your practices.

Ingredients:

*Choose quantities according to the strength of purification and ritual needs.

- Basil
- Rosemary
- Yarrow
- Cumin
- Cypress essential oil

Mix herbs and essential oil in a bowl and allow to rest for about an hour. You may wish to light some incense and candles appropriate the rituals you will be preparing for to help you get centered and grounded. Spend as little or as long as you need in the bath to prepare.

New Moon Ritual Bath

To honor the moon as she becomes new again, and to purify after the dark time of the waning moon, try this bath ritual to help you prepare for the growth ahead in conjunction with the phases of the moon's energy in your life.

Ingredients

- 1 Tbsp Rue
- 2 Tbsp Mugwort
- 1 tsp Valerian
- 3 Tbsp Sage
- Several whole Bay Leaves
- 7 drops of Frankincense Essential Oil
- ½ cup Epsom salt

Mix the herbs together in your bowl. In another bowl, mix the salt and essential oil and let sit for at least two hours before your bath. Add the salt to your bath water. Add the herbs to a muslin bath bag and tie off. Add the bag to the salt bath.

Light a silver candle for the moon energy, if desired. You can also bring a piece of moonstone into the tub with you. Spend time reflecting on what moon rituals you want to prepare for as she waxes in your life.

Chapter 7: Magical Oils

Using magical oils in your sacred work is something of great value and any magical oils can be successfully incorporated into a number of spells and rituals. The way you make oils depends almost entirely on the kind of practice you have and there are only a few simple rules to help you get going with this energy.

A majority of magic oils will combine a carrier oil with a few to several different essential oils, or herbs, to create the aroma and energy of whatever spell work you are trying to do. Magic oils can be added to baths, used for consecrating ritual tools, and for anointing candles for candle magic work. You can also simply rub the magic oil into your skin to absorb the overall energy and infusion of power that you are trying to work with.

Essential oils are not easy to make on your own at home, and you can find a majority of them in online shops or in local health food or healing stores that provide a wide assortment of choices. You can also use loose herbs and infuse oils over several weeks, with the energy of the herbs before using it for magical purposes.

Magic oils bring yet another fantastic element to your herbal practice and can give you the aromas and magical vibrations you need to connect with your spells, rituals, and healing intentions.

Making Magical Oils

Your oils can be as simple or complex as you want or need them to be. Some recipes might be just 2-3 essential oils, while another might have 10 or more varieties. Some will ask for 5-10 drops, while others require 20 or more. A lot of it depends on tastes, preferences and magical intentions, so it really is about your own judgement and intuition when you are making these potions for your own specific purposes.

It is best to start with less and add as you go, pausing to sniff and smell along the way to make sure it has the right energetic "bouquet" for your manifestation needs.

Blending Your Oils

Blending your oils is easy and straightforward when you have all of the ingredients that you need. You will need the following items to get you started:

- A glass jar to add oil and herbs to
- Carrier oil (ex: safflower, grape seed, jojoba or apricot kernel)
- Small funnel (to pour oil into small dropper bottles)
- Small dropper bottles and droppers (usually in blue or brown glass colors)
- Desired essential oils

The amount of oil you choose to use will depend on your ritual and spell needs. For the sake of the following recipes, we will only use a single batch which will only need about an ounce of oil or 2 tablespoons.

Make sure all of your tools, like jars, funnels, and dropper bottles are clean and sterilized before adding your ingredients. The following recipes use essential oils, and you may find that this is the most natural choice for your spell work. Keep in mind that you can also brew magical oils with the same tools, but instead of adding essential oils, add fresh or dried herbs to the carrier oils and let the herbs to stand in the oil for two weeks, or more, to infuse it with herbal magic.

Many people use this technique to flavor their olive oils for cooking, to add more flavor to their dishes. Some folks will add garlic, rosemary, and peppers to cooking oils without realizing that they are making a magical, herbal oil. The same principles apply when making and herbal extract of your own in this way.

Purification Oil

As a general rule of thumb, use your creative visualization powers to concentrate and focus on your intentions while you are blending your oils. This purification oil can be used in a variety of spells and rituals.

Ingredients:

- 6 drops juniper
- 4 drops cedarwood
- 2 drops lavender

Mix ingredients. You may want to start with what the recipe calls for and then swirl the essential oils into the carrier oil and test the aroma. Depending on your preferences, you may wish to add more drops. If it feels too pungent with what you already have, balance it by adding a drizzle more of your carrier oil.

Consecration Oil

Useful for consecrating sacred or ceremonial tools. Excellent for all ritual and spell work.

- 6 drops frankincense
- 6 drops myrrh
- 3 drops cinnamon

Use your judgement and intuition with how much more or less you need of each essential oil. Focus your intentions into the oil as you are creating and blending it.

Prosperity Oil

Prosperity oil is an excellent thing to have on hand for any luck, money, abundance, wealth, good fortune, and even love spells. Prosperity spells are thought to work well on Thursday nights, but you can use your intuition to guide you in your practice. Waxing moons are the best time to create prosperity magic. Sometimes, it is best to wait for a whole moon cycle to pass before you begin to use your magical prosperity oil, giving it time to rest and enhance the energies you have concocted with your focus and with the herbs in the bottle.

Some of the main prosperity oils are: cinnamon, myrrh, sandalwood, ginger, patchouli, sweet orange, bergamot, frankincense, clove.

Prosperity Oil

This prosperity oil will utilize mostly fresh herbs rather than essential oils; however, you can add more essential oils to it to make it more intoxicating to your needs.

Ingredients:

- Sunflower seeds
- A coin
- Bay leaves

- Allspice
- Bay berry
- Bergamot essential oil
- Your ingredient mixing tools (jars, funnels, etc.)
- Carrier oil

Mix the ingredients in a bowl. As you mix the herbs, visualize your wealth and prosperity. You can use affirmations to help your intentions. You may want to clean your coin with some baking soda salt before adding it to your bottle of oil. Add the herbs to the oil. Keep in a dark area for several weeks. Use this oil for prosperity spells by anointing your candles, or add oil to a cloth and rub it on your purse, wallet, or wherever you put your cash. You can also use it as a perfume, or before a job interview.

Love and Attraction Oil

Attraction Oil

To attract love into your life, this oil can help you in any spell to encourage that energy to come forward for you. Attraction spells are best on a waxing moon, and so making and blending your oil should happen at the same time. This oil calls more for loose herbs, but you can add some essential oils.

Ingredients:

- Roses (petals and buds)
- Lemon Balm or Lovage Herb
- Lemon zest
- Rose quartz
- Olive oil, or other oil

Add the ingredients to oil. Include the rose quartz as well and let the oil sit on your altar next to a candle colored for love magic and set the intention of attraction. It can be specific or general. Keep the rose quartz in the bottle throughout the use of your oil magic.

New Love

This oil will help to attract a new love into your life. This recipe calls for essential oils.

Ingredients:

- 6 drops Ylang-ylang
- 2 drops Ginger
- 2 drops Rosemary
- 2 drops Cardamom
- 5 drops vanilla
- Carrier oil

Mix the essential oils and the oil together. Use for your sacred love spells and rituals to anoint your candles, put on your body, or add to your holy baths. Waxing crescent moons and full moons are great times to use this oil.

Energy and Empowering Oils

All of the following essential oil blends are meant to be uplifting, energizing, and empowering. They will bring a lot of pizazz to any spell that you need to add more power to, or if you need to energize yourself through your spells and magic work.

All you need for these next three recipes is your preferred carrier oil and all of your mixing tools. You may also want to add crystals and gemstones or use some sacred ritual work as you create your oil potions. Apply these to your candles, magic tools, crystals, bath salts, and more!

Energizing Blend #1

- 2 drops bergamot
- 2 drops cedar wood
- 1 drop frankincense
- 1 drop orange

Energizing Blend #2

- 2 drops cedar wood
- 2 drops fir
- 1 drop basil
- 1 drop rosemary

Energizing Blend #3

- 2 drops peppermint
- 2 drops orange
- 2 drops grapefruit
- 2 drops lavender

Enjoy playing with these recipes and change them to suit your needs and aromatic preferences. There are so many essential oils to choose form and for a complete list, see the Table of Correspondence at the end of this book to give you an idea of what to look for.

Also, remember, that you don't have to use essential oils in order to make a potent oil potion. You can use loose herbs and infuse the oil with their energies and allow for more magical brewing before using it.

Any oils that you create can complement your rituals, spells, and healing practices. There are tons of ways to apply this tool to your craft, so get creative, use your intuition and have fun!

Chapter 8: Herbal Magical Creations

There is a wide variety of possible uses for making magic with herbs. So far you have learned about herbal magic that you can imbibe, apply, or soak in with your ritual baths, and there are also assorted charms, pillows, sachets, talismans, amulets, and other magical creations that can incorporate herbs to further impower your work.

With all of your magical creations, you can get really crafty and imaginative. Afterall, Wicca, spell craft and magic are all creative arts and so it is a brilliant way for you to explore your creative self with the creations you make for your manifestations and magical purposes.

If you don't consider yourself artsy or crafty, that is ok! These simple creations are not for anyone else but you (unless you are doing spell work for another person) and so it doesn't really matter if has perfect seams. Even if you are making a sachet or pillow for someone else, the beauty is in the magic and the powerful intention behind the creative construction, and so you don't need to be a talented "crafter" in order to make a magical creation.

The following section will give you a few essential pointers about making a magical creation successfully, and the most important part of it is that you have a good time getting to know your own magic as you explore the herbal bounty you will be adding to these charms.

Making Magical Creations

Making any magical creation is just like casting a spell. You are working with sacred materials that you have collected while you are putting them together in a practical and useful form. Many charms take the form of a sack, pouch, sachet, or pillow, as a creative way to store herbs and magical elements for long-lasting manifestation and use.

What you will need for these projects is a small amount of fabric, sewing materials, like a needle, thread and scissors, and the herbs you want to incorporate. You can also add other magical elements, like gemstones and crystals, feathers, essential oils, and even small pieces of paper with incantations and spells written on them that will be sown into the pillow, sachet, or other charm creation.

If you have never sewn before, don't fret! All of these creations are very simple and straightforward and can be accomplished with minimal sewing experience, or none at all.

For a sachet, you are basically sewing a small pillow case that you can add the herbs to and then tie off the top of to keep them inside. A sachet is handy for short term needs and if you are adding additional charms and stones, they will be easier to remove when your spell or ritual is done and you no longer need the charm. To sew a sachet, follow these steps:

1. Cut your fabric so that you have two identical pieces that can be anywhere from 4x6 inches to 5x7 inches. (You can go bigger if you need a larger charm, or smaller if you want. These sizes are suitable to start)

2. Put the pieces of cloth face to face. You will sew the long sides and the bottom in one continuous thread to create a seam.

3. Leave some room at the edge (about 5/8 inch) so that your stiches aren't too close to the edge which will cause holes when you turn the pouch right side out.

4. You only need a simple in and out stitch and just sew in a straight line.

5. Leave the top open to put herbs in after you turn your little sachet right side out.

6. You can tie it off with a ribbon, cord or string.

7. To turn it into a necklace, make the string longer.

These simple steps will help you build a general sachet, or pouch, to contain your spells and herbal magic. You can find plenty of online sewing tutorials if you need more of a visual explanation for how to sew a simple stitch.

You can use these same steps to make your pillow, the only difference being that you will sew the top closed after you add your herbs, rather than tying it off. The reason for this is so you can use it regularly without herbs falling out. Many pillow creations are used under the pillow you sleep on, or as a comfort for the eyes and head while relaxing during meditations or astral projections.

The following magical creation recipes are examples to get you started with making your own. As always, have fun and get creative with what you put inside and how you want to manifest some magic with these beautiful tools!

Luck Charm Sachet

For sachets, you can play around with what quantities of herbs you will want to use. All of the herbs listed will make for a powerful luck charm when added together.

Ingredients:

- Chamomile
- Nutmeg
- Star Anise
- Dandelion seeds
- Honeysuckle
- Rose Hips
- Rosemary
- Sandalwood
- Thyme

Make a standard sachet with your chosen fabric (it can be anything from velvet or satin to muslin or cotton). Mix all of the herbs in the bowl and charge the herbs with your intentions for luck energy. You can use an anointed luck candle and/or a prosperity incantation to help you improve the energy of your manifestation. If you want to cast a circle and use your altar and ritual space from this part of your creation process, you absolutely can as it will add even more potent energy to your spell.

You can carry this sachet in your purse, keep at your office to help with your promotion, or bring it with you to your job interview. Set it on top of your lottery tickets, or next to an object or symbol that represents what you are trying to manifest luck for.

If you want to add some additional items, like one of your gemstones that represents luck, or some runes, you can do this too. Writing down what you want to manifest on paper and then folding it up into a small piece to put into your sachet, will really empower the message of your spell.

Prophetic Dream Pillow

Dream work is very powerful and having some herbs contained in a magical charm under your pillow at night is a great way to keep dark dreams and nightmares away and invite the lucid and prophetic dreams.

- A small charm (like a silver moon, or some small gemstones)
- Chamomile
- Mugwort
- Wild Asparagus Root
- Peppermint
- Burdock
- Rose Petals
- Anise
- Hops
- Cloves
- Jasmine

Make a larger sachet (square or rectangular) by sewing all sides except for about 2 inches of the top, so that all of the edges are almost completely sewn together leaving only a small 2-inch opening. This opening is where you will turn your fabric right side out and you will also use the opening to spoon or funnel your herbs into it.

Mix the herbal ingredients as you visualize and concentrate on what you want the herbs to represent and help you manifest. Give plenty of time to charging your sacred herbs. If you're going to do this through a ritual circle at the altar, you can include some mugwort incense and a purple candle to help cast the magic of divination and prophecy while you create your pillow. Place your unique charm or ornament that represents night magic into the mixture.

Fill the pillow as much as you can with the mix; you don't want to stuff it though, as the herbs will need a little bit of breathing room. The quantity of herbs you use will be determined by the size of the pillow you are going to sew. Once you have filled the hole in the top with your herbs, you can close the hole with your needle and thread and try to finish it off as neatly as possible with the rest of the seams.

Place under your pillow at night after sipping a dream tea and awaken your subconscious with the powerful and intoxicating aromas of this herbal dream pillow.

All magical creations are a fun and creative magical process. Explore what kinds of pillows and sachets you can make and remember that just about anything goes as long as you harm none and are having fun. The next chapter will involve some more magical creations that are slightly more advanced spells and rituals that include sewing a magical charm.

Chapter 9: Magical Herbal Creation Spells

This chapter will build upon what you learned in the last chapter, opening you up to the process of using your herbal magical creations in more formal spell casting and manifestation work. You learned about how to sew herbs into a sachet or a pillow and that creating these charms can have a strong impact on your practice, or your overall health and well-being.

This chapter will expand upon those concepts by showing you how to make a poppet, which is a sewn doll to represent something or someone, and how to make an herbal pouch. Pouches tend to be worn around the neck, like a medicine bag, while poppets are something that you will carry with you.

The Uses of a Poppet

Poppets tend to represent another being, like a friend, family member, loved one or pet. You can make a poppet to express your inner spirit, or inner child as well, to help you do personal healing magic. A word of caution: never cause harm to another. Poppets are not intended to cause ill injury. If you are a practicing Wiccan, then you know the law of 'harm none' and this goes for making and using poppets as well.

Make wise choices when constructing your magical poppets if they are intended for others. Use this magic purpose for good, healing, love, and peace, rather than curses, hexes, or ill-intent.

You may make a poppet to reduce worry and anxiety in a person, or to help them heal after a major surgery. Poppets are intended to contain the herbs that will help the person, or self, with whatever matters are needing healing or adjustment. Poppets can be used to help luck and good fortune come into a person's life, or to bless them with life-long love.

If you are looking for the healing magic from a poppet, make yours represent you and your needs as it will act as a constant daily reminder of what your magical purpose and intentions are. The following section is a spell to help you create a poppet for prosperity. You can use it as an example for making other types of poppets.

Prosperity Poppet Spell

The poppet you make is a figurine, or doll, to represent a person (including the self) or an animal. Traditionally, they are made from fabric, cut into a shape to represent a human or animal form. Think of a cookie cutter for a gingerbread man: you would simply draw a similar shape on the fabric you want to use and have two identical pieces to sew together to make your doll. The same idea works for creating an animal shape.

The sewn figure is stuffed with herbs, powders, crystals and stones, and so on. Sometimes people will add pieces of hair of their own, or another person's, or even fingernail cuttings to add the personal essence of the person. A photograph is also just as useful.

This prosperity spell will be to make a poppet of yourself so that you can draw prosperity into your own life.

You will need the following items for this:

- Fabric and materials for sewing your poppet (needle, thread, scissors)
- Mixing bowl
- Green Candle
- White Candle
- Angelica
- Basil
- Bay leaves
- Cinnamon
- Honeysuckle
- Thyme
- Tiger's eye
- Sunstone
- Citrine

1. Cast your circle at your altar or work space.

2. Light your green prosperity candle and your white candle for faith and purity.

3. Burn some incense to purify your space.

4. Place your herbs in the mixing bowl and mix together.

5. Smudge the herbs with the incense and concentrate on what you want to stuff your poppet with- in this case, prosperity and abundance.

6. Add the gemstones and let the mixture sit with the crystals on the altar between the candles.

7. Cut your figure out of the fabric, as you would to make a pillow or sachet. In this case, cut it in the shape of a gingerbread man, or human form (or animal).

8. Sew the pieces together leaving an opening at the top of the head to turn the poppet right side out.

9. Once the poppet is right side out, you can begin to fill it with the herbs and small crystals. As you fill it, imagine filling yourself and your life with prosperity and abundance. Concentrate and focus on your intentions while you do this.

10. Once the poppet is full of herbs, sew the opening shut. You can dress your poppet in hand made clothes or wraps as you desire.

11. Set the poppet on the altar and let it sit there while the candles burn out. If you have left over herbs, sprinkle them around your poppet.

12. Once you are finished, close your circle. Keep your poppet close to you or and your altar.

**Note, if you want to stuff the poppet with any personal items, including your hair, a picture of yourself, or your name written on paper, this can be an additional step to include.

Protective Power Pouch

A pouch is a lot like making a sachet, except you will wear it around your neck at all times. It can be minimal, or larger, depending on your needs and tastes, or preferences. Often, they are sewn out of leather, but any kind of cloth you like will work.

Making a pouch casts a spell for the wearer to receive specific energies as long as they are wearing it. It is something that can alter over time, depending on what you want to put in it, so sew your pouch to be a long-lasting charm that you can refill, and re-bless, over and over again.

You will need the following items for this:

- Materials of your choice to sew your pouch (leather, canvas, velvet, etc.)
- Long cord to tie the pouch shut, and long enough to hang down over your heart when worn around the neck
- Rosemary
- Angelica
- Sage
- Cloves
- Mugwort
- Wormwood
- Tourmaline
- Onyx
- Hematite
- Mixing bowl

- Black candles

1. Cast your circle and make sure you have all your ingredients inside with you.

2. Light your black candles of protection. (you can also burn incense, like sage or mugwort, for security)

3. Mix your ingredients in a mixing bowl on your altar. Connect to the powers of protection, and speak to each herb of its protective powers as you add it to the bowl.

4. Add the gemstones and let them imbue the herbs with additional protective powers. While your herbs charge with the stones and candles on the altar, you can sew your pouch.

5. Cut the fabric to the size you want. You will need to cut two identical pieces of cloth to sew together, exactly like you are making a sachet.

6. Once you have sewn the sachet, you can add your herbal mixture, including the stones.

7. Tie off the pouch with the cord and wear around your neck (you can also sew your pouch to be a drawstring bag and just sew the long cord to the edges of the bag instead of using it as the tie)

8. Close your circle and wear your pouch every day.

There are endless applications for how you can use poppets and pouches to enhance your herbal magic practice. Enjoy the art and craft of magic by playing around with some new spell ideas to help you embrace these fun and exciting techniques for manifestation.

Chapter 10: Magical Incense

Incense is as old as antiquity. It is a combination of spices, herbs, resins, oils, and tree barks, used to create a sacred atmosphere and enhance relaxed and meditative trances and states of mind. It has been known as a holy ritual tool for many ages and is still prized for its ritual uses today. Incense helps you to communicate with the divine and brings the element of air and that of fire into your spells and rituals.

This section will give you an introduction to incense, how to use a loose herb incense, as well as a few recipes to make your own.

Introduction to Incenses

The best and most traditional way to use incense in your magical practice is to burn the loose herbs. Typically, as you may have seen in a religious practice, a censer, or hanging incense burner, is swung around the space to let the smoke waft through the air. The censer hangs from a chain or rope and is filled with the dried herbs and resin granules. Many Wiccans will use a cauldron to burn their incenses, instead of censer, so that they can use their hands for other spell work, instead of swaying the censer around.

Incense has also been traditionally used as an offering during spells and rituals, not just for cleansing and purification of your circle. It can be burned before, during, and after your spell work to continue the energy of intention you are trying to create.

Some incenses are also used to create a different state of mind or consciousness. An example of this would be burning mugwort to induce divination and scrying by awakening and opening the third eye. It has an impact on the third eye chakra, asking it to open as you smell and see the smoke rising in front of you. Some will even see visions in the smoke, or use the smoky shapes and curling for readings or divinations.

Store bought incense sticks can have a lot of synthetic ingredients and flavorings, so be careful with what you purchase. Spells and rituals need natural, earthly items, and so when you choose pre-made incense sticks, read the label and make sure you understand what ingredients you are getting.

Another form of incense can come from heating or diffusing essential oils as aromatherapy for your rituals. You can purchase diffusers from a variety of shops and online stores and it will help the essential oils permeate the air all around you.

However, you use incense, keep in mind its main uses in magic: purifying sacred spaces, cleansing and consecrating tools and energy, divination, meditation and scrying, aromatherapy, and as a representative of air and fire in your circle.

Loose Incense

A lot of people these days will just use incense sticks or cones due to loose-incense being a bit more labor intensive, however loose incense is the way to go if you want to connect with herbs and practice their magic.

Loose incense requires some kind of a heat proof dish, like a cauldron, and other burning apparatuses, like charcoal disks. Charcoal, when lit and smoldering, will help ignite the dried, loose herbs and give them the smoking that they need. Basically, you light the charcoal disk (sold at many incense shops and herbal apothecaries) and place it in your cauldron. Let it burn for a little while to catch fire and then blow at the flame. You basically now have an ember to put your herbs on so that they can smoke.

Making your loose incense is another fun part of the process. You need to decide what your magical intentions are before you create your blend. It might be just about the magical purpose, or you may be wanting to build an incense to fill you home with certain aromas, like fruity, floral, woodsy, etc.

Making incense is just another fun creative process as you work with herbal magic, so think of it like brewing a dry potion that will eventually turn into fire and smoke.

Herbs and Spices

Just about any herb or spice can be used to make an incense. A mortar and pestle is a traditional tool, or you can use a coffee grinder to make them into fine powders that will burn better. Dried is best with almost any of these, but you can always try a fresh burn which may need more flame than ember to get going.

Gums and Resins

These can be sticky and tricky to work with and should not be put in a coffee grinder- you'll never get the stick out! Mortar and pestle is the best way to crush these up and you can even freeze them first to make them slightly less sticky and gummy. They have a beautiful musky and rich fragrance and are an excellent addition to any loose incense blend.

Wood and Bark

If they aren't already processed this way, you will have to grind your woods and barks into chips that are easy to burn. They don't need to be powdered, but they do need to be widdled down into small pieces to add to your incense blends. Try getting them into smaller pieces with a chisel, or hatchet first, and then grind them more in a food processor.

The work may seem like a lot compared to buying a box of pre-made sticks at the store, but this is wonderful to get a lot closer to your herbal magic practices and will infuse your spells and rituals with a whole lot more power, intention and purpose.

Meditation and Visualization Incense

Both of these recipes can be tweaked to your liking and the herbs used are meant to help you achieve a state of relaxation to open your mind and your ability to see visions. Let them transport you with every waft of smoke as you inhale the sweet and smoky aromas.

Meditation & Vision Incense:

The following combination of herbs is meant to transport you into a state of calm, but also to awaken your third eye and connect you to the seat of your inner vision. With these ingredients, you will need to work with quantities that feel right for you. Before burning them, try smelling each one to see which resonates with you the most. Add more of that one than these others. Use your intuition to help you decide on what amounts you prefer.

You can add resin if so desired and you will need to make sure that they are well-ground and mixed together before burning

Ingredients:

- Frankincense
- Bay Leaf
- Damiana
- Mugwort
- Charcoal disk
- Cauldron

1. Light the charcoal and place in the cauldron.

2. Wait until it is a glowing ember and then sprinkle herbs on top.

3. Seat yourself near the cauldron or put it directly in front of you.

4. Sit in a comfortable position and allow yourself to disappear into your vision state.

5. You may need to continuously sprinkle more onto the charcoal while you are working.

Tranquility Incense:

Use the same practice of intuiting what you want to the most of in your incense by sniffing the ingredients first. In this case, the sage, rose petals and meadowsweet will be the strongest scents and then the benzoin and rose oil will complement the other herbs.

Ingredients:

- Sage
- Rose
- Benzoin
- Meadowsweet
- Rose oil
- Charcoal
- Cauldron

1. Grind herbs and mix together.

2. Add benzoin and a few drops of rose oil. Mix thoroughly.

3. Place lit charcoal into the cauldron and sprinkle herb mixture on your ember.

4. Lie down in a sacred and comfortable space and focus on restoring your energy and your health while you meditate on the aromas.

House Blessing Incense

House Purification Incense:

- Frankincense Resin
- Myrrh Resin
- Sandalwood
- Cedar
- Dill Seed
- A few drops of Rose Geranium Oil
- Charcoal
- Cauldron

1. Grind resins with mortar and pestle.

2. Mix with other herbs and oils.

3. Add to charcoal ember.

4. Carry through the home and take into every corner. Waft into every room while you imagine cleansing and purifying it with this sacred scent.

House Blessing Incense:

- Lavender
- Basil
- Hibiscus
- Grapefruit Oil
- Charcoal disk
- Cauldron

1. Grind herbs and mix them together.

2. Add a few drops of the oil.

3. Sprinkle herbs on top of charcoal ember and carry through every doorway, blessing every entrance and exit of every family member and guest.

Incense for Love

Draw and Strengthen Love Incense:

- Sandalwood
- Basil
- Bergamot
- Cinnamon
- Chamomile
- Rose Oil
- Lavender Oil
- Charcoal disk
- Cauldron
1. Grind herbs and mix.

2. Add a few drops of any of these oils to the mix and stir together.

3. Burn with charcoal and waft over your body.

4. Add this to a love spell or ritual on a waxing moon, or burn before a date comes over.

Love Incense

- Resin of your choice
- Cinnamon
- Rose Petals
- Vanilla
- Amber Oil
- Patchouli
- Charcoal disk
- Cauldron

1. Grind loose herbs and roots. Grind resin with mortar and pestle.

2. Mix ground herbs and resin together.

3. Add a few drops of each oil and stir.

4. Add to the charcoal ember and carry through your space, or add to your current love spell or enchantment.

5. Burn while making love charms, pillows and sachets.

6. Present as a gift to your loved one.

Making incense is a lovely, creative experience and is a large part of working with all herbs and plant materials. If you are wanting to become more aware of herbs and their magic, working with loose herb incenses is an excellent path to take. Use the recipes you found here to give you a launch pad to experiment with other incense concoctions and brews and enjoy the pleasure of this sacred and aromatic smoke magic!

Tables of Correspondence: Herbs

This list offers some, but not all magical properties of herbs. Further research may be required.

Acacia

Friendship, platonic love, psychic work

Acorn

Wisdom, personal power

African Violet

Healing, protection

Agar Agar

Success, opportunity, joy

Agrimony

Removing inner blocks, removing unwanted energies

Alder

Poetry, music, divination

Alfalfa

Prosperity, abundance, money

Almond

Prosperity, wisdom, abundance

Aloe

Good luck, protection

Amaranth

Healing a broken heart, healing

Amber

Protection from harm, protection for outside influences

Anemone

Protection, healing

Angelica

Attracts positive vibration, protects against negative energies

Anise

Psychic work, happiness

Apple

Friendship, love, immortality

Apricot

Love

Arnica Flowers

Enhancing psychic power

Arrow Root

Healing, purification

Ash

Invincibility, protection, sea magic

Asparagus

Male sex magic

Aspen

Healing, clairvoyance,

Astragalus Root

Energy, protection

Avocado

Beauty, lust, love, sex

Azalea

First loves, high spirits, do not eat

Balm of Gilead Tears

Healing grief, manifestation, love

Bamboo

Luck, wishes, protection

Banana

Fertility, prosperity, potency

Barberry

Atonement, cleansing

Barley

Harvest, protection, love, abundance

Basil

Dispels, fear and weakness, wisdom

Bay Laurel   /Leaf

Good fortune, success, strength

Bayberry

Healing, relief of stress

Bee Pollen

Love, happiness, joy

Beet

Love

Belladonna

Letting go of past love

Bergamot

Memory, rest, healing

Birch

Purifying, protecting

Black Cohosh

Courage, potency

Black Pepper

Removing unwanted/ negative energies

Black Walnut

Wishes, divine communication

Blackberry

Money, protection

Blessed Thistle

Protection against negative energies

Bloodroot

Purifying, protecting, love

Blue Cohosh

Money, empowerment

Blue Violet

Good fortune, inspiration

Bluebell

Friendship, truth

Boneset

Exorcism, removing unwanted energies

Borage

Psychic work, courage

Brazil Nut

Love, luck

Buckthorn

Elf magic, removing enchantments

Buckwheat

Treasure, wealth, riches

Burdock

Cleansing unwanted emotions

Butchers Broom

Psychic work, divination

Cabbage

Moon, money, fertility

Cactus

Protection, banishing, protecting

Calamus

Healing, money, luck

Calendula Flowers

Psychic and spiritual work

Camellia

Riches, wealth

Camphor

Psychic and dream work, divination

Caraway

Memory, mental work, passion

Cardamom

Lust, love, and fidelity

Carnation

Balance, strength, healing

Carob

Protection, health

Carrot

Fertility, lust, love

Cascara Sagrada

Legal issues, money

Cashew

Money

Catnip

Cat spells and rituals

Cat's Claw

Shaman work, vision work

Cayenne

Healing from divorce/ separation, cleansing, purifying

Cedar

Money, power, strength

Celandine

Victory, joy, success

Celery

Psychic work, lust, male potency

Chamomile

Healing, love, stress reduction

Cherry

Happiness, love, divination

Cherry Bark

Frugality, direction

Chervil

Divine communication, spiritual support

Chestnut

Love

Chia

Good health, protection

Chickweed

Love, fertility

Chicory

Removing obstacles, removing frigidity

Chili Pepper

Breaking hexes, fidelity, love

China Berry

Luck

Chives

Weight loss, protection

Chrysanthemum

Protection

Cilantro

Garden magic, home blessings

Cinnamon

Luck, strength, love, lust

Cinquefoil

Power, health, wisdom

Citronella

Business, persuasiveness

Clover

Protection, fidelity

Clover, Red

Financial magic

Cloves

Gaining what you wish for

Coconut

Purifying, protecting

Coltsfoot

Love, prosperity

Columbine

Courage, love

Comfrey

Money, safety during travel, and any Saturnian purpose

Coriander

Love, health, immortality, and protection.

Corn

Divination, good luck

Cotton

Protection, healing, fishing magic

Cowslip

Business blessing, treasure finding

Coxcomb

Protection

Cramp Bark

Female energies

Cucumber

Fertility, chastity

Cumin

Protection, fidelity

Curry

Protection from negative forces

Cyclamen

Lust, happiness

Cypress

Overcoming grief and loss

Daffodil

Fertility, love, good luck

Daisy

Innocence, babies, love

Damiana

Sex, attraction, lust

Dandelion Leaf

Summoning spiritual energies

Dandelion Root

Wishes, divinations

Devil's Claw

Banishing unwanted company

Devil's Shoestring

Career, power over the opposite sex

Dill

Money, fortune, luck

Dogwood

Health, wisdom, protection

Dragon's Blood

Purifying, protecting

Dulse

Home harmony, sea magic

Echinacea

Draws money

Elder

Sleep, wisdom, home and business blessings

Elecampane

Removing angry, violent energies

Elm

Elves, love

Endive

Sex, love

Epsom Salt

Cleansing, purifying

Eucalyptus

Protection, healing

Evening Primrose

Calling faeries, love

Eyebright

Memory, logic, psychic advancement

Fennel Seed

Virility, vitality, strength

Fenugreek

Attracts money, fertility

Fern

Cleansing, clarity

Feverfew

Protection, especially from illness/ accident

Fig

Love, divination, fertility

Flax Seed

Money

Fleabane

Protection, exorcism, chastity

Foxglove

Visions, protecting the home/ garden

Frangipani

Love trust, attraction

Frankincense Resin

Consecration, meditation

Galangal Root

Legal matters, hex breaking, doubling riches

Gardenia

Dispels strife, brings peace

Garlic

Protecting, purifying, healing

Gentian

Strength, power

Geranium

Happiness, removing negative thoughts

Ginger

Adventure, confidence, success

Ginkgo Biloba

Fertility, aphrodisiac

Ginseng

Beauty, lust, love

Goldenrod

Money, divination

Goldenseal

Business, finance, healing

Goosegrass

Good dreams, tenacity, luck

Gorse

Romance, weddings, love

Grape

Mental work, garden magic, money

Grape Seed

Fertility, garden magic

Grapefruit

Purifying, cleansing

Hawthorn

Career, rebirth, fertility, fishing magic

Heather

Immortality, luck

Heliotrope

Joy, happiness

Hemlock

To end something, do not consume.

Henna

Love

Hibiscus

Love, divination, dreams

Hickory

Protection, lust, legal dealings

Holly

Marriage, love, dreams

Hollyhock

Material success, gain

Honey

Sun magic, attraction, binding

Honeysuckle

Fast abundance, money

Hops

Dreams and sleep

Horehound

Creativity, inspiration

Horseshoe Chestnut

Healing, money

Hyacinth

Peace of mind, sleep, love

Hydrangea

Attracting love, breaking hexes

Hyssop

Purifying, cleansing

Iris

Courage, faith, wisdom

Irish Moss

Luck

Ivy

Fertility, love, healing

Jamaican Ginger

Gambling luck

Jasmine

Charging crystals, protection, divination

Juniper

Attracting good vibrations, male potency

Kava Kava

Visions, astral travel

Knotweed

Binding, healing

Kola Nut

Calming, soothing, dispels depression

Lady Slipper

Protection against hexes

Lady's Mantle

Aphrodisiac, transmutation.

Larch

Protection, anti-theft

Larkspur

Protection, health

Laurel

Long and happy marriage

Lavender

Sleep, healing, peace, calm, love

Leek

Strengthen existing love

Lemon

Spiritual cleansing, removing internal blocks

Lemon Balm

Psychic work, heling, love

Lemon Grass

Psychic work and cleansing

Lemon Verbena

Attractiveness, prevent nightmares

Lettuce

Love and sex magic, lust

Licorice

Attraction, love, fidelity

Lilac

Memory, wisdom

Lily

Renewal, marriage, happiness

Lily of the Valley

Tranquility, peace

Lime

Purifying, tranquility

Linden Flowers

Love, protection

Lobelia

Attracting love

Lotus

Spiritual awakening and growth

Lovage

Energy, dreams

Lungwort

Travel blessings

Mace

Self-discipline, concentration, focus

Magnolia Flowers

Love, loyalty, beauty, peace

Magnolia Bark

Love, fidelity

Maidenhair Fern

Attracts love and beauty

Mandrake

Prosperity, protection, fertility

Maple

Money, wealth, luck

Maple Syrup

Love, longevity

Marigold

Admiration, respect, legal, matters

Marjoram

Purifying, cleansing

Marshmallow Root

Psychic work

Meadowsweet

Career, stress relief

Mesquite

Healing

Milk Thistle

Perseverance, wisdom, good decisions

Mimosa

Love, dreams, purifying

Mint

Vitality, business, communication

Mistletoe

Creativity, prevents misfortune, protection

Monkshood

Protection from unwanted energies

Morning Glory

Attraction, binding, banishing

Motherwort

Success, confidence, healthy ego

Mugwort

Lust, fertility, scrying, divination

Mullein

Courage, protection, banishes unwanted energies

Musk

Self-esteem, attractiveness

Mustard Seed

Faith, endurance, courage

Myrrh

Psychic work, spiritual awakening

Myrtle

Peace, youth, love, money

Narcissus

Harmony, tranquility, peace

Neroli

Confidence, courage, joy

Nettle

Strength, removes unwanted energies, protects

Nutmeg

Prosperity, luck, love

Oak

Sacred wood for altar tools

Oak Moss

Strength, power, luck

Oatmeal

Brighid worship

Oatstraw

Abundance, wealth

Olive

Marriage, love security, fruitfulness

Olive Leaf

Peace, fertility, potency

Onion

Endurance, stability, protection

Orange

Happiness in marriage, romance

Orange Bergamot

Attracts money

Orange Blossoms

Harmony, peace, open heart

Orange Peel

Home blessings, luck, love

Orchid

Memory, focus, will power

Oregano

Vitality, energy, strength

Osha Root

Protection from unwanted energies

Palm

Focus, divination

Palo Santo

Cleansing, purifying

Pansy

Relationships, love, divination

Paprika

Energy

Papyrus

Protection

Parsley

Prosperity, attracts money, home blessings

Parsnip

Male sex magic

Passion Flower

Friendship, prosperity

Patchouli

Love, money

Pau d'Arco

Healing diseases

Peach

Wisdom, love, fertility

Pear

Lust, love

Peas

Love, money

Pennyroyal

Tranquility, calm, peace

Peony

Prosperity, business, protection form negative forces

Pepper, Black

Courage, banishing

Peppermint

Purifying, protecting, healing

Periwinkle

Marriage, grace

Persimmon

Luck, healing, sex change

Pimpernel

Health, protection

Pine

Prosperity, success, new beginnings, clean breaks

Pineapple

Luck, chastity

Pink Rose Buds

Long-lasting relationships, love

Pistachio

Breaking love spells

Plantain

Home blessing, healing, removing unwanted energies

Plum

Love, peace, healing

Plumeria

Eloquence, success with others

Poke Root

Obtaining lost items

Pomegranate

Wishes, divination, fertility

Poppy

Abundance, love

Poppy Seeds

Visions, pleasure, awareness

Potato

Money, luck

Prickly Ash Bark

Breaking unwanted energies

Primrose

Secrets, revealing hidden truths

Pumpkin

Moon magic

Pumpkin Seed

Health

Quince

Happiness, love, luck

Radish

Lust, protection

Ragwort

Fairies, charms, attraction

Raspberry Leaf

Love, protection

Red Clover

Domestic animal blessings, love

Red Willow Bark

Cleansing, clearing, meditation

Rhubarb

Protection, fidelity

Rice

Money, fertility, rain

Rose

Happiness, domestic love and peace, relationships

Rose Geranium

Avoids gossip

Rose Hips

Luck, spiritual energies

Rosemary

Protection, health, memory, love

Rowan

Psychic work, protection

Rue

Freedom, mental powers

Rye

Self-control, fidelity

Saffron

Strength, lust, love

Sage

Wisdom, healing grief, memory

Salt Petre

Fidelity

Sandalwood

Purifying, cleansing

Sanicle

Safe travels

Sarsaparilla

Sex, love, money

Sassafras

Overcoming addictions

Savoury

Passion, sex, love, lust

Saw Palmetto Berries

Spiritual awakening, protection

Scullcap

Fidelity, relaxation, peace

Sea Salt

Cleansing, purifying

Senna

Love, lust

Sesame

Passion, lust, money

Shallots

Luck

Shave Grass

Fertility

Sheep Sorrel

Heart health

Shepherd's Purse

Healing

Skunk Cabbage

Legal matters

Slippery Elm

Stopping gossip, protection

Snapdragon

Purifying, protecting, exorcising

Snowdrop

Aids with grief and loss

Solomon's Seal Root

Cleansing, protecting

Sow Thistle

Stamina, strength

Spanish Moss

Opening and clearing blockages

Spearmint

Healing

Spiderwort

Love

Spikenard

Luck, protect against illness

Squaw Vine

Childbirth, fertility

St. John's Wort

Prophetic dreams, romantic visions, happiness

Star Anise

Psychic work

Straw

Luck

Straw Flower

Protection, longevity

Strawberry

Good fortune, success, love attraction

Sugar

Sex, love

Sugar Cane

Sympathy, lust, love

Sulfur Powder

Protects against someone's power over you

Sunflower

Wisdom, wishes, energy

Sweet Bugle

Love, marriage prospects

Sweet Pea

Friends, allies, loyalty

Sweet Potato

Image magic

Sweetgrass

Calling spirits

Tamarind

Love

Tangerine

Joy, strength, energy

Tansy

Longevity, immortality

Tarragon

Compassion, healing abusive situations

Tea Leaves

Strength, courage

Tea Tree

Clarity, harmony

Thistle

Protection, healing

Thyme

Affection, loyalty

Toadflax

Breaking hexes, protection

Toadstool

Rain magic

Tobacco

Personal strength, confidence

Tomato

Love

Tonka Bean

Courage, wishes, love

True Unicorn Root

Breaking hexes, protection

Tuberose

Serenity, calm

Turnip

Ending relationships

Uva Ursi

Intuition, psychic powers

Valerian

Dreams, harmony, peace, love

Vanilla Bean

Lust, passion, love

Venus Flytrap

Protection, love

Vetiver

Attraction, prosperity, breaking hexes

Vervain

Youth, peace, healing, sleep

Vetch

Fidelity

Vinegar

Binging, banishment

Violet

Dreams, visions

Walnut

Divine communication, blessings

Watercress

Moon and sex magic

Wheat

Conception, fertility, money

White Sage

Purifying and cleansing

White Willow Bark

Protection against negative energies

Willow

Moon, love, healing, overcoming sorrow

Wisteria

Psychic awareness

Witch Hazel

Protection, healing grief

Witches Grass

Love, lust, happiness

Wood Aloe

Success, prosperity

Wood Betony

Protecting, purifying, banishing unwanted energies

Woodruff

Money, victory

Wormwood

Inhibit violence, remove anger

Yarrow Flower

Weddings, love, luck

Yellow Dock

Money, fertility, healing

Yerba Mate

Love, lust, fertility

Yerba Santa

Psychic work, healing, beauty

Tables of Correspondence: Essential Oils

This list offers some, but not all information about the benefits and uses of essential oils. Further research may be required.

Allspice Berry

Anti-depressant, digestive aid, warming, and anesthetic

Angelica Seed

Sedative, relieves many ailments, helps with digestion

Anise Seed

Respiratory ailments, balances hormones, helps relieve flatulence and indigestion

Basil

For treating fever and colds, anxiety aid, stimulant, antiseptic

Bay Laurel

Respiratory issues, sedative, analgesic properties

Bergamot

Digestive issues, dispels fear, good for urinary tract, antidepressant

Blood Orange

Neurological health, digestive remedy

Camphor

Stimulating, anti-inflammatory

Caraway Seed

Digestion, disinfection, insect repellent

Cardamom Seed

Aphrodisiac, circulation

Carrot Seed

Stimulating, muscle relaxer, skin rejuvenation

Cassia

Antidepressant

Catnip

Sedative, anti-inflammatory

Cedarwood

Stimulant, cellulite reduction, sedative

Celery Seed

Arthritic relief, lowers high blood pressure, anti-inflammatory.

Chamomile

Boosts immunity, sleep, relaxation

Cinnamon

Antidote to poison, aphrodisiac, antiseptic

Citronella

Insecticide, antispasmodic

Clary Sage

Helps hair grow, creates euphoria, scalp tonic

Clove Bud

Anti-viral, anti-tumor, antioxidant

Coriander Seed

Purifying, detoxifying

Cypress

Breaks down cellulite, deodorant, help with rheumatic conditions

Eucalyptus

Immune booster

Fennel

Weight loss, digestion

Fir Needle

Antiseptic, relieves cough

Frankincense

Human growth hormone stimulator, anti-cancer, wrinkle reduction

Geranium

Antidepressant, fungicide, can relieve irritated skin

Ginger

Antioxidant, aphrodisiac, relief of arthritic pain

Grapefruit

Lymphatic and digestive stimulant, reduction of cellulite

Helichrysum

Anti-allergenic, helps to heal scars

Hop

Helps support menopausal symptoms, diuretic, antispasmodic

Hyssop

Digestion, fever reduction

Juniper Berry

Sedative, detoxification

Lavender

Antidepressant, sedative, sleep, reduces stress

Lemon

Cleansing, detoxifying

Lemongrass

Reduces fever, deodorant

Lime

Antidepressant, antioxidant

Magnolia

Antidepressant

Marjoram

Help heal from sickness, oxygenates tissues, vasodilator

Melissa

Mood booster, uterine health, balances hormones

Mugwort

Stimulates appetite

Myrrh

Tonic for aging skin, regulates cholesterol, revitalizes

Neroli

Anti-inflammatory, aphrodisiac

Nutmeg

Digestion and gastric juice secretion, aphrodisiac, hypnotic

Orange

Antidepressant

Oregano

Anti-parasitic, antioxidant, antiviral

Patchouli

Immune booster, thyroid health, anti-depressant

Pennyroyal

Stimulant, emmenagogue

Peppermint

Neurological health, headache relief, digestion

Pine Needle

Restorative, uplifting, cleansing

Rose

Skin health, uplifting, anti-depressant

Rosemary

Memory enhancement, restorative

Sage

Anti-inflammatory, memory enhancement, concentration

Sandalwood

Calming, hydrates skin, emollient

Spearmint

Energizing, relief of menstrual pain

Star Anise

Stimulating, antiseptic

Tea Tree

Anti-fungal, anti-viral

Thyme

Stimulates digestion, respiratory health

Verbena

Detoxification

Vetiver

Hydrates skin, stimulates nervous system

Wintergreen

Pain relief, respiratory health, diuretic

Wormwood

Narcotic, deodorizing

Yarrow

Regeneration, anti-infection

Ylang Ylang

Euphoria, aphrodisiac

Tables of Correspondence: Incense

This list of incenses offers some but not all of the effects of burning them. Further research may be necessary.

Acacia

Psychic work

African Violet

Home blessings and spirituality

Allspice

Money, luck

Anise Seeds

Meditation

Basil

Attract love, fidelity, luck, sympathy, wealth, protection against negativity

Bay

Psychic powers, prophetic dreams

Bayberry

Money attraction

Benzoin

Purification, prosperity

Cedar

Purification, psychic powers, love, curing illness

Cinnamon

Protection, money, stimulate psychic awareness, healing

Clove

Purify, remove negative energy, money attraction, prevent gossip

Copal

Love, purifying

Damiana

Psychic work

Dragon's Blood

Dispel negative energies, protection during spells and invocations, add to other incenses for extra power

Elecampane

Clairvoyance, scrying, divination

Frankincense

Purification, protection, meditation, psychic visions, luck

Gotu Kola

Meditation

Heather

Conjuring helpful spirits

Hibiscus Flower

Love

Jasmine

Love, money, inducing prophetic dreams

Juniper

Psychic power, breaking curses and hexes

Lavender

Love, rest, sleep

Lilac

Increase psychic powers, attract harmony

Mace

Increase psychic powers

Mesquite

Added to other incenses to increase powers

Mint

Increase sexual desire, money attraction, protective powers, high vibrations

Myrrh

Consecration, healing, purification, meditation, rituals

Nutmeg

Meditation, prosperity, increase psychic powers

Patchouli

Attracting, money, wealth, and fertility

Pine

Purification, banishing negative energies, money attraction

Poppy Seeds

Fertility, love, luck

Rose

Love romance, courage, prophetic dreams

Rosemary

Purification, prevention of nightmares, dispels depression, fairy magic, restful sleep

Rue

Helps restore health

Sage

Protection against negative energies, purification of sacred spaced, wisdom, money, healing body, mind and soul

Sandalwood

Promotes spiritual awareness, healing rituals, wish magic, exorcising demons

Star Anise Seeds

Psychic awakening and awareness

Strawberry

Love

Sweetgrass

Conjuring helpful spirits before a spell

Thyme

Purifying, pre-ritual purification, healing, attracting good health

Vanilla

Love, increase passion and sexual desire, improve mental power

Vervain

Exorcise unwanted spiritual energies

Vetivert

Breaking curses, protection

Willow

Averting negativity, attracting love, promotion of healing

Wormwood

Stimulates and increases psychic powers

Conclusion

What a wonderful journey it has been through the magical world of herbs! This book is your beginner's guide to help you really get involved with the various processes involved with herbal magic. All of the information and recipes in this book are meant to help you understand your own Wiccan, or magical practice more and to help you bring the medicine and magic of plants into your world.

Throughout these pages, you have discovered the ancient world of herbal medicine and plant lore as well as the use of herbs for medicinal and magical purposes in shamanism and other practices. In so many of those religions and philosophies, the idea of wholeness with the universe is presented and relates to the concept of correspondences. Each plant knows what it has to offer and so communicating with each one like a friend and ally is part of what this book wants to teach you, as well as how they correlate with the seasons, planets, sun and moon cycles, and elements.

The biggest take away in this book is most likely to have a list of all the most common and essential herbs and what their magical and medicinal energies are. You can refer back to this book as often as you need to look up these plant and herb properties to help with your spells and rituals.

Knowing what herbs to use is a huge part of the lesson of practicing herbal magic and what this book has also shown you is how to ask the herbs what they want to offer, how to collect them at the right time, and how to prepare and store them for future uses. All of the methods in this book are tried and true ways to honor the magic of herbs and incorporate them in your everyday life through remedies, spells and craft work.

You can enjoy many delightful recipes and instructions for teas, baths, making sacred oils, charms, poppets, and pillows, and expand upon all of them in order to design and create your magical practices.

Herbs are a major tool for health, healing, wholeness, and so many possibilities of drawing powerful energy into your life. This book wants you to have all of the tools that you need in order to practice with herbal medicine and magic responsibly, creatively and with and attitude of love and reverence for every one of Mother Nature's gifts.

Moving forward, spend time getting to know the herbs in your neighborhood, in your garden around the shops that you like to visit, and begin to create your very own herbal practice at home. Start using the spells and the recipes in this book and find your inner herbal shaman to help you stay balanced in your practice of magic.

If you have found this book helpful and useful in any way, a review on Amazon.com is always a blessing. May you enjoy the magic and medicine of herbs. And so it is!

Made in the USA
Coppell, TX
20 August 2021